BYGONE BRIT.

AT PLAY
1900–1970

LONDON: HMSO

Researched and prepared by Publishing Services, Central Office of Information.

© Selection and introduction Crown copyright 1995

Applications for reproduction should be made to HMSO

First published 1995

ISBN 0 11 701895 3

Published by HMSO and available from:

HMSO Publications Centre
(Mail, fax and telephone orders only)
PO Box 276, London SW8 SDT
Telephone orders 0171 873 9090
General enquiries 0171 873 0011
(queuing system in operation for both numbers)
Fax orders 0171 873 8200

HMSO Bookshops
49 High Holborn, London, WC1V 6HB
(counter service only)
0171 873 0011 Fax 0171 831 1326
68-69 Bull Street, Birmingham, B4 6AD
0121 236 9696 Fax 0121 236 9699
33 Wine Street, Bristol, BS1 2BQ
0117 9264306 Fax 0117 9294515
9-21 Princess Street, Manchester, M60 8AS
0161 834 7201 Fax 0161 833 0634
16 Arthur Street, Belfast, BT1 4GD
01232 238451 Fax 01232 235401
71 Lothian Road, Edinburgh EH3 9AZ
0131 228 4181 Fax 0131 229 2734
The HMSO Oriel Bookshop
The Friary, Cardiff CF1 4AA
01222 395548 Fax 01222 384347

HMSO's Accredited Agents
(see Yellow Pages)
and through good book sellers

Acknowledgments

We would like to thank the staff of the British Library Newspaper Library at Colindale
for their ready and cheerful assistance and co-operation, and for their expertise in problem
solving. The staff at the British Library at Bloomsbury have also helped in turning up rare
and distant journals. We are also indebted to the National Magazine Company, to the
National Federation of Women's Institutes, and to the Thomas Cook archive, who so kindly
allowed us access to their archives. Copyright in the extracts quoted generally belongs to the
newspapers and the magazines concerned, and to their successors in business. Present owners
have been most kind in granting permission to quote. In spite of all our efforts, it has not
been possible to trace all present copyright owners in the extracts featured.

We would like to thank our colleagues in COI Pictures Section for helping us to choose the
photographs for this book.

The cover illustrations are by courtesy of the National Museum of Photography, Film and
Television in Bradford (top), Paul Popper Limited (right) and COI Pictures Section (left).

The Cup Final photograph on page 34 is by courtesy of Paul Popper Limited.

PREFACE

By Sir Harry Secombe

There's nothing quite like coming across a 50-year-old newspaper or magazine – when you're moving house, perhaps, or having a particularly vigorous spring-clean. The shape and size of their yellowing pages may look familiar, but their contents seem to come from another world.

The Bygone Britain series explores our past through the pages of these old newspapers and magazines, which were only ever meant to be bought, read for a day or so and thrown away, but often end up lining people's drawers or wrapped round their crockery.

I find them endlessly fascinating. On the one hand here are events familiar through the reasoned analysis of history – battles, political upheavals – reported with vivid immediacy. Yet news items such as Chamberlain's successful appeasement mission to Berlin can only be viewed through the lens of hindsight. There are also the news stories that took a long time to happen: the earliest of many items about the Channel Tunnel in Bygone Britain is dated 1907!

Quite unselfconsciously, the articles, letters and advertisements reveal completely different priorities from our own. It is quite shocking that a small and ostensibly sentimental item about the discovery of an abandoned baby finishes with the casual disclosure that the infant was then consigned to the workhouse. Conversely, the behaviour of these aliens from another age has the power to amuse us in a way that would make them quite indignant: the excruciating niceties of visiting cards are surely no laughing matter, and what on earth is wrong with attempting to banish grey hair with radium? Likewise, in these knowledgeable days of niche marketing and core business, we find it absurd to see an advertisement urging hairdressers to sell the odd bicycle on the side.

But there are many hints that the people who populate these pages are not such strangers to us after all. Get-rich-quick schemes and dubious books already feature prominently in the small ads, and the slimming advertisements seem as widespread as in our own press. Some of the ideas voiced in the articles are ones that we thought our own generation had come up with: domestic science as a subject for boys, the dangers of too much exposure to the sun. And, needless to say, affairs of the heart loom large across the pages, whatever the decade.

The things that we can recall ourselves exert their own particular attraction. Coverage of events we remember, pictures of celebrities, advertisements for objects we coveted excite a warm glow of recognition and affection. Other pictures may arouse quite opposite emotions: horror and self-loathing to think that we ever went around with lapels like that! Our reactions to our memories are as much a gauge of how we as individuals have changed as of how society has changed.

So what conclusions can we draw from leafing through the pages of the Bygone Britain books? The increasing pace of technological change is evident, as is the growing informality – in manners, in language, and in address to the readers. The problem page letters confirm this. Early in the century, the letters themselves do not appear; all we see are the replies, addressed to a mysterious correspondent with a fanciful name: Heart's Ease or Sapphire. Fifty years later many writers think nothing of revealing their true identities along with their troubles. (In passing, let us be thankful for the demise of the enterprising service offered by the *Hairdressers and Toilet Requisites Gazette*, whereby people sent in samples of falling hair – and worse – for trichological analysis.)

Does the very different look of the articles in the 1900s and those of the 1960s – tiny, dense text with small headlines giving way to more spacious type with *Sun*-style screamers – mean that our powers of concentration are declining? That papers and magazines have to try harder to wrest our attention from television is obvious, but modern technology, availability of newsprint, and more widespread literacy have all played their part in shaping our contemporary press.

Whether you have a serious interest in British history and society, or you're an avid consumer of trivia; whether you can remember most of the first seventy years of this century, or you weren't even born, you will find plenty to wonder at, to mourn and to laugh about in the Bygone Britain series.

INTRODUCTION

Britain at play is a kaleidoscopic subject: sport, music, socialising, fashion, literature, theatre, radio, TV, film, pop. We focus on the country enjoying its leisure, whether decorously or energetically, and on the personalities – artists, musicians, sportsmen and women, actors, writers – whose achievements and catastrophes have enthralled the public.

The book provides not only glimpses of the big events in the broad stream of Britain's sporting, cultural and social traditions through the years, but also covers the British at play in a more private environment, and offers unusual slants on distinguished careers. For example, it features the very young Janet Baker, making one of her first public appearances, at York in 1953, and the Grimsby press reflecting on local girl Norma Procter's latest success, at Covent Garden in 1961.

A quick glance through some of the items can give us an idea of what made life fun for our grandparents and parents. In 1900 *Queen* was giving its readers ideas about what to wear for the theatre on winter evenings – and no half measures. Extreme formality and elegance were essential for the respectable. By 1931, when *Harper's Bazaar* was advising a woman on how to conduct herself when lunching with an older man or a younger man, things had become more relaxed. The lure of forbidden fruit was powerful: *Shadow of her Sin* was the title of the serial in the *Evening News* in spring 1902, and *The Granta* relished a review of the film *Sodom and Gomorrah* in 1924. In 1914 public indignation led to a boycott of the tango because of its supposed immorality.

For tamer souls, a temperance public house opened in London in 1904 and the *Bucks Herald* reported a Band of Hope social evening with an acetylene lantern in 1911; the *Croquet Association Gazette* for May 1910 covered the thrilling end to a unique croquet match; and *Retail Credit World* in 1928 provides an unconsciously comical account of a staff outing.

What comes across from these pages is the wide spectrum of live entertainment available at the beginning of the century. Theatrical, concert and opera life was just as rich as it was in the 1960s. (There was no television to keep people at home.) Music halls enjoyed enormous popularity, and their stars were stars indeed: Marie Lloyd ('with a heart as big as Waterloo station'), Dan Leno, Harry Lauder, and George Robey had to work hard for demanding and critical audiences. Musical comedy flourished at Daly's, the Gaiety and the Adelphi. Gilbert and Sullivan had struck a happy mean of words and music – not too demanding, but highly professional and always delightful. The plays of Wilde and Shaw were providing an intellectual dimension which those of Pinero, for example, had possibly lacked – but all entertained superbly. By the 1890s Edward Elgar, after an initial struggle, had broken through as the foremost British composer of the day, and the world of serious music was to expand as the new century progressed.

With Marconi's introduction of regular broadcasts in 1921, the electronic media began their merciless invasion of our homes. A 1939 edition of *The Gramophone* carries record reviews for Adelaide Hall and a young Vera Lynn. It is somewhat alarming to discover that television was giving us Sabrina, Bill Haley, *Six-Five Special*, and the Platters with hardly a pause as long ago as 1957, while on radio, there were the Goons – the zaniest of comic creations – and Tony Hancock and Kenneth Horne – both masters of hilarious understatement.

British humour, whether broad slapstick, satire, or unnerving understatement, has always been with us and has helped to create an international image, sometimes baffling to foreigners. Perhaps unconsciously, we have also drawn out the paradox: the contrast between the continuing British contribution to global artistic and cultural life and a national reputation for philistinism; Britain as a great cultural centre, but the majority of the British unaware or uninterested.

Britain was once the world's foremost exporter of sport. Many of the games played throughout the world with such zest and in such earnest, and with ever increasing speed and strength, originated in Britain. At the threshold of the twentieth century the British love of sports and pastimes was never more marked: not only were they considered healthful, but they also allowed a flutter or gambling for high stakes – another British passion. The Queensberry rules of the late 1860s had eliminated the barbarities of prizefighting, and both boxing and horseracing were avidly followed by all classes. The skills of football teams which sprang up in industrial areas throughout Britain quickly outran those of the public schools. (The FA Cup competition was introduced in 1871; the English football league in 1888; the goal net in 1891. The number of Rugby clubs had risen from 31 in 1872 to 481 by 1893.)[1] Although rugby came late to Wales, the Welsh soon stamped their dominance on it. Cricket, golf and tennis had a more limited appeal, but all had begun their triumphant progress abroad before 1900.

Among sporting highlights, we have covered the legendary Olympics of 1908 and 1924, and the crowded year 1933 – trouble at Manchester United; a Welsh win at Twickenham; bodyline; floodlit football. From 1932 comes an interview with Gordon Richards and from 1935 an appreciation of 'The Master' – Jack Hobbs. Post-war sports papers have much about speedway, and we are in time to catch David Hemery and Ann Jones in 1968–69.

We have not overlooked the exploits of visitors from overseas, whether Madame Wallruga von Isacescu, who made an attempt on the Channel in 1900; Suzanne Lenglen, the Wimbledon star of the 1920s; Nellie Melba and Joan Sutherland, Australian opera divas the British took to their hearts; or the first performance of Stravinsky's *Petrouchka* in London in 1913.

In 1924 Edith Evans took audiences at the Lyric Theatre, Hammersmith, by storm as Millamant in Nigel Playfair's production of Congreve's *The Way of the World*, the finest comedy of wit and manners of the English Restoration. She 'emerged as our greatest actress in a single night', said one critic. 'One of the most blinding visions of character that have ever been dramatized', wrote another. Arnold Bennett, one of the play's promoters, thought that Edith Evans had given the 'finest comedy performance' he had ever seen. He went backstage to tell her so. Surely this extraordinary woman had profoundly studied her great part, and would have something to say about its subtleties, contradictions and inner meaning. But no. She seemed to have no idea what she had created. 'How exciting', she answered, and moved on.[2]

Here, perhaps, is a clue to the British character: understatement, a fear of being thought too serious, a dislike of fuss. Keenness, ability, offhandedness and modesty are all part of the tradition of Britain at play.

John Collis
COI
August 1995

1 Keith Robbins, *The Eclipse of a Great Power: Modern Britain 1870–1975* (London, 1983), p. 66.
2 Kenneth Muir in Brian Morris (editor), *William Congreve,* New Mermaid Critical Commentaries (London, 1972), pp. 133 ff.

1900 ▮ 1909

INGENIOUSLY DEVISED COIFFURES AT M. JEAN STEHR'S

IN these days, when the hairdressing ordained by fashion demands the hand of a skilled expert, the woman who is out of reach of her coiffeur would often be in sorry plight were it not for the many convenient devices by which art steps in to the aid of nature. The accompanying sketches illustrate some of these at their best as produced by M. Jean Stehr, of 235, Oxford-street. One is a coiffure de l'opéra, arranged in so naturalistic a manner as to defy a critical

Coiffure de l'Opéra.

eye to detect that it is produced by means of an entire transformation headdress. The hair is arranged in loose ondulations, without any exaggerated fulness, and gathered into a light knot fastened with small tortoiseshell combs, and finished with a curl set rather high at the back of the head; the wearer's own fringe can be brought out beneath the transformation so as to avoid any line on the forehead.

Queen 1900

DOUBLE ACROSTIC NO. 1715.

[SIXTH OF THE QUARTER, ENDING SEPT. 29.]

Across the border and across the sea
  Of kindred origin, first cousins we.
The latter some would have us teach their young;
  With tongue contending, 'tis a living tongue.

1. Security upon my house and field.
2. To him the Greeks at Cranon had to yield.
3. A man-of-war that hasn't ship'd a crew.
4. Than Katharine a more outrageous shrew.

                MINT (slightly altered).

[It may interest solvers of long standing to learn that the above was, in substance, communicated to our columns three decades ago by a talented solver of that period. Answers within thirteen days will be welcome.—ED.]

Queen 1900

JEFFRIES STILL CHAMPION.

HE DEFEATS CORBETT AFTER A TERRIFIC FIGHT

Jeffries beat Corbett on Friday night in a match for the heavy-weight boxing championship of the world at the Seaside Sporting Club, Coney Island, New York, with a knock-out blow in the twenty-third round. The stakes were 5,000dols. a side and the "Police Gazette" belt, which carries with it the championship of the world, and in addition the winner was to receive ten per cent. of the gross receipts.

Corbett was always the cleverer boxer, but Jeffries showed wonderful stamina, and took tremendous punishment without flinching. In the end he won by sheer strength, Corbett tiring after the twentieth round. The blow which finished the contest in the twenty-third round was a swinging right-hander which landed on Corbett's jaw, and sent the great boxer down like a log.

After the match Jeffries said: "Corbett gave me the best fight of my career. It was really a surprise. I think I would have whipped him sooner had not my left arm given out early in the fight."

Daily Mail 1900

OPENING OF THE IMPERIAL THEATRE.

"A ROYAL NECKLACE."

Upon the site of a theatre, gone and unregretted, has sprung up a magnificent playhouse, radiant with marble pilasters and gorgeous embellishment. The phœnix must not be mentioned in connection with the new Imperial. It arose from no ashes, save the ashes of mournful memory. For five-and-twenty years, in spasmodic and erratic fashion, the old house pursued a generally uneventful career. Its window-bill orders and complimentary ticket hunters had a natural home it was rarely at the vanished establishment near St. James's Park. Charles Kemble, in the days of direst straits at Covent Garden, never flooded the town with his "paper" to such an extent as did some managers of Westminster's dramatic temple. Yet there are cherished recollections in connection with it, especially of Marie Litton and her delightful companions, of Phelps and his last appearances on this earthly stage. Mrs. Langtry has wiped away a structure which had fallen upon evil times, and last evening another Imperial threw open its doors. "Double-tides" of workers had striven their hardest to complete the building in the stipulated time, and, considering all things, the arrangements were fairly well forward. Suggestions of Quince, the carpenter, and Snug, the joiner, were impossible of total suppression, but there was little need for Mrs. Langtry's apologies at the termination of the performance. She hopes to make the theatre more comfortable. It would be difficult to render it more handsome.

Daily Telegraph 1901

The Earl of Coventry, Master of the Queen's Buckhounds, visited Ascot kennels and the Cumberland Lodge Stud yesterday, in anticipation of the opening of the hunting season. Goodall, the recently appointed Queen's Huntsman, has charge of the pack, which commences forest practice about the 9th of October.

Queen 1901

Games at Montem School, c. 1900: reaping peasants . . .

. . . and alternate knee-bends

Queen 1900

THEATRE DRESS FOR WINTER WEAR.

LOW VANDYKED BOLERO, with three-quarter sleeves and oval tablier slightly draped on right hip in white taffeta, sprinkled with Venus pink spots in velvet. Folded belt in pink silk, matching the bracelets, encircling the muslin sleeves with deep frill edged with lace. Irregularly draped berthe in white silk muslin, which extends at the back as a kerchief and droops down the front as a pouch. Wreath of monthly roses on left side, opposite a band of fur, terminating with a natural sable head and three tails. Muslin puffings across the shoulders. Appliqué of lace or embroidery on points of vest and on sleeves. Pink frill edges the tablier, and finely pleated muslin skirt composed of two deep flounces, each, however, simulated by the centre frill. Three clusters of sable heads and tails.

THE ATTEMPT TO SWIM THE CHANNEL.

Madame Wallruga von Isacescu, the Austrian Amateur Champion swimmer, started yesterday morning on her attempt to swim across the Channel from Calais to the English coast. The morning was beautifully fine, with bright sunshine, and there was only a very light air from the east, the sea being almost smooth. The weather conditions, therefore, could not have been more favourable. The swimmer entered the water from a bathing-machine near the Casino at 7.30 a.m. attired in a tight-fitting lady's bathing costume, the arms and the lower part of the legs being left bare, her body having been well covered with grease before starting. Only a few people saw her start, but she was watched from the shore at Calais until she had got several miles out into the Channel. Starting on the flood tide, she drifted in an easterly direction up Channel, until between nine and ten o'clock, all the time making headway across the current. Then the ebb tide set, and for about six hours drifted in the opposite direction. She was accompanied by a steam tug, and had arranged that her nourishment when in the water should consist of simple food and warm tea, no intoxicants being taken. Lanterns are carried by the tug, and other provision is made for the swim extending into the night. Madame Isacescu calculated before she started that she would be able to cross the currents at the rate of two miles an hour, but our Correspondent says that this reckoning is regarded as much too confident. The late Captain Webb swam the Channel from Dover to Cape Grisnez in 23 hours, and very little beyond an average of one mile an hour has been accomplished by any swimmer who has since unsuccessfully undertaken the same task. Last night there was haze in the Channel, and, as the air was chilly, it was regarded as doubtful whether the lady could remain long enough in the water to complete the swim. It was also thought that she had made a mistake in selecting Calais sands for her start instead of Cape Grisnez, which point would have shortened her passage across the Channel by nearly four miles.

A Calais telegram received at Dover this morning states that Madame Wallruga von Isacescu, the Austrian lady swimmer who yesterday essayed to swim the channel, gave up after accomplishing nearly 20 miles and was taken on board the tug which had accompanied her.

A Press Agency telegram states that Madame von Isacescu left this morning for Paris. She will probably make another attempt next week if the weather conditions are favourable.

Evening Standard 1900

LISTENING yesterday afternoon to the Elgar Symphony for the sixth time, it occurred to me that a potent attraction in the work is the calming effect it exerts on nowaday nerves. This soothing influence makes itself felt at the opening, and although there is much subsequent agitation and strenuousness, there is a paramount suggestion of nobility and strength that seem to banish querulous thoughts and petty anxieties. That music has this power is admitted, and I am inclined to believe that the Elgar Symphony possesses it to an exceptional degree, and that it is this which makes the music grateful to so many ears. Be this as it may, the work given under the direction of the composer attracted another large audience yesterday, was most attentively followed, and was obviously enjoyed. The interpretation was, in my opinion, the best conducted by Sir Edward Elgar, and the beautiful instrumentation was finely played by the Queen's Hall Orchestra. The only other performance calling for notice was the captivating playing of Miss Kathleen Parlow in Mendelssohn's violin concerto. The gifted Canadian imparts a delightful personality to her interpretations, and this was pleasingly prominent on this occasion. So vivacious and buoyant was her rendering of the last movement that she was recalled four times. This and Svendsen's "Carnival in Paris" and the orchestral arrangement of the Song of the Rhine Maidens from Wagner's "Götterdämmerung" were conducted by Mr. Henry J. Wood.

Referee 1909

CHEAP OSTRICH FEATHERS.

"FINE feathers make fine birds," and the demand for these graceful adjuncts to millinery, notwithstanding leagues and societies which we all uphold and respect, was never greater. The main supply comes from South Africa, and they must of necessity be costly. Like many other wares, they are cheaper when bought direct from the provider, and a lady—Mme. Aline, 6, Gloucester-terrace, Queen's-gate, London, S.W.—is the sole agent of the Imperial Ostrich Co., the Park, Worcester, South Africa. Buying in this way, in the bulk, a few shillings is made to do duty for a great many more. They are sold in cases, for which a definite sum is charged, containing four large white feathers, four drab ones, and four black, the lengths ranging from 10 to 24 inches. They have, of course, to be dyed or blanched and dressed, but they can give a liberal choice, and possibly last for years. Usually such feathers pass through six different hands before they reach the purchaser. A vast number of people are profiting by the opportunity, and the success of the arrangement is proved by their recommending friends to do the same.

Queen 1900

Imperial Theatre.
"A ROYAL NECKLACE."

Mrs. Langtry opened her beautiful theatre with a success that is a bright omen for the future. It is beautifully fitted up, and reveals perfect taste in every detail. It is not spacious, but it is cosy in the extreme, and no part of the house could be called anything but comfortable. The last thing that has been consulted in the creation of this fine theatre has evidently been expense. The glitter of the Pavonazetta marble, the sheen of the pilasters, the curtain, the velvet hangings, all harmonise perfectly, all produce an atmosphere such as even a Greek or Roman architect might have envied, or an Egyptian taken a tablet of. But, after all, we come to see the play and not the theatre.

Dramatic World
1901

OUR AMUSEMENT GUIDE
For Residents and Visitors in London.

THEATRES.

APOLLO, Shaftesbury Avenue. — "Kitty Grey." Evenings at 8. Matinées, Saturdays, at 2. Miss Edna May and Mr. G. P. Huntley.

AVENUE, Northumberland Avenue.—Last weeks of "The Night of the Party." Evenings at 8.30. Matinées, Wednesdays, at 2.30. Miss May Palfrey, Miss Mina Blakiston, and Mr. Weedon Grossmith. Preceded at 7.45 by "Between the Dances."

COMEDY, Panton Street, Haymarket.—"When We Were Twenty-One." Evenings at 8.15. Matinées, Wednesdays and Saturdays, at 2.15. Miss Maxine Elliott and Mr. N. C. Goodwin.

COURT, Sloane Square.—"Charles I. & II," at 8. An Olio Entertainment at 8.30, and Princess Lolah at 10.

CRITERION, Piccadilly Circus. — "The Undercurrent," at 8.30. Matinées, Saturdays, at 2.30. Mr. Arthur Bourchier.

DALY'S, Cranbourn Street, Piccadilly. — "San Toy," at 8.15. Matinées, Saturdays, at 2.30. Miss Ada Reeve, Messrs. Huntley Wright, Rutland Barrington, and Hayden Coffin.

DRURY LANE.—"The Great Millionaire," at 7.45. Matinées, Wednesdays and Saturdays, at 1.45. Miss Mary Brough and Mr. Charles Fulton.

DUKE OF YORK'S, St. Martin's Lane.—"The Sentimentalist," at 8. Mr. Lewis Waller.

GAIETY, 345, Strand.—"The Toreador," at 8. Matinées, Saturdays, at 2.

GARRICK, Charing Cross Road.—"Iris," at 8. Matinées, Saturdays, at 2. Miss Fay Davis and Mr. Dion Boucicault.

HAYMARKET.—"The Second in Command," at 8.30. Matinées, Saturdays, at 2.30. Miss Winifred Emery and Mr. Cyril Maude.

HER MAJESTY'S, Haymarket. — "The Last of the Dandies," at 8.15. Matinées, Wednesdays and Saturdays. Mr. Beerbohm Tree.

LYCEUM, Wellington Street.—"Sherlock Holmes," at 8. Matinées, Saturdays, at 2. Mr. William Gillette.

LYRIC, Shaftesbury Avenue.—"The Silver Slipper," at 8. Matinées, Wednesdays, at 2.30. Miss Winifred Hare and Mr. Willie Edouin.

PRINCE OF WALES', Coventry Street, W. — "Becky Sharp," at 8. Matinées, Wednesdays and Saturdays, at 2. Miss Marie Tempest and Mr. Leonard Boyne.

PRINCESS'S, Oxford Street.—"The Two Little Vagabonds," at 8. Matinées, Wednesdays, at 2.15. Miss Sydney Fairbrother.

ROYALTY, Dean Street, Soho.—"The Second Mrs. Tanqueray," at 8.30. Matinée, Wednesday, at 2.15. Mrs. Patrick Campbell.

ST. JAMES'S, King Street.—"The Likeness of the Night," at 8.15. Matinées, Wednesdays and Saturdays, at 2.15. Mrs. Beerbohm Tree and Mr. and Mrs. Kendal.

SHAFTESBURY, Shaftesbury Avenue.—"Are You a Mason?" at 9. Preceded at 8 by "Charity Begins at Home." Matinées, Wednesdays and Saturdays, at 3. Miss Ethel Matthews and Mr. Paul Arthur.

STRAND.—"A Chinese Honeymoon," at 8. Matinées, Wednesdays and Saturdays, at 2.15. Miss Louie Freear and Mr. Lionel Rignold.

TERRY'S, Strand.—"A Tight Corner," at 8.15, followed at 10.15 by "Sheer-Luck Jones." Miss Sarah Brooke and Mr. George Raiemond.

VAUDEVILLE, Strand.—"Sweet and Twenty," at 9. Preceded at 8 by "Scrooge." Matinées, Wednesdays, at 3. Preceded at 2 by "You and I." Miss Ellaline Terriss and Mr. Seymour Hicks.

WYNDHAM'S, Charing Cross Road. — "The Mummy and the Humming Bird," at 8.30. Matinées, Saturdays, at 2.30. Miss Mary Moore and Mr. Charles Wyndham.

Lady's Gazette 1901

ARRIVAL AT TOTTENHAM

A CHAT correspondent informe[s] that the scene at South Tottenham Saturday night previous to the arriv[al] the team, and on the early Sunday [morn]ing, when the team arrived, was beyond the expectations of the mo[st en]thusiastic Spur. Bands and firev[orks] galore greeted the players, and the [size] of the Cup itself, though so insignif[icant] in size, created enthusiasm of the extraordinary character. The hou[rs did] not appear to have affected the desi[re of] the inhabitants of the Tottenham di[strict] to show honour to the Spurs; but, some dozen or two rounds of chee[r] the players were taken to their house, and the enthusiasts separate[d] again show up in even stronger forc[e] Monday night at the Spurs' ground. the latter celebration the enclosure packed with a dense throng, and proceedings arranged by the Spurs' [com]mittee were capitally carried out. T[hese] consisted of animated pictures of the Final games, fireworks, music, various other attractions. The proc[eed]ings commenced at 8.30, and termin[ated] about midnight, though many kep[t up] the merriment and rejoicing proceed until Tuesday was well advancing. the afternoon the Spurs team had [been] to Luton, and defeated the home tea[m in] a Southern League match by 4 t[o 1] Seven of the Final team took part in game.

Football Chat and Athletic World 1901

Mr. Choate, the United States Ambassador, arrived at Carlton House-terrace, yesterday, from Cromer.

Dr. Howard Tooth has returned by the transport Canada from South Africa, after eight months' service as Physician to the Portland Hospital.

Sir Philip Fysh, the Agent General for Tasmania, who is staying at Frinton, near Walton-on-the-Naze, will return to London early next week.

Princess Soltykoff, accompanied by Mlle. Olga Alberdinski, Maid of Honour to the Czarina, left King's-cross last night for Braemar Castle.

Evening Standard 1900

Cardiff and District Notes.

—o—

The committee dinner was duly held at the Grand Hotel on the 7th inst., and in the absence of Mr. Huxtable, Mr. Jno. Webber took the head of the table, and very ably conducted. About fifteen members sat down to a very good repast, and a most enjoyable evening was spent. After dinner several of the company obliged with some songs, Mr. Alfred Lewis being in good form, as was also Mr. Allen (Reynolds and Co.), Messrs. J. H. Davis, G. Jennings, and A. J. Curtis. Those that would not sing had to make a speech, Messrs. J. C. Cobb, Howard Lewis, J. H. Merrett, and W. T. Bustand being in good fettle. The absence of Messrs. Travers, Huxtable, and Brind was keenly felt, but in spite of all it was a good dinner, and a wish was expressed that more social evenings of the kind should be spent.

—o—

British Baker 1903

LACE ROBES AT MESSRS D. H. EVANS'S, OXFORD STREET, W.

R OBE OF FRENCH FIGURED NET, trimmed with gathered satin, with material and ribbon for bodice, in black and also cream.

No. 2. MAURESQUE LACE ROBE, in ivory, cream, and beige, including sleeves and corsage.

ueen 1900

Westminster Cathedral—that great fact—was bound, sooner or later, to make an appearance in fiction. Just as Charlotte Bronte led her heroine into a Catholic church in Brussels, Disraeli a hero of his elsewhere abroad, and Mrs. Craigie a hero of hers at Farm-street, so now, in "The Day's Journey" does Miss Netta Syrett send Cecily—another overburdened outsider—to sanctuary : "She went to the window and pushed it wider open. Before her, springing like a long-stemmed flower towards the blue of the sky, was the campanile of Westminster Cathedral. It was a tower that Cecily had learned to love. It was an exotic flower blossoming radiantly above the grey heart of London. She looked at it to-day with a fresh sense of its beauty."

❖❖

Tablet 1905

OUR SERIAL STORY.] [All Rights Reserved.

THE SHADOW OF HER SIN.

"Fate is a creditor who signs his receipts in his debtors' blood."

By EDITH and ARTHUR APPLIN.

CHAPTER XLV.—(Continued.)
Halbert Leaves for Paris.

Yes, life was very generous, giving Edith all the heart of woman could desire—all save the greatest of all gifts, love. Love of a kind she received, it is true ; the love of many men was offered her again and again—good, bad, and indifferent ; but the love of the one man had gone, perhaps for ever. She dared not think of it. But his companionship, his friendship ; she did think of that and long for that, and anxiously await his return. But he did not come, nor did he even write one line. He had disappeared, leaving nothing behind for her to cling to, nothing save her work.

So, with the reopening of the Electric Theatre in November, Edith gladly found herself once more in harness. It was good to greet each member of the company at rehearsal again ; even to speak the well-known lines and rehearse the well-known scenes ; and though others grumbled—as is the way of actors—she was grateful.

Halbert returned from the land of the Midnight Sun with tanned cheeks and a 40lb salmon—in a glass case.

"Well," he said, when he had time to speak to her alone. "You mustn't turn away from me and look unhappy. I've fished and smoked my passion away among the fjords of Norway, and so you can safely regard me in the light of a father now !"

Edith always felt tears in her eyes when Halbert spoke lightly of his own feelings. She knew he sacrificed himself to others.

"My best pal," she answered. "How much longer do you think the play will run ? What are you going to produce when it is finished ?"

"I've got another success up my sleeve," he smiled.

"And will there be a part for me ?"

Halbert nodded. Then, as a thought struck him, he frowned, and said, more seriously, "I had forgotten, there is the epilogue of this play to be written first ; you'll have to help me."

"The epilogue ! What do you mean ?"

"Have you forgotten so soon what I promised on Dartmoor, after I'd made a silly old fool of myself ? But perhaps I only made the promise under my breath to my own bit of hardened conscience."

"Oh, hush," she cried.

"Dear friend, I can't hush. Do you think I'm blind ; can't I see that you're not happy ?—you, the rich, popular, beautiful Mary Marton, are not happy. And I know the reason !"

She tried to stop him, in vain.

"Well, I'm going to make you happy. There's a 'Mr. Right' wandering about somewhere, fooling his time away, when he ought to be by your side. I believe I met him, at Edinburgh, on that great first night."

Edith's colour changed, and she hid her face.

"Ah, I'm not wrong then ! Well, I want you to tell me all about it. Ah"—as Edith moved away—"don't think me impertinent or prying, though if you do I sha'n't care, for you've got no father and you've got no mother, and some one ought to put things straight for you. No woman yet ever managed her own love affair successfully. Unless her lover hauls her to the altar with a mental six-inch cable she never gets there. Now your lover is—away. Something's wrong ; tell me, and I'll haul him back—for I know he wants to come—only something's gone amiss."

Evening News 1902

ASCOT—THE ROYAL PROCESSION

AMONG those who are away, or going, are the Dowager Lady Strathmore and Lady Maud Lyon, who are spending some weeks at Glamis Castle. Lady Kilmorey and her daughter, who have been away some time, are returning, but Lord Kilmorey's house in Aldfort Street, is let. The Duchess of Abercorn will probably go to Venice for a week or two. Both she and the Duke are very fond of Italy. Lord Curzon, who is suffering from neuritis, will take a complete rest for some time.

THE opening day of Ascot Races was the most brilliant that can be remembered. The lawns were crowded with a fluttering mass of beautifully gowned women and men in frock coats and top hats, and when the King and Queen arrived it would be difficult to imagine a more beautiful scene than was presented to the eye; the moving mass of human beings resolving itself into a veritable kaleidoscope of brilliant colour.

TOBOGGANING has its very attractive charms. It also has its dangers. The sad death of Captain Henry Singleton Pennell, V.C., who was killed by a most unfortunate accident on the Cresta Toboggan Run at St. Moritz Dorf on January 19th, cast a gloom over the whole of Switzerland. It speaks well for the care of the officials and the accuracy with which the course was constructed that there has been no fatal accident till this. It seems that the tobogganer who went down the slide in front of Captain Pennell fell over a bank which guards the right side of the course at a point where it turns somewhat sharply to the left. This bank follows almost immediately after one which guards a sharp turn to the right, and the two were christened " Battledore " and " Shuttlecock " by Lady Bancroft many years ago. This tobogganer who fell did not sustain any injury. A number of spectators out of the crowd, who were watching this interesting part of the Run, rushed to his assistance, and trampled down the deep snow which usually lies all round the outside of " Battledore," and forms a complete protection from the rocks and stones in case of a fall. When Captain Pennell came down in his turn he fell at exactly the same spot with such violence that he ruptured the internal organs.

Health Resort 1907

The Bodleian Library once possessed an original first folio of Shakspere's Plays, which, unfortunately, passed out of its possession not many years after its purchase. Some time ago the present owner of the book, who wishes to dispose of it, offered Bodley's Librarian the refusal, stating that the price was £3,000. The Bodleian, as all the world should know, is deplorably poor, and to pay such a sum as this for a single book is a thing quite out of the range, either of its experience or of its powers. Mr. Nicholson accordingly published an appeal to old Oxford men, and we are glad to see that it has been almost completely successful. But the last £400 have to be contributed by to-morrow, after which date the owner withdraws his offer to the Bodleian. Unless, therefore, Mr. Nicholson finds himself to-morrow with £3,000 in hand, we may expect to see the folio shipped over to America to swell the treasures of some millionaire. But we hope that Bodley's Librarian, having come so near to the goal of his desire, will not **now** have his hopes dashed at the last moment.

Church Times 1906

Banbury Guardian
1905

MRS. BROWNING'S PEKINESE SPANIELS AT TURWESTON RECTORY.

Years before the little Chinese dynasty had attained its present eminence at the Northamptonshire Rectory over which Mrs. Browning presides, she became possessed of her first pair, which her brother, Commander Guy Gamble, R.N., brought over in 1889 from the Celestial Empire. Strangely enough one of the pair, Fantails, was presented to him by Mr. George Brown. This gentleman, who has spent long years in China, is an authority on the breed, and since his return from there his advice and influence have been most beneficial to the club which now looks after the interests of the breed. Unfortunately, " the call of the East " has been too strong for him, and within recent days he has once more turned his face towards the grim inscrutability of the Imperial Dragon. The dog shows of that period ignored the little Oriental, which has now proved a little gold-mine to them, and, though isolated specimens have for forty years occasionally graced the foreign dog classes, it was not till 1902 that the breed received official recognition. But Mrs. Browning had been breeding from her importations, and in 1889 Erh-Shih, a brindled fawn with a very profuse coat and a granddaughter of Fantails, made her first appearance in public. Her sire is Pekin Peter, the noted dog imported by Mrs. Loftus Allen. Out of doors Erh-Shih's instincts are sporting, and she may be constantly seen emulating the accomplishments of the pea and thimble gentlemen of the racecourse by endeavouring to locate the whereabouts of a rat in a woodpile. Indoors she is supernaturally intelligent, and willingly displays quite an assortment of " parlour tricks," such as shutting doors, dancing, &c., while playing the piano denotes that she has developed musical talent. Two small daughters of Erh-Shih are Chinchilla, a light fawn brindle, and Cha-Nii, their sire being Tau-chi, bred by Mrs. Albert Gray from her Tai-Tai and Mrs. Douglas Murray's celebrated Ah Cum. Tau-Chi is little brother to Chi-Fu and half-brother to Mrs. MacEwen's Ch. Gia-Gia. This is, indeed, illustrious lineage. Chinchilla's fascinating little personalty gained for her the challenge prize and many specials at the last show of the Ladies' Kennel Association (Incorporated) at the Botanic Gardens. Cha-Nii elected to take up maternal duties, and is the mother of a litter of puppies by Miss Davis' Kia-Mien. Watching a group on the lawn, a big dog, Brackley Boxer, took our fancy; certainly his nose might be a little shorter, but his type of head is decidedly good, and his coat is profuse. He is a son of Brackley Mu Kwan and Goodwood Ming, and was bred by Lady Algernon Gordon-Lennox. Brackley Tarsa, by Brackley Pekoe ex Brackley Mu Kwan, is another dog of similar type. Mrs. Browning has besides these many other specimens of this fascinating breed, of all colours—light fawns, brindles, and reds—and varying in weight from 4½lb. to 16lb., and as she has mated her bitches to the best stud dogs their pedigrees are most distinguished. Besides this, they are extremely healthy and lively, as they should well be with their freedom to roam about the gardens and fields of the Rectory, and they enjoy life to the uttermost.—*The Ladies' Field.*

Public Opinion 1903

Medical and Scientific.

Athletic Training.

THE trainer of a generation ago would simply have stood aghast at the sweets and other savoury food stuffs eaten by your modern rowing or running collegian. Yet it may be doubted if the physique either of the individual athlete or of the nation ever stood at a higher general standard of "fitness." . . . . One pertinent fact with regard to training is that both past tradition and present practice condemn with emphatic voice the use of tobacco and alcohol and other indulgences to which healthy man—wonderful animal that he is—is unhappily prone. So long as the main principles of temperance, plain living and abundant exercise are carefully applied to the man in training, so long will the results be likely to succeed. . . . Every human being living under reasonably good conditions of environment ought to be, like the healthy schoolboy, always in a state of "training."—*Medical Press.*

THE NATURALIST.

A NEW DOG SOAP.—A few weeks ago Spratt's Patent submitted to us a new dog soap which was said to be fatal to fleas and other similar pests which trouble dogs, especially during the summer months. The soap is beautifully scented, remarkably nice to use, and we have found it answer all the purposes its manufacturers have urged in its favour. Properly used it kills both lice and fleas, and, moreover, can be applied to the most delicate toy dog, as well as to terriers and other animals—not excepting cats. Of course, dog owners must recognise the fact that the unpleasant little vermin are to be found in the dog kennel or other sleeping cabin, and they must be got rid of there as well as from the dog, or they will reappear on the latter. The difficulty with most dog soaps has lain in the fact that they were not nice to use, but this new concoction from Messrs Spratt appears to be as pleasant as the best toilet soap.

DOG SHOW AT THE ALEXANDRA PALACE.—It is some years since this unfortunate building was utilised for the purposes of a dog show. However, next month an exhibition on a very large scale is to take place there, when well-nigh a best on record is expected to be scored. Mrs E. Stennard Robinson, the energetic secretary of the Ladies' Kennel Association, is promoting the function, and we believe its success is already guaranteed, although it precedes the annual show of the Kennel Club only three weeks. The schedule of prizes for the Alexandra Palace fixture, issued the other day, contains very nearly 2000 classes, which, should each receive but one special contributory, a colossal gathering would be the result. All varieties of the dog known will have an opportunity to compete; many of the prizes will be extremely valuable, and the show is open to all, men and woman alike. Even a special feature is being made of some of the sporting classes; indeed, such a schedule of prizes has never previously been issued. Many special judges have consented to be present, including Lieut. Emil Ilquer, the German authority on dachshunds, and several ladies will also officiate in the ring, Miss Amyne Gordon judging Chow Chows, Mrs Houldsworth Italian greyhounds, Mrs Jenkins toy spaniels and toy terriers, and Mrs Hughes Skye terriers. The show, which will be held under Kennel Club rules, opens on Tuesday, Sept. 25, entries closing on the 17th of the same month, but if made prior to Thursday, the 13th, a reduced fee is allowed.

The Rev. Stanley Parker of Brighton has been visiting the public-houses of that city on Saturday evenings, not clad in clerical dress. His revelations are awful. In one public-house he found in an upper room 50 young men and women. "And the sights we saw and what we heard I should not dare to describe or repeat. Neither should I care to say much about the overtures made to us by women in some of the public-houses. It made my heart bleed to see young women of 15, 16, 17, and 18 being dragged down into the deepest depths of degradation in the places we visited." That scenes similar are going on in all our large cities and towns only makes the matter worse, and calls aloud for renewed effort, and the spirit of prayer.

Scottish Women's Temperance News 1908

Queen 1903

MARATHON RACE.

PRINCESS OF WALES
STARTS THE CONTEST.

AMERICAN VICTORY.

HAYES THE WINNER.

DORANDO, THE ITALIAN,
DISQUALIFIED.

THE QUEEN
AT
THE STADIUM.

Yesterday the Marathon Race, run from Windsor Castle to the Stadium, a distance of some twenty-six miles, produced as dramatic and unexpected a finish as any lover of sensation might desire. The British representatives were strongly in front for half the course; then the running was taken up by Hefferon, the South African. Longboat, the much-fancied Canadian athlete, retired at the twentieth mile, and Appleby, one of the best of the English contingent, gradually disappeared from the contest. Just before the Stadium was reached, Hefferon, who was leading at this point by a few yards, was passed by Dorando. The Italian entered the enclosure amid a scene of wild excitement, followed by Hayes, a representative of the United States, the latter having succeeded in passing the South African, after a gallant struggle.

Then ensued the most remarkable, and also the most painful scene of a day which had obviously tried the strength of the competitors to the uttermost. Dorando, in going round the Stadium enclosure, fell through sheer exhaustion, more than once. Helped by the officials, who immediately came to his rescue, he managed to breast the tape somehow. But as it was due to the assistance of others that he finished first, the race was very properly given to the American representative, Hayes, and Dorando was disqualified.

The scene in the Stadium, during the conclusion of the struggle, was absolutely unparalleled. Every seat was occupied, and every spectator seemed to be adding his quota of enthusiasm to the deafening roar of applause which greeted the conquering heroes. The magnificent organisation of the race from start to finish reflects the greatest credit on Lord Desborough, whose prodigal exertions in the interest of the Olympic Games will not soon or easily be forgotten. The Princess of Wales started the competitors at Windsor, and the finish was witnessed by her Majesty the Queen.

Under the presidency of the Right Hon. Lewis Harcourt, First Commissioner of Works, the official banquet to the representatives of the Athletic world took place last night at the Grafton Galleries.

Daily Telegraph 1908

CORRESPONDENCE.

[NOTE.—*The Editor does not hold herself responsible for the opinions expressed by her Correspondents.*]

ON COACHES.
To the Editor of THE HOCKEY FIELD.

DEAR EDITOR,—I hope you won't mind this long letter, but I want to tell you how very difficult hockey is to play properly. I have never been to a boarding school before this term, but have always had a governess at home. It's great rubbish having a governess like that, because you never get any decent games. My sister Marjorie and I used to play a little tennis and golf, but we had never played cricket or hockey in our lives. Consequently we felt awfully stupid when we went to school this term, and found that little girls, ever so much younger than we, were able to be quite good right wings, and left half-backs, and all the rest of it. However, there is no nonsense of that sort about us, and Marjorie said at once that we could not play hockey at all, and we were told that a coach was coming to teach the new girls. We did not quite know what a coach was, but were very glad someone would show us how to play, and were very excited when the afternoon came. Now it is over, however, Marjorie and I are nearly sure we shall never be able to be hockey players, as we have not got enough brains. I knew I was rather stupid at lessons, but did not think this would matter much for hockey. But it does.

The coach—she was quite a young-looking lady, and she could run very fast—said all kinds of things which I could not understand at all. She told me I was a " right half-back," and said that a girl with a thick red pig-tail of hair was the left wing on the other side. " Now you are never to leave that girl for a moment," she said. " Wherever she goes you must go." She then blew her whistle, and all the girls began running about. I think the red-headed girl must have been new too, as she did not seem to play very well. She ran all over the field, and I had to run after her. Presently the coach said to me : " What are you doing over here on the left ?" I did not like to say it was because the red-headed girl was there, as she did not seem to notice her ; but we both went back to the other side of the field. Soon the red-haired girl started off again, but I said to her politely, " Do you mind staying here by me, as the coach scolded me for going over there after you, and she told me at the beginning that I was to stick to you all the time." The red-haired girl was very nice about it, and promised not to run off like that again, so we stood together by the white line and had a talk. I found she was very keen on stamps, and had quite a good collection. We planned to do some swopping on Saturday, as you can only have your albums out on Saturdays at this school.

Hockey Field 1906

DORANDO (Italy) reaches the Finish. *Inset :* DORANDO being brought to at the last bend.

DUKE OF YORK'S THEATRE.

"PETER PAN;

Or, the Boy who Wouldn't Grow Up."

A Play in Three Acts,

By J. M. Barrie.

Peter Pan	Miss Nina Boucicault.
Mr. Darling	Mr. Gerald du Maurier.
Mrs. Darling	Miss Dorothea Baird.
Wendy Moira Angela Darling	Miss Hilda Trevelyan.
John Napoleon Darling	Master George Hersee.
Michael Nicholas Darling	Miss Winifred Geoghegan.
Nana	Mr. Arthur Lupino.
Tinker Bell	Miss Jane Wren.
Tootles	Miss Joan Burnett.
Nibs	Miss Christine Silver.
Slightly (Members	Mr. A. W. Baskcomb.
Curly of Peter's	Miss Alice Dubarry.
1st Twin Band)	Miss Pauline Chase.
2nd Twin	Miss Phyllis Beadon.
Jas Hook (the Pirate Captain)	Mr. Gerald du Maurier.
Smee	Mr. George Shelton.
Gentleman Starkey	Mr. Sydney Harcourt.
Cookson (Pirates)	Mr. Charles Trevor.
Cecco	Mr. Frederick Annerley.
Mullins	Mr. Hubert Willis.
Jukes	Mr. James English.
Noodler	Mr. John Kelt.
Great Big Little Panther Redskins	Mr. Philip Darwin.
Tiger Lily	Miss Miriam Nesbitt.
Liza (Author of the Play)	Miss Ela Q. May.

Redskins, Pirates, Crocodile, Eagle, Ostrich, Cat, Pack of Wolves, by Misses Mary Mayfren, Victoria Addison, Moira Creegan, Gladys Stewart, Kitty Malone, Marie Park, Elsa Sinclair, Christine Lawrence, Mary Maddison, Gladys Carrington, Laura Barradell, Daisy Murch ; Messrs. E. Kirby, S. Spencer, G. Malvern, J. Grahame ; Masters S. Grata, A. Onker, D. Ducrow, C. Lawton, W. Scott, G. Henson, R. Franks, F. Marini, P. Gicardo, A. Biaccra.

Act I.—Our Early Days.
Scene 1.—Outside the House. (Painted by Mr. W. Hann, designed by Mr. W. Nicholson.) Scene 2.—Inside the House. (Mr. W. Harford.)
Act II.—The Never, Never, Never Land.
Scene 1.—The House we built for Wendy. (Mr. W. Hann.) Scene 2.—The Redskins' Camp. (Mr. W. Hann.) Scene 3.—Our Home under the Ground. (Mr. W. Hann.)
Act III.—We Return to our Distracted Mothers.
Scene 1.—The Pirate Ship. (Mr. W. Harford.) Scene 2.—A Last Glimpse of the Redskins. Scene 3.—Home, Sweet Home.

In "Peter Pan" Mr. Barrie again relies not on any real dramatic interest but on his marvellous powers of keeping you amused in the theatre. The story is of the simplest. Peter Pan is a boy who ran away from home the day he was born because he heard his parents discussing what he should be when grown-up, and he did not want to grow up. He appears, however, to be anything up to fifteen, and is the head of a fairy colony of boys who have fallen out of their perambulators when their nurses have been looking the other way, and have not been claimed within seven days. He flies by night around the houses and catches what he can of the fairy stories told to the children within, and retails the same to the members of his Band on his return home. He has already visited the night-nursery of the Darling household. Mrs. Darling has seen him and has closed the window so rapidly as to cut off his shadow, which she rolls up and puts in a drawer. Peter comes again in search of his shadow, attended by Tinker Bell, a flitting light which enables him to locate the whereabouts of his shadow. Peter cannot, however, fix his shadow on again. There are three children asleep in the room. Wendy awakes, and is soon sewing his shadow on to him. The two talk, and Peter comes to the conclusion that what the Band wants is a mother, and invites Wendy to fill the position. The younger brother and sister are awakened, and in the end all three determine to accompany Peter back home.

Morning Post 1904

---

* * *

Last night Mr. Charles Frohman presented Mr. J. M. Barrie's play "Peter Pan" for the five hundredth time at the Duke of York's Theatre. For the past five years this play has constituted Mr. Frohman's Christmas annual at the Duke of York's, and business during the past weeks has, I am assured, been as great as in previous years. The present season concludes on Saturday, Feb. 13, and on the following Monday Miss Pauline Chase and the Duke of York's Theatre company will appear at the King's Theatre, Glasgow, for two weeks. This is the fourth year in succession that Mr. Barrie's play has visited Scotland.

* * *

Miss Marie Tempest and company have scored a great success in Mr. W. Somerset Maugham's new play, "Penelope," at the Comedy Theatre. The booking has exceeded the most sanguine expectations of the management.

* * *

Mr. Frohman announces that he will present Mr. G. P. Huntley and Miss Julia Sanderson in "Kitty Grey" at the Amsterdam Theatre, New York, to-morrow week, for a season.

* * *

"What Every Woman Knows," which Mr. Frohman presents at the Hicks Theatre, reached its hundred and fiftieth performance last Tuesday.

* * *

Old Drury's gorgeous and gay "Dick Whittington" pantomime is still being given twice daily—namely, at 1.30 and 7.30—and big is the booking.

* * *

At the Adelphi Messrs. George Edwardes and Robert Courtneidge are giving ten performances per week of their bright and beautiful "Cinderella" pantomime—that is to say, there are matinées on Mondays, Wednesdays, Thursdays, and Saturdays at 1.45.

* * *

Last week of the capital "Babes in the Wood" pantomime at the Shakespeare, Clapham, as "The Merry Widow" is booked there for to-morrow week. Matinées of the pantomime will be given to-morrow, and on Wednesday, Thursday, and Saturday at 2.15.

* * *

All playgoers will be glad to learn that Mr. Charles Hawtrey is now recovering from his severe illness. His season with Mr. Tom B. Davis at the Royalty will, in all probability, start with a revival of "Jack Straw."

* * *

Mr. Lewis Waller announces the last fortnight of "Henry the Fifth" at the Lyric. On Tuesday, Feb. 2, he will produce

"The Chief of Staff."

the four-act drama written by Mr. Ronald Macdonald, son of the late Dr. George Macdonald. As before noted, the scene is laid in a South American Republic.

* * *

Referee 1909

FAMOUS TEMPERANCE PUBLIC-HOUSE IN EAST LONDON.

The Red House of Stepney.

"A public-house without beer"—these, in large, bold letters are the words inscribed over the front of the famous Red House, Stepney. It is hoped the number of such public-houses may be very soon greatly multiplied. Only in some such way is the influence of the flaring, deadly gin-palace to be combatted.

THE RED HOUSE, STEPNEY, A FAMOUS TEMPERANCE PUBLIC-HOUSE IN THE EAST-END OF LONDON.

The Morality in Mixed Clubs.

The Modern Tendency.

There is an ever-growing tendency among middle-class women to abhor the woman's club, and, upon some pretext or another, to join one of the clubs for both sexes which are springing up, not only in London but in the Provinces. Some of these clubs have club premises, some have not : in none of them is the moral tone particularly good.

Advice 1908

Sunday Circle 1904

THE KING OPENS NEW MUSEUM.
A BRILLIANT SPECTACLE.

The King and Queen, in the presence of various members of the Royal Family, the Archbishop of Canterbury, the Premier, and several other Ministers of the Crown, of members of the Diplomatic Corps, and of a great general assembly, opened the magnificent building known as the Victoria and Albert Museum yesterday at noon.

The opening ceremony was performed in the Octagon Court of the new Museum. The scene was one of the most brilliant that could possibly be imagined. The marble floor and bare white walls of the chamber formed a perfect setting for the brilliant uniforms, the summer dresses, and the bright red cloth with which the seats and platform were covered. In a prominent position, facing the daïs, were a number of Hindoo gentlemen, attired in flowing robes and turbans of the most delicate hues. In a gallery the band of the Irish Guards discoursed music, while at intervals the students from the Royal College of Music, the girls dressed in white, sang selections.

At the close of the ceremony their Majesties drove back in State to Buckingham Palace, being enthusiastically cheered all along the route.

Before leaving the building the King conferred the honour of knighthood upon Mr. Cecil Smith, the director and secretary of the Museum. Later in the afternoon the King left town for Halton House, Tring, on a week-end visit to Mr. Alfred de Rothschild.

Referee **1909**

MR. L. MACDONALD MACLEOD,

The Scottish International Rugby player, who has just died. Mr. Macleod was captain of the Cambridge University Rugby fifteen of 1905-6.

Reynolds Newspaper **1907**

An ingenious exhibit was that of Mr. A. Hopkins, M.V.O., who is probably the champion camper-out of the world. He was formerly an officer in the navy, and, like most naval men, he seems to have no difficulty in solving the problem of *Multum in parvo*. He is a cyclist, and carries the whole of his elaborate camp equipment on his machine. His beautiful little green union silk tent, which flew the white ensign and also the Club pennon, was a model of neatness and compactness. He has invented many wonderful devices for ensuring the maximum of comfort with the minimum of inconvenience, and one hears with surprise that the tent, the mattress, and the scores of necessaries laid out in perfect order on the ground all go into three little leather cases.

World of Travel **1908**

PRIMA DONNA'S FAREWELL.

LONDON, *December 31.*

Madame Patti will give her inaugural farewell concert on New Year's Day. The series will terminate eventually.

Clarion **1907**

Taxis in Drury Lane

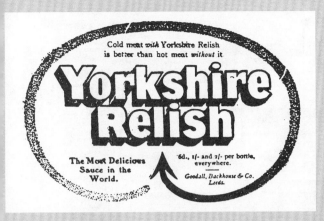

a balloon meeting at Ranelagh, 1906.

Early in the week at Roxton, just where the Ivel joins the main river, Mr. Smelt, legering very deep with a worm, caught a fish weighing 3¼lbs., which he thinks is a roach. This opinion is shared by Mr. Barker, at whose shop a cast of the remarkable capture can be seen. Other local anglers maintain that it is a hybrid between a roach and a bream, an impression, doubtless strengthened by the slightly bronze colour of the fish, though this may be due to great age. The arguments in favour of its being a roach are that:—(1) Very large roach are frequently caught in the Ivel; (2) the fins and scales of the specimen are those of a roach; (3) there is a good breadth across the back (hybrids usually run thin). We thought the head was a roach's. If it is a roach, it is probably the finest specimen ever caught in the British Isles, but to settle the dispute the cast is to be sent to the Editor of the "Fishing Gazette," and his decision will be awaited with much interest.

Ampthill and District News **1908**

BISHOPMILL MOTHERS' MEETING.—Under the above auspices very successful meetings are carried on in Bishopmill Hall during the winter months, and every year about Christmas time a social gathering is held. The function took place on Monday evening, Mr W. Rose Black, Hythehill, presiding over a large audience. After a splendid tea a lengthy programme was gone through. A few remarks by the Chairman preceded an interesting address by Rev. John Mair, New Spynie. Songs, recitations, readings, and instrumental music prolonged the evening's entertainment, those who contributed being Mrs MacBey, Miss J. K. Smith, Miss K. Welsh, Mrs Maclean, Mr and Mrs Johnston, Miss Crissy Shiach, Mr D. Inglis, the Chairman (Mr Black), and Mr John Macphail. Fruit was served out, and a very enjoyable gathering was brought to a close by the usual votes of thanks.

Northern Scot **1908**

PROMENADE PIER RE-OPENS.

SPLENDID CONCERT BY AUSTRALIAN ENTERTAINERS.

After having passed through a long period of many vicissitudes, the Promenade Pier was re-opened on Monday for the season, when the Australian Entertainers commenced an eight weeks' engagement, under the direction of Mr. Lightfoot. The programme submitted was in every way attractive, and proved most enjoyable to the large audience that had assembled. With the necessary public support, Mr. Lightfoot assured our representative that he would present some really magnificent programmes, in which some of London's leading artistes would appear. Therefore, it behoves townspeople and visitors alike to do their utmost to give the organisers every possible support.

The company consists of six artistes, who includes Miss Eva Dickson, Miss Lilian Graham, Miss Christine Birkett, Mr. Hector Lightfoot, Mr. Reginald Goond and Mr. Pownall, and their repertoire consists of duets, quartettes, ballads, humorous selections at the piano, choruses, etc. We can assure our readers that each one is an accomplished and clever artiste, and are possessed of very fine voices, that can scarcely fail to secure them the favour of their listeners. The programme is interspersed with bioscopic pictures of a remarkable character, which receive the rapt attention of the audience.

There will be a sacred concert on Sunday evening, when an exceptionally fine programme has been arranged, and it is hoped to see the Pavilion crowded.

Dover Telegraph **1909**

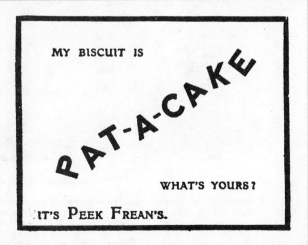

Egyptian Hall, Piccadilly (d. 1905).

Referee 1909

Referee 1909

Vesta Tilley.

* * *

Miss Vesta Tilley's return to the Palace proved very welcome, so vivacious was she. She sang among other things a song called "Naughty Boy," and her and everybody's old favourite, "Jolly Good Luck to the Girl Who Loves a Soldier," which again went splendidly. Mr. Herman Finck's new musical pot-pourri, entitled "A Jumble Sale," is very exhilarating. It ranges from "Walking in the Zoo" to Wagner.

* * *

Dan Leno as Mother Goose

1910–1919

FUNNY GAMES FOR WINTER PARTIES

Fifteen impromptu laughter-making games for the holidays

Needle-threading. The game is to thread the greatest possible number on a reel of cotton in a given time

"How is this forfeit paid?"

Picking up peas with two pencils and putting them into a cup. It is far more difficult than it sounds

Walking past at a *brisk* pace, each competitor tries to knock the cork off the bottle, with one flip of a finger

Tailing the Manx cat. Blindfolded players have to pin a paper tail on to the cat. Some results are very laughable

Fortune-telling by cards. "Your Past, Present, and Future are : you have sat down in the ring—you are still sitting— and will have to get up"

A contortionist competition. The men have to pass under a girl's arm, held straight out, by bending backwards. The lower the arm is held the better

Amateur Sherlock Holmeses. The players smell a number of liquids in bottles, and write down the supposed contents of each on a card

Music from France.

In Cambridge there is a growing interest taken in Modern French Music, which Dr. Vaughan Williams, with his splendid and astounding innovations in the "Wasps," has perhaps done a great deal to awaken among the less expert. There is now announced a concert for next Wednesday, February 9th, at 5 p.m, given by Miss Newton and Miss Wood, consisting mostly of piano and vocal music of this school, little, if any, of which has been performed in Cambridge before. The "Air and Variations" from Op. 63 by Vincent d'Judy has only once been performed in England before this, and on this occasion the performer has had the advantage of playing it to the composer and verifying her interpretation. The programme includes songs by Gabriel Fauré, Reynaldo Hahn, and Claude Debussy, all taken from the verse of Paul Verlaine, and Maurice Ravel's setting of "Le Paon," one of the humorous "Histories Naturelles" of Jules Renard; and is completed by Old French and Italian music, and by Chopin's Ballade in F minor, Op. 52, which is performed less frequently than it deserves. This is, in fact, an opportunity which will rarely be repeated.

Gownsman 1910

* * * * *

The following account of a unique finish was unavoidably crowded out last month. It is taken from the report of the Costebelle Club tournament :

"In one of the games of the last Monthly Handicap the finish was probably a record one.

Mr. R. C. Longworth, playing Blue and Black, was for the penultimate and rover hoops respectively.

Playing Blue, from a spot between the turning peg and one back, he shot at Yellow, which was near the right upright of the penultimate hoop, missed the ball, but hitting the inside of the left upright, ran that hoop, the rover hoop, and hit the winning peg in the one stroke!

Next turn, with Black a little to left of the penultimate, he shot at the rover hoop, made that, and hit the winning peg, also in one stroke!"

* * * * *

Croquet Association Gazette 1910

CUDDINGTON.

Band of Hope.—A lantern lecture on Poultry was given to the members of the Band of Hope and adult friends on Wednesday, 8th inst. The Rev. A. C. Alford manipulated the acetylene lantern, and Mr. T. J. Frost gave the lecture, which was a little above the heads of some of the younger members, but the seniors thoroughly enjoyed the instructive views of the various incubators, rearers, and stock.

Bucks Herald 1911

TO ELECTRIFY A KNITTING-NEEDLE OR PIECE OF BROWN PAPER.

Instead of a comb, an ebonite knitting-needle, a piece of sealing-wax, or a strip of brown paper folded twice and made scorching hot, may be used, and, in place of being rubbed in the hair, can be stroked quickly with a piece of hot flannel or fur, or even with the dry hand.

Each will quickly become electrified and can be tested in the same way, by attracting pieces of bran or paper.

TRICK WITH A PING-PONG BALL.

A light ball, such as a celluloid ping-pong ball, can be made to follow an electrified comb. It is best to place the ball on rails. Two blind rods fixed side by side about an inch apart answer the purpose. A ball can easily be induced to run up and down these rails by the invisible electric force.

Electricity can also be obtained by rubbing a hot glass tube or a flint glass tumbler with a piece of silk made into a small pad, and the same experiments can be performed as with the ebonite comb.

Pearson's Magazine 1910

* * *

Can You Do Phonologues ?

An Interesting Competition for Shorthand Writers.

We have coined the word "Phonologue." A Phonologue is an arrangement of shorthand signs in the form of a sketch, the signs being at the same time an accurate rendering in shorthand of the words of a sentence, or a combination of sentences.

We offer a prize of 10s. 6d., or a Swan or Waterman Fountain Pen, each week for the best Phonologue sent in. You stand a better chance if it is original, as we cannot, obviously, give you the prize if someone else sends the same Phonologue as yourself.
Pitman's Shorthand only may be used.

Below we give an example of a Phonologue. It is based on the famous Shakespearean phrase, "A horse! a horse! My Kingdom for a horse!" (*Richard III.*)

* * *

Start at top of nose, and read : "Rarely will Richard's rage be spent on a (old sign for "a ") nag of this kind."
Then go back to same point, and read downwards : This animal neither eats nor drinks.
"Here's his eye."
"And his nose."

Latest 1910

OUR DRAMATIC DIARY.

THE air is full of pantomimes and children's plays, further notices of which will appear next week. There are few novelties to announce in the immediate future. The next production of the Incorporated Stage Society is to be a new three-act play by Norman McKeown, entitled "Travellers."

Jan. 18 is the date fixed for the production of "Billy" at the Vaudeville. The leading parts will be played by Mr James Welch, Miss Audry Ford, and Miss Iris Hoey. "Baby Mine" is to be withdrawn on Jan. 12.

Jan. 15, "Œdipus Rex" at Covent Garden is likely to create as much interest as Professor Reinhardt's other production at Olympia. Mr Martin Harvey and his strong cast are hard at work on rehearsals.

"Kismet" reached its 300th performance on Thursday last. "Fanny's First Play" started at the Kingsway on Monday. "Charley's Aunt" is drawing large audiences to the Whitney Theatre. "The Glad Eye" is also doing well at the Apollo Theatre.

"The Blue Bird," revived at the Queen's, is as delightful a performance as ever. Mylyl and Tyltyl, as played by Dorothy Burgess and Mallie Block, are perfect in their way, as also is Mr Ernest Hendrie as the dog Tylô.

"Eager Hearts" will give a dramatic performance at the Passmore Edwards Settlement Hall, Tavistock-place, W.C., on Jan. 12, at 8.30, when they promise to produce an original comedy with songs by M. Gabrielle Urwick, entitled "The Passing of the

[Daily Mirror Studios.

MR GEO. GRAVES AS KING OF MNEMONICA AT DRURY LANE.

Flappers"; the music will be by Mrs Fredk. Urwick. The entertainment is organised by the Lady Rachel Byng in aid of the "Eager Heart Fund" for Cinderellas (Destitute Children of London).

Queen 1912

ATHLETIC NOTES.

THIS year's athletic season opens at Fenner's on Tuesday next, with the first instalment of the Freshmen's Sports. The second day is Thursday, and the Sports begin each day at 2.30. The entries seem to be larger than usual, and certainly the racing will be both better in quality and in keenness than for some years past. It is impossible to spot the probable winners of any events, except the Weight and the High Jump—the former should go to R. S. Woods (Downing) and the latter to A. C. Straker (Jesus). Among others, J. G. Will, D. G. Davies, and H. M. Macintosh will be prominent in the sprint, with the odds on Davies: the Quarter should go to the first of these three. The Half is very open: C. N. Lowe would win it if he were fit, which he is not: probably under the circumstances F. G. Heap, of King's, will be successful. The Mile again is doubtful, but R. A. Peters looks likely, with strong opposition from E. P. Turner and others; and Turner should win the long distance event, with Bock close up. The Hurdles will be one of the best races, and the finish should be close. J. C. de V. Biss seems to have the best chance in the Long Jump.

The match between Peterhouse and Magdalene also begins next week, and people are busy training for it. With the approach of college matches, the fortnightly membership is increasing rapidly. It is not very long, but a very fair modicum of training can be done in a fortnight—enough to make all the difference.

The Granta 1911

LITTLE TICH AT THE TIVOLI.

MISS VIOLET BLYTH-PRATT

Mr M. V. ESMOND

News of the World 1912

Billiards 1912

JOHN ROBERTS PLAYING.

I do not know much about the firs billiard champion, John Kentfield, o Brighton—not more than I have read. B all accounts he was a deep student of his ar

and a good practitioner. He helped the practical side along in no small degree, as regards both his doings upon the table and the excellent technical hints he gave in improved construction to the pioneer firm of Messrs. Thurston. We owe to Kentfield, I am assured, the billiard slate, thinner cloths, and, above all, perhaps, the resilient rubber cushion. The more one looks into " the Kentfield period," the clearer is his influence on the billiard material since provided to be noticed. He left a great legacy to the game, and endowed it with two superlative strokes in the shape of the " short-jenny " and the "spot-stroke."

TRINITY FOOT BEAGLES.

FRIDAY, OCTOBER 24TH.

The Slow pack met at the Observatory. A weak hare was found in a root-field close to the meet and killed after a hunt of about ten minutes. The University Farm was next drawn, and a hare found; unfortunately she ran into some rabbit-wire and was chopped. Another was shortly found opposite Girton College, and after a circle she ran into some gardens at Girton village, where scent failed. A fourth hare found close by ran up to Mr. Saltmarsh's farm and back to where we found her : she was then hunted slowly to Girton cross roads, where we could do no more. Scent very poor, particularly late on.

The Granta 1913

THE VOGUE IN FUR.—A woman of fashion requires a g deal of fur to complete her toilette. Her hat is either comp of it entirely, or trimmed with it. A leader of fashion just been wearing a toque, the crown ermine bordered skunk, with tall mounts—a couple—in front. Entire ma of black fox are among the novelties, and a costume ermine is by no means a rarity, bordered with black Such mantles entirely envelop the figure, and are cut straight lines, draped on one side. The wide sleeves often of black fur. These *vêtements* cross in front, and caught up on either side, so that the figure seems to s from a most spidery foundation, and to grow out on the hip some bulk. Such a cloak leaves not an atom of the dres view. A collarette of skunk is fastened with a white came and a muff to match completes the effect. Perhaps the ra fur there is is black sable. A very large cape-shaped stole a huge muff, big enough to hide the arms, was worn of at a recent fashionable meeting, and was greatly admi With a black charmeuse dress and a necklace of pearls whole effect was quite delightful. Sable fitch is another co fur. A small cape of this, fastened on one shoulder wit violet chrysanthemum, was decidedly *chic*, the flower repeated the large muff. On many of the cloaks and furs appear the tassels, made of knotted silk, with wooden beads in wonde colouring ; they are mostly very large. The wooden beads ar many colours, some round, some oblong. Intermixed with th are strings of paste or pearls, and silk, and sometimes fringe leather, metallic threads, and crystal balls. They are o half a yard in length, and some are attached to the end a sash swathed to the figure. They are decorative, exceedingly costly.

Queen 1914

Daily Sketch 1914

THE BOMBARDIER TO "WIN OR QUIT."

He's never felt fitter.

Daily Herald 1912

ASCOT SCANDAL

Lady Who Trafficked in Tickets for the Royal Enclosure.

A mysterious lady was the defendant in a curious case in which Viscount Churchill asked for an injunction to prevent the trafficking in badges for admission to the Royal enclosure at Ascot.

Counsel for plaintiff explained that the badge was also not transferable and had to be worn on the course.

The defendant, he said, was a lady in London, and it had come to the knowledge of the authorities that in May and June two tickets had been sold and the badges transferred.

Lady Detective Investigates.

On Thursday a lady detective was employed to investigate the matter. She went to the defendant and was referred by her to another lady. This second lady on Wednesday telegraphed and wrote to Viscount Churchill asking for the return of a voucher which had been sent back to him on the ground that it would not be required. The two motored to Ascot and there received a voucher, which was exchanged at the office for the badge, which the lady detective wore in the enclosure on Thursday.

The injunction was granted.

"PARSIFAL" AT COVENT GARDEN.

"Parsifal" has come to Covent Garden. The question which a great many people were asking—very prematurely, it would seem—is whether, in the common phrase, it has come to stay. Of course, answers will differ very widely, but it is a curious fact, and one which is almost equivalent to an answer, that the same question is being eagerly asked in all the places where "Parsifal" has been heard in the last few weeks.

To-day our concern, however, is with last night's performance rather than with speculations as to the future.

Take it all in all, Covent Garden may look back on it with justifiable pride. Let me say at once that there were two hitches: the moving scene, having behaved very well in the first act, grew recalcitrant in the third, and caused a stoppage; and in the last scene at one place the chorus got out of hand. Of course, these things are not as important as some people will pretend (though regrettable enough), but if one does not mention them one will be accused of not having noticed them. Apart from these, though, we had a splendid frame for the great pictures which Wagner has drawn. The Temple of the Grail is beautiful in design and colour, and gives the right impression of vastness and mystery. The scene of the Flowery Mead appeals to the imagination in the right way, except that the flowers are a little too obtrusive. In Klingsor's Magic Garden Mr. Harker might, I think, have left a little more to our imagination, and the austerity of the Castle itself seemed a little out of place. I thought that both the scenes in the Temple and the opening scene would have been better for more light. Semi-darkness is not necessarily poetical. The moving scenery is as well done as is possible, but a little more of awe and mystery might be imported into it by means of lighting. It hardly seems likely that it could be done better as long as the attempt is made to follow the letter of the stage directions of Wagner; but there are other ways in which the right effect could be achieved, and I cordially agree with those who suggest that it should be done in much the same way as Siegfried's journey to the Rhine is done in "Götterdämmerung." The music makes a far greater effect if the eye is not distracted by the moving panorama. The music is, after all, the thing, but many people talk as if everything mattered more than the music or the way in which it is played or sung.

Star 1914

Daily Sketch 1914

HER FIRST BIG PART.

Although Miss Hermione Gingold is only sixteen and has just been given her first "grown-up" part—that of Jessica in Philip Carr's production of "The Merchant of Venice"—she has had considerable stage experience. She appeared at His Majesty's in "Pinkie and the Fairies" when she was eleven, and she has played in Shakespearean Festivals both in London and at Stratford-on-Avon.

For the last two years she has studied with Miss Rosina Filippi, who thinks a great deal of her capabilities.

PAID TO DRIVE AUDIENCES AWAY.

How Really Bad Performers Can Earn High Salaries.

"CHASERS."

If you are a music-hall artist and your "turn" is really very, very bad—so bad, in fact, that managers will not give you an engagement, even as an "extra"—do not despair.

There is a lucrative livelihood awaiting you, an absolutely up-to-date profession born of the latest form of public entertainment—the continuous show.

And the secret of the new profession is that you are not required to entertain people, but to drive them away!

Ever since American theatrical and "vaudeville" managers started the continuous shows which have become so popular in this country, those managers have been faced with a very difficult problem.

That problem is not how to get patrons into those continuous shows, but how to get them out!

For large numbers of those patrons, having paid a certain sum (often a small sum) for admission, refuse to leave when they have seen the "round" of the show.

In fact, women bring their knitting or their novels, and even the men bring their meals and, indeed, adopt all sorts of devices so as to stay and get all the entertainment they can for their outlay.

HIGH SALARIES.

At last certain managers began to adopt a scheme which is now general throughout America and is being arranged for England, especially in the provinces.

They engage certain actors, actresses, reciters, knockabouts and cross-talkers, and at a given time they send them on the stage. The effect always proves magical. The hitherto loitering audience simply melts away.

Now, many American managers, visiting England year by year, spend part of their time in going around our theatres and halls to select "Chasers," as these bad performers are called, and many an alleged comedian, comic singer, "serio," and so forth has gone to America and received high salaries.

Of late several English managers, especially those controlling a certain class of cheap provincial music-halls, have found it useful to go to America or around these islands in order to find the best-worst "Chasers."

AUDIENCES FLEE IN THOUSANDS.

"There was a pretty little English serio-soubrette who came over to New York some time ago," a well-known American manager told The Daily Mirror. "She was really clever, but through being too local and so on, her songs did not 'get over,' as we say.

"In one way and another I saw that she was worth money as a 'chaser.' She was heartbroken by her really shocking failure and resolved to start back to England on her own account.

"I got introduced to her, tried to persuade her to stop, got her to stay a few days at her hotel to think it over.

"But, no, sir! She was obdurate. She would not consent to stay longer than the time for the next boat after the one I had made her miss.

"At last, determined not to lose such a top-line 'chaser' as that, I did a desperate thing. I married her!

"And, sir, my wife is one of my most profitable vaudeville assets. The audiences flee in thousands when she starts!"

Another striking instance of the value placed on really powerful "Chasers" is provided by the experience of two English cross-talkers and step-dancers, who, after they had made a disastrous debut in New York, at £16 a week, were engaged as "Chasers" for a lengthened term at £60 a week, with promise of a periodical increase!

Daily Mirror 1913

Musical Opinion 1913

A CUTTING taken from *The Daily Mail* gives an amusing chat with Igor Stravinsky, the composer of some extraordinary ballet music now being played at Covent Garden. He finds little to interest him in the music of the past. Bach is too remote and Beethoven too thoughtful, though he handsomely admits that there is something pleasing in Schubert and Mozart. He dislikes opera and considers that Wagner sounds best in the concert room. Russian musical life he declares to be stagnant and naively adds: "They cannot stand me there." The Viennese, he holds, are barbarians,—apparently because the orchestras there could not play his "Petrouchka" and also because they hardly know Debussy and chased Schönberg away to Berlin. Now Schönberg, says Stravinsky, is one of the greatest creative spirits of our era. He finds his only kindred spirits in France, which in Debussy, Ravel and Florent Schmitt, possesses the foremost creative musicians of the day. These three with Schönberg make four of the greatest creative, &c. As they are his only kindred spirits, Stravinsky makes the fifth, which completes the tale, though he is modest enough not to say so. His new ballet, he goes on to tell us, has no plot. I can already hear in advance some of the audience declaring that it also has no music. If it has not, it will not be for want of material; for, says the young composer, the score includes five trumpets, eight horns and all the woodwind in families of five, and a hundred and twenty-five rehearsals will be required before it can be produced.

A perusal of this somewhat hysterical interview leaves one with the feeling that Stravinsky does not suffer from the fault that he finds in Beethoven who, by the way, like Schubert and Mozart, managed to write some tolerable music employing only two trumpets and a couple of brace of horns, and called for no happy families of five in the woodwind department. It is a pity that these clever young composers cannot write without demanding abnormal resources. Greatness in music depends upon ideas, not upon the size of the band or the dimensions of the full score; and time has a way of relentlessly proving this, among other things. That is why some gigantic scores produced during the last fifty years are already beginning to collect the dust, while works by the old composers who are too "remote" or "full of thought" for our Stravinskys are still in constant demand; not, be it noted, because they are old or because they are scored for a small band, but in spite of those facts, and because their composers had something to say and knew how to say it. There is never room on the shelf for the works of such men.

REPLY TO TANGO BOYCOTT.

Peeress Critics Have Not Seen It Danced Properly.

To demonstrate that the tango is *not* immodest, as many of the peeresses and other leading hostesses have declared in placing a boycott upon it, the Queen's Theatre management are inviting society leaders and others to a special tango matinée on Monday. Every person in the theatre is to be asked to vote "Yes" or "No" to the question "Is the tango immodest?"

Miss Clayton, who tangoes at the Savoy Hotel every night with her partner "Marquis," replies to the peeresses in a *Daily Sketch* interview:—

"The criticisms appear to be from people who have never seen the tango danced as it is taught by the best teachers, or they are the descendants of those who, when the polka was first introduced, attacked that dance as a vulgar and indelicate one.

"Any dance can be made vulgar. The tango is the *one* dance which is nearer to the old English gavotte and minuet. It is so graceful that it is leading people's thoughts in that direction rather than to the excitable and boisterous dance of the ragtime type."

From her own friends and pupils Miss Clayton hears exactly the opposite to what others say of the tango.

Daily Sketch 1914

TENNIS AND CROQUET TOURNAMENTS
CANCELLED.

COUNTY CRICKET is now practically the only game that is carrying out its fixture list. In the week before last the usual summer tournaments in other games were very little interrupted. The war had come so suddenly that there was hardly time to cancel engagements for that week, and they were therefore held to, although interest in them was inevitably rather small. Last week the case was quite different. The lawn tennis tournaments, of which the principal ones were those at Buxton, Felixstowe, Folkestone, and Scarborough, have mostly been abandoned. It is still uncertain what will be the case with the September tournaments, but it is hardly probable that many of them will be held. The foreign ones which usually attract interest, like those at Le Touquet, Thun, Les Avants, Territet, and Montreux, must certainly go by the board; and if a few seaside fixtures are carried out it will only be in the hope of helping the holiday season not to fail entirely at these places.

The same is the case with croquet. Already the various committees have announced the abandonment of the tournaments at Roehampton, Coventry, Tavistock, and the Monmouthshire Tournament, which were due this week; the tournaments at Horsham, Leamington, and Torquay for next week; those at Hunstanton and Paignton in the week beginning Aug. 31; and those at Northampton (Sept. 7) and Portsmouth (Sept. 14).

Queen 1914

DRINK AND MARKMANSHIP.

EFFECT OF ALCOHOL AND HUNGER.

Details of shooting experiments carried out by men both before and after taking alcohol are supplied by the True Temperance Association. The tests were made on miniature rifle ranges.

In each instance twelve shots were fired, on the first day under normal conditions of health and habits, before taking any alcohol, immediately after drinking a measured quantity, and in half an hour later.

On the second day the same number of shots were fired while the men were tired and hungry, first without alcohol, then after drinking a quantity, and again half an hour later. Altogether 31 results are tabulated.

"B.W." scored 69 on the first day, without drink. Then having consumed four pints of ale and a bottle of Guinness's stout, he scored 93, and half an hour later 82. When tired and hungry his score before a drink was 71; after four pints of ale and a stout it was 79, and thirty minutes later 94.

Without drink "G.R." scored 117. Having drunk six-pennyworth of Scotch whisky his score was 119, and half an hour later 120. When hungry and tired and without drink he scored 112, and after a similar amount of whisky 116, repeating the score half an hour afterwards.

In the case of "E.P." the score without alcohol was 63, after taking a moderate dose of brandy and water it was 61, and 82 half an hour later. Hungry and weary, he scored 77 without drink, and on brandy and water 83, the final score half an hour later being 87.

Vine and Spirit Gazette 1915

The crack Irish stallion, King Hummer, the greatest son of George Hummer, is to serve a few mares at Audenshaw before going back to Ireland. The pacer is with Jack Skinner, with whom arrangements must be made. The fee is five guineas, with five shillings stud fee, all to be paid at time of service. This is a capital opportunity for north country owners to get the use of this great stallion.

* * * * *

Trotting World 1916

BRINGING DOWN THE HOUSE.

MISS VESTA VICTORIA, of "Daddy wouldn't buy me a bow-wow" fame, helps to demolish the old Tivoli, where she achieved some of her greatest successes. (Photo Clarke.)

THE DUKE OF WELLINGTON'S HEIGHT.

[TO THE EDITOR OF THE "SPECTATOR."]

SIR,—As a boy I lived with an officer who had been through the Peninsular War and also at Waterloo under the Duke of Wellington. He said if you met the Duke walking he was a little man, but the Duke on horseback was a big man. In other words, he had a long body and short legs, just as some men have short bodies and long legs, and are tall when walking and comparatively small when sitting. There is a well-known picture of the Duke and Sir Robert Peel standing side by side, in which Peel appears tall and the Duke beside him small.—I am, Sir, &c.,
P. W. C.

The Spectator 1915

"NEVER PUT OFF TILL TO-MORROW——"
Some time ago, after many hours of perseverance and deep thought, I solved a very difficult problem set in a certain competition. I felt very proud of my abilities, and although I had finished it and prepared the same ready for despatch some days previous, I had decided not to post it until the closing date. Unfortunately, pressure of business detained me from home on the very evening it should have been sent. The next day was too late, and my labour of love had been wasted. The correct solution, which was identical with mine, was duly published. Imagine my chagrin when I found not a single competitor had forwarded the absolute correct answer. I had lost a most valuable prize.—Miss Ethel Hardy, 66, King Edward Road, Coventry. (5s.)

Home Companion 1916

BRITISH PIANOFORTE INDUSTRY

THE days when German street musicians contributed to the melancholy of our thoroughfares are fortunately gone, and it is to be hoped that the fashion of purchasing German-made pianos will depart also, although, with the restrictions of the Government in regard to the importation of component parts, British manufacturers are not altogether sanguine on this point.

Time was when we were infatuated by German musical products, and a music teacher from the " Fatherland " was frequently followed by a piano from the same source, notwithstanding that the British manufacturer was able to produce instruments which cannot be surpassed by Germany, or any other country in the world. The German has scorned the idea that we are musical. Perhaps that was because we purchased mouth organs from him to the extent of £32,900 annually. Nevertheless, in 1912 Germany exported to this country pianos and piano parts of the value of over £600,000, while within the British Empire as a whole, she did an immense business, Australia being her best customer outside of Great Britain. Germany sent to the Commonwealth pianos and parts to the amount of £383,500.

The total value of German and Austrian exports of musical instruments and parts thereof to the United Kingdom in 1912 was £748,200. Therefore, had we the capacity, there is trade to be captured in musical lines within the Empire, and in the countries of our Allies.

British Manufacturer
1916

Nottingham Evening Post 1917

DIVED INTO CANAL.

NOTTINGHAM YOUTH'S DESPERATE EXPEDIENT.

There was an element of humour in an incident, which occurred on Saturday during a round-up of youthful Nottingham gamblers by the local police. Ten youths, including Arthur Gregory, of Red Lion-street, and Albert Hopkins, of an Aberdeen-street lodging-house, both labourers, were playing pitch and toss under the canal bridge, London-road. The advent of Sergeant Grevatt and P.c. Salisbury, caused consternation among them, and Hopkins, in his eagerness to avoid capture, dived into the canal, fully clothed though he was. For about ten minutes he defied the police, swimming about and refusing to come out of the water but finally gave himself up.

At the Nottingham Police-court to-day the youths named were fined 5s.

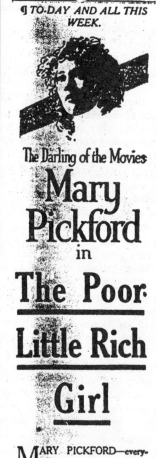

¶ TO-DAY AND ALL THIS WEEK.

The Darling of the Movies

Mary Pickford in The Poor Little Rich Girl

MARY PICKFORD—everybody's sweetheart—in a graphic and soul-stirring dramatic story of a rich child who finds real happiness amidst the most poverty-stricken surroundings.

ORCHESTRAL MUSIC. Varied Programme. Comedy. Interest and Current Event Items. Luxurious comfort, a well-ventilated Theatre, and everything that can be done to add to the enjoyment of patrons.

The Picture House

LONG ROW, NOTTINGHAM.

" THE DAILY NEWS & LEADER "

Football Annual

NOW READY.

1d. everywhere.

London Signal
1916

The Great Adventure.

The other day my younger son and I ran away. The daring idea was his, not mine. Everyone in the house had been on pilgrimage with me, he never. It was to be strictly a voyage à deux. Mild hints that it might be accompanied by other members of the family were tactfully but firmly rejected. This was a purely masculine enterprise. We were to wander where we would, have lunch out, and get back when we felt inclined.

We tried it first—I say we, but the younger adventurer's share was a passive one; he looked the part, that was all—with the pert and bustling lady in the X.Y.Z. shop where we had lunch. We explained elaborately to her that we had slipped away from the hands of detaining authority, and that we wanted to eat all the things we were not allowed to have at home, the things we were always told were not good for growing boys. How would she advise us to deal with the menu? Which were the really dangerous and deadly dishes upon it? We smiled, as though to take her into our conspiracy; and she smiled, the regulation X.Y.Z. smile, but she did not understand a bit. She was a giddy, frivolous young miss, who probably thought it was a great thing to be grown up, and did not know that the glory of life is to be young and to keep young even when time is trying to make you old. And we saw her giggling afterwards with the other waiteresses in a way that showed she thought we were rather silly. I fear she had forgotten how to make-believe, and knew nothing about the spirit of adventure.

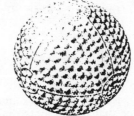
Believes in Children Seeing Plays

A thorough believer in the importance of children seeing good plays, Miss Horniman is severe in her condemnation of the grown-ups who scant the trouble of seeking a suitable play for their children. She tells me of some unfortunate dozen or so of children who were taken by their astounding parents to see Ibsen's "The Dolls' House."

Could anything be more indicative of ignorance and carelessness?

She believes equally as much in the wisdom of allowing children to act, and for the unbelievers Miss Horniman suggested this remedy: "Just let them have an office under the dressing-room of a dozen children, and listen to their dancing, singing and laughter after giving two performances. They would have little reason to complain either of their health or spirits."

Dame Tatler

Mother and Home 1916

Stamp Collectors' Fortnightly 1918

The Finding of the "OFFICIAL" Error.
By H. A. KING.

This unique stamp was found in May, 1917. The owner, a friend of mine, while home on leave from his military duties, was looking through a number of envelopes bearing Official stamps, which he had obtained many years previously through an acquaintance in London.

Of the stamps, 75 per cent. were "Army Official", the others "I.R. Official".

Unfortunately, my friend tore the stamp off, before noticing the error: he told me of it at once, but I could hardly credit him until I had seen the stamp, as it had been

twelve months in my care, without being noticed.

Many collectors doubted its genuineness, until they saw it.

The present owner of the stamp acquired it during the current year.

In my opinion, the overprint should be "ARMY OFFICIAL", and many theories have been advanced to account for the omission of the first word.

So far as I have been able to learn, the copy is absolutely *unique*.

05565. "*Le Carillon de Cythère*" (*Chimes of Cythera*). *Paderewski. Couperin.*
12-inch Record, 12s. 6d.

One of Couperin's gems with chime imitations, old-fashioned embellishments of trill, shake, etc., beautifully rendered by the magic of Paderewski. This disc represents a perfect example of the exact manner in which this type of old-world composition should be played. Every note and shade of expression has been caught by the recording machine with an effect that is enthralling. The personality of Paderewski has never shone more brightly than at the present time in the passionate endeavour he is making in England in the direction of mitigating the terrible sufferings and agony of his co-patriots in Poland, a trait of character of which a noble reflection is found in all phases of his art and life-work.

2-3107. "*Old Folks at Home*" (*Swanee River*). (*With Dvořák's "Humoreske," as violin obbligato.*) *Gluck and Zimbalist.*

Pianomaker 1915

Truth on Ladies' Golf.

If you want to get a line as to the superiority of ladies' golf over that of the mere male you have only to take the two rounds qualifying scores at St. Annes for the first thirty-two places in the English Championship. First came Miss Cecil Leitch 84, then a 91, 92, two 95's, six 99's, and the rest wandered up to 108. Goodness only knows what the other scores must have been like. Well, Miss Leitch simply jazzed home in the final against Mrs. Dobell, a round and a half (10 up and 8 to play) sufficed, and there you are. It is inconceivable that under such circumstances thirty-two scratch male players would have returned such duffing scores. But I wish to goodness ladies would run the men's Open and Amateur Championships. The success of their meeting, the numbers of players and spectators, all showed that only forethought and energy were required to have carried through the competitions for the males. The ladies may not be proud of their scores, but they may be proud of their initiative. It is nothing else than scandalous laziness that has been the cause of nothing being done for the men. The professionals should have held the pistol at the head of Dilly and Dally, and they would have surrendered at discretion.

The Lady Golfer 1919

┌─────────────────┐
│   FIXTURES   │
│   AT   │
│   OLYMPIA.   │
└─────────────────┘

Traveller's Gazette 1919

THE International Horse Show, which has been suspended during the war, will open at Olympia on Monday, June 9, and close on Saturday, June 14. The Secretary of the War Office has announced that the Royal Naval, Military and Air Force Tournament will now be held from June 26 to July 12, instead of May 15–31, as originally arranged. Londoners will rejoice to see once more the famous musical ride of the Household Cavalry, the musical drive of the Chestnut Battery, the demonstrations of the Army Service Corps and other items of a programme which year after year drew crowded houses—the attendance in the spring of 1914 constituted a record—and contributed so materially to the Service charities.

THE BLUE GUIDE TO LONDON

"Half-crowns and florins are sometimes confounded, and it is just as well to say 'half-crown' in tendering that coin for payment."

"Careful people make a habit of jotting down the numbers of bank-notes, as this may conceivably help their recovery in case of loss or theft."

"The streets of London are scantily lighted after nightfall, and the stranger is strongly recommended to provide himself with an electric torch."

On the risks of colds in London the editor speaks with wisdom and prudence. "Chilly weather is by no means unknown even in summer. . . . Waterproofs and umbrellas are indispensable." Strangers accustomed to warmer houses than those of England must be on their guard against illness.

The climate of London is not much safer than that of Madrid, where no traveller dare sally forth after sundown without his greatcoat.

A mass of information is given with regard to hotels, boarding-houses, shops, amusements, luncheon and tea rooms, the postal service, tourist offices, picture galleries and museums. The tourist is advised to allot not less than three weeks to his itinerary. Two pages are occupied with details about church services, and it is a mark of the up-to-date character of the work that Dr. Jowett is mentioned as the minister of Westminster Chapel. The leading Baptist, Congregational and Presbyterian churches are named, though not in order of pre-eminence. St. John's Wood Church should have been mentioned under the last of these headings. I am not sure that "Marylebone Chapel, Seymour-place," should be put first among Primitive Methodist centres. There is no reference, I think, to St. George's Hall, Old Kent-road. Is there a touch of humour, perhaps, in the editor's reference to a secularised Sunday? Strangers who do not care to attend any of his long list of churches "may pay a morning visit to the animated Jews' market in and about Middlesex-street (beware of pickpockets!)."

LAMBERT & BUTLER'S
WAVERLEY
Straight Cut Virginia
CIGARETTES

Your friends judge you by the cigarettes you offer them. Give them Waverley Cigarettes to smoke and you cannot fail to be regarded as a man of discriminating taste.

10 FOR **5½**D.
20 FOR **11**D.

The Imperial Tobacco Co. (of Great Britain and Ireland). Ltd.
W 148

Cornish Guardian 1919

THE RACECOURSE PLUNGER.

Most people are wondering says a gossip writer in the "Sunday Express," how long the Earl of Wilton will last on the Turf. He who sups with the devil needs a long spoon, and the young man with little experience of racing who battles with the bookmakers needs a longer purse. Lord Wilton, they say, is the biggest Turf plunger since that unfortunate Marquis of Hastings of whose exploits Lord Chaplin may tell us something new in that interesting book they say he is preparing.

There are not so many gay young gamblers nowadays. Half a dozen years ago Mr. James de Rothschild used to adventure large sums—did he not lay £10,000 to £1,000 on Snow Leopard at Epsom and lose his money?—but marriage and the war—he had seen a good deal of service in Paris and elsewhere—have tempered his enthusiasm, and he has lost his old inseparable friends, Neil Primrose and "Tommy" Robartes—both killed in action.

THE KAISER'S EFFIGY.

After the concert the crowd thronged the streets, and made merry to their heart's content. As is became dark, the streets were illuminated, and riots of fireworks burst forth in all directions. Early in the evening the proceedings were further enlivened by a procession headed by young Davey, Hitchins, Merrifield and Smale bearing an effigy of the Kaiser holding aloft the white flag on which was emblazoned: "Kamerad!" Followed by a great crowd they bore the "Kaiser" to the Recreation Ground, where his paraffin saturated "corpse" was ignited and consumed by the flames to the evident satisfaction of the onlookers. The air balloons sent up by Mr. Spalding, the manager of the Picture Theatre, during the day and in the evening added to the variety of the day's entertainment.

STREET MERRYMAKING.

Then the crowd gave themselves over to merrymaking in the streets, which presented an animated scene until a late hour. The Stenalees Band added to the liveliness by playing the Flora backwards and forwards with young people dancing and jumping in their wake. At 10.30, the Stenalees Band, who under Bandmaster Lennon, had served the committee well right through the day, finished by playing the National Anthem, but it was not for an hour or so after that that the crowds finally dispersed after a memorable day's festivities.

NO HITCH.

The day's programme was carried through without a hitch, which, considering the magnitude of the task, especially on the catering side, reflected great credit upon the committee, who were excellently organized by the Chairman, Mr. N. F. Bellamy; the general hon. secretaries, Messrs. Vowles and Dobell, upon whom the brunt of the work fell; Mr. S. Chapman, who rendered splendid service as tea secretary; and Mr. A. E. Gaved, hon. treasurer.

Cornish Guardian 1919

FREE
Pattern!

VERY little material. . . . VERY easy to make. . . . VERY nice when you've made it. It LOOKS nice, and you can walk about in it COMFORTABLY.

Given away with this week's "Home Chat," 1½d.

If your newsagent has sold out, ask him to order a copy for you.

"Home Chat."

On Sale Everywhere. 1½d.

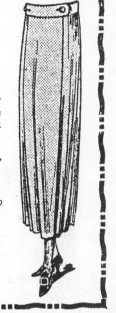

THE LETTING OF GROUSE MOORS.

Food Controller's Important Notice to Sportsmen.

The Food Controller is informed that the letting of grouse moors and shooting properties is being prejudiced at the moment by uncertainty as to the probable supply of cartridges. Lord Rhondda, therefore, desires to state that the Minister of Munitions has placed at his disposal a certain amount of lead specially to be used for shooting game, and it is hoped that the supply so authorised will suffice for providing this valuable supply of food. The necessary forms of application for cartridges under this scheme will be ready at an early date, and due notice will be given.

The Food Controller is further advised that a considerable quantity of .22 ammunition will be available through the ordinary trade sources in time for rook shooting, and he hopes owners of rookeries will so far as possible use this ammunition for rook shooting, in order to conserve ordinary shot cartridges for other purposes.

Belfast Weekly News 1918

Tavistock Gazette 1919

PEARLS IN THE THAMES.

While playing on the beach at Allhallows, at the mouth of the Thames, a little boy picked up a large mussel, from which his father extracted four pearls. Two are black and perfectly spherical, and two white. All four are very small, the largest being about the size of the head of a large pin.

There are heaps of pretty pictures like this in the "Children's Fairy."

Buy
YOUR Children

the CHILDREN'S FAIRY. See how they will linger over every page of COLOURED pictures, and every jolly story in this fascinating weekly paper which they love so much. This week there is a Working Toy Model of the Fairy Cinema Given Free with every copy. Ask for

THE
CHILDREN'S
FAIRY

Out on Thursday.

The New Fourpennies.

I can very thoroughly recommend the new numbers of the "GIRLS' FRIEND" 4d. LIBRARY, which are now on sale at all newsagents':

"Her Lord and Master!" (No. 311).
"Billy the Orphan!" (No. 312).
"Postman's Knock!" (No. 313).
"She Wouldn't be a Servant!" (No. 314).

Each has a plain but tasteful pink cover.

OXFORD PAGEANT, 1919.

A PAGEANT lasting over a week will be held at Oxford this summer, beginning on 26th of this month. The Duke of Marlborough is chairman of the executive committee, and the Prince of Wales, the Earl of Jersey and Viscount Valentia are among the patrons. The pageant will illustrate numerous episodes in English history, and Mr. Ben Greet has undertaken to fill the post of stage-manager. Mr. Martin Harvey is to sustain the part of St. George.

Traveller's Gazette 1919

THE ANCIENT GAME OF HURLING.

[TO THE EDITOR.]

Sir,—Partial as we are to games in which a ball of some kind is used, it is singular that one of the most ancient games, the Cornish game of hurling, is so seldom played outside the Western county.

The game is followed without difficulty, no great outlay is required, and few games are more interesting to players and spectators.

J. W. TICKEL.
18, Victoria Street, Plymouth.

Cornish Guardian 1919

1920–1929

F.A. CUP FINAL.

Aston Villa Victorious for the Sixth Time.

Huddersfield Present the Only Goal.

By WANDERER

The Sportsman
1920

Aston Villa F.C. on Saturday enjoyed the satisfaction of establishing a new record, as at Stamford Bridge they became the holders of the Football Association Challenge Cup for the sixth time. Strictly speaking they have, as the outcome of those successes, held the three different trophies that have been associated with the competition. In 1886-7 they were the first to take in the Midlands the original trophy won outright by the Wanderers in 1877-78, and returned by that famous club of the infant days of Soccer, and it was when again in their custody after the season of 1894-5, their only failure in the Final intervening three years earlier, that the Cup was stolen from a tradesman's window in Birmingham whilst on exhibition there. In 1896-7, after one of the finest struggles of the series, now numbering forty-five in all, they became holders of the replica by victory over Everton by the odd goal in five, and again triumphed at the expense of Newcastle United in 1904-5. Later, when the copying of the design was resented and a third trophy provided, the old Cup being presented to Lord Kinnaird to celebrate his twenty-one years as President of the Association, they became the holders in 1912-13 by lowering the colours of Sunderland, and now they have achieved yet a further victory by disposing of Huddersfield Town. It is a record that eclipses the five wins to the credit of both the Wanderers and Blackburn Rovers, though each of these clubs secured the Cup three seasons in succession, of which they may deservedly feel proud.

In tackling Huddersfield Town they were up against a very stiff proposition, and my prophecy in Saturday's SPORTSMAN of a strenuous game and a narrow margin for the Midlanders was accurately borne out. Under the rules in force until shortly before the war the clubs would have had to meet again at Old Trafford next Wednesday, as at the expiration of the regulation ninety minutes neither team had scored, although there had been hair-breadth escapes and missed chances galore. The fact of a replay being necessary three successive Aprils led to the stipulation by the F.C. Council, in whom the power of altering the Cup rules is vested, that an extra half-hour must be played, and it was some seven or eight minutes after the entry on this additional period that the only goal of the game was registered, enabling the presentation ceremony to be duly performed by Prince Henry. The manner in which it was obtained was somewhat galling to the Yorkshire team, for the ball, following a corner-kick, was deflected into the net by their own centre-half. We members of the Fourth Estate located towards the back of the Grand Stand were almost unanimous in the opinion that it had been shouldered through by the Villa inside-right, Kirton, though I noticed that Bullock appeared to be condoling with Wilson after the ball had been netted. Enquiries of the losers at the close of the game elicited the true fact, which they took philosophically, but the victors' own officials were in the dark at first, and clarification was only forthcoming after enquiries had been set on foot. The two rival players were close together, and the mistake was a most reasonable one.

Dame Melba's Visit.

The great event of the week was the visit to the Opera House, on Sunday, of the famous prima donna, Dame Nellie Melba. Her artistry was superb, and only in the slightest degree was there a difference in the richness of her tone, a slight huskiness suggesting itself in the deeper sustained notes, but the purity and sweetness of tone were as of old, with all their magic power. Her personality as an artiste had all its potency and bewitchment upon her charmed hearers. The diva wore a modish robe of ceil blue panne velvet, draped to a tablier point at the hem in front over the underskirt of charmeuse worn short to the ankles.

Blackpool Gazette 1920

Pearson's Magazine
1921

" And how about young men ?"

" Ah, there you touch on a difficulty. I am afraid we shall be dependent for a long time, in England, on foreign male dancers. The normal temperament of the Englishman does not seem to take kindly to ballet dancing."

" Can you wonder—so long as tradition decrees that the male dancer, at all events in ' classical ' ballet, shall wear a long wig and a boy's tunic and float sighfully about like an indeterminate neuter ? At the best he is a figure of fun, at the worst a picture of effeminacy !"

" I entirely agree with you. But there's no reason why an English ballet should be obliged to adopt so un-English a convention. It isn't a necessary one."

" And you think that when it does come it will have a great future before it ?"

" I am sure of it. It's a case of the Sleeping Beauty, only awaiting the right managerial kiss to come to life. The English are a jolly people—the stupid old notion to the contrary has been exploded at last— and if the present popularity of dancing means anything, it is that English people are finding out the way to give expression to their jollity . . ."

" Apropos of that, Miss Bedells, I wish you would tell me what you think of modern ball-room dancing."

" Personally, I love the modern dances. They require a considerable amount of skill to be done well, of course, and syncopation being the basis of all of them, I'm not surprised that people with a defective sense of rhythm find them difficult. But what a relief from the monotonous ' one, two, three, one, two, three,' of the old-fashioned waltz !"

This photo, taken fourteen years ago, obtained for little Phyllis her first engagement at the London Empire.

The Oxford and Cambridge Boat Race, 1921. Cambridge won.

The Cup Final, 1921. Tottenham Hotspur's Bliss takes an extraordinary overhead shot at the Wolverhampton goal.

SCOUT CHARTS

These Charts are approved by The Chief Scout, Sir Robert Baden-Powell, Bt.

Here is a complete list:

1 How to be Healthy
2 Wrist and Arm Exercises
3 Leg and Trunk Exercises
4 Abdomen and Leg Exercises
5 Dumb-Bell Exercises
6 Indian Club Exercises
7 Ju-Jitsu
8 Rescue from Fire
9 Rescue from Drowning
10 How to Act in Emergencies
11 How to prevent Consumption
12 Quarter-Staff Play
13 Knots, Hitches, and Bends
14 Morse Signalling Code
15 Semaphore Signalling Code
16 Simple Bandaging
17 Sick Nursing
18 Swimming
19 Figure Carving
20 Boxing
21 Stencils and Stencilling
22 Hammock Making and Netting
23 Bugle Calls
24 The Scout's Staff and its Uses
25 Fretwork
26 Camp Cookery
27 How to make a Model Aeroplane
28 Badges of Rank in the Army
29 Badges of Rank in the Navy
30 Club Room Hints
31 Tentmaking
32 Camping Hints

PRICE 3d. EACH. (Postage 1d. extra.)

Three for 11d. (post free). Six for 1s. 8d. (post free). Complete set of 32, 8s. 3d. (post free).

From the Editor of "THE SCOUT," 28 Maiden Lane, London, W.C. 2.

Scout 1921

For the first time in his long and successful career Mr. A. J. Fright, a member of the Ramsgate H.S., is offering for sale stock from a very choice collection of stock birds, the parents of which he purchased from Mr. E. G. Rigby, who, it will be remembered, won the Great Northern Marennes Race in 1910 with his good hen, " Miss Bouchier." With such antecedents as the famous bird mentioned in Mr. Fright's advert., it is no cause for wonder that he has had more than his share of prizes racing in the H.P. National, N.F.C. and Ramsgate H.S. Situated as his loft is out on the East Coast, his winnings are all the more creditable. Mr. Fright offers for sale squeakers from a stud of well-bred stock birds at prices from £1 each, and no fancier in want of reliable stock need hesitate to purchase at such nominal prices.

Homing Pigeon 1921

HOW SUZANNE WON.

"Veritably Queen of the Game."

It was worth it all, the long wait, the hours of standing, the aggravation of the rain, all the discomfort.

Lenglen, in a flame-coloured bandeau, gave the most magnificent exposition of ladies' lawn tennis that the world has ever seen. Such anticipation, such perfectly executed strokes, such control of the ball and command of the court!

She proved herself veritably a Queen of the game.

Suzanne took the first game to love on her service, and Molla also acquired one. At 3–1 the champion conceded another, after which she was right away to the end of the match, taking all nine games in succession. The scores were 6–2, 6–0, and they represented the game well.

The American fought every inch of the way, but neither she nor any other woman is in the same class with Lenglen. The victory was entirely conclusive.

Kissing the Champion.

When it was over and the shouting from the stand had subsided, Suzanne was seized in the dressing-room corridor by a crowd of French enthusiasts. She was embraced and kissed.

Mère Lenglen loudly exclaimed concerning the wonderful match. Père Lenglen permitted a jubilant kiss.

The *Illustrated Sunday Herald* asked Lenglen if she was satisfied.

" Perfectly," she said. " I have reserved myself all the way through in order to play my very best in this match, my hardest. Yes, I am satisfied."

Mrs. Mallory was not so satisfied. " Your length was at fault," said an admiring supporter.

" I am not satisfied," she said. " Do I want to play her again? You bet. She (Suzanne) said to me after the match, ' Now you see that I was ill when I played you in America.' I said, ' You have done to me here what I did to you in America.' "

Illustrated Sunday Herald 1922

Your Summer Clothes

Your summer clothes soon soil and crumple. They can be quickly restored to their newness by sending them to Clark's Dye Works, Retford. If *prepaid* they will be returned cleaned and pressed in 56 hours, postage paid.

CHARGES FOR CLEANING.

Summer Dress	6/6	Flannel Trousers	1/6
Skirt (including repleating)	3/9	Flannel Sports Coats	3/9
Jumpers	3/-	Suits	6/6

CLARK'S·DYE·WORKS,
RETFORD.

Lenglen at Wimbledon

1922

CHARLIE'S GUESTS.

They Find He Went to Bed at 7 a.m.

Fifty boys and girls from Hoxton paid a visit to the Ritz Hotel yesterday to present Charlie Chaplin with small gifts " in appreciation of the joy and laughter you have brought into our lives."

Arriving at the Ritz at noon they found that Charlie was fast asleep. He retired at 7 a.m. Eventually Charlie was called and, hurriedly dressing, received the party in his sitting-room.

After accepting a box of cigars from the boys and a bouquet from the girls, Charlie handed each child a packet of candy, gave an exhibition of " What an old man looks like when visiting a picture gallery," and spoke many happy words to the children.

At New York yesterday Judge Hough granted Charlie Chaplin a temporary injunction to restrain the Rollo Corporation from distributing pictures of Chaplin or parts of films which he has discarded. The judgment also required the Corporation to give an indemnity of 20,000 dollars.

Illustrated Sunday Herald 1921

THE QUEEN OF COMEDIENNES

Vaudeville Loses a Wonderful Artist by the Death of Marie Lloyd: How She Sang Her Way to Fame.

Marie Lloyd, Queen of Comediennes, who has charmed audiences the world over, has gone from us. The news of her death, which occurred yesterday at her home in Woodstock-road, Golders Green, London, will be felt as a personal loss by the many thousands of her admirers.

A tremendous worker during the whole of her long music-hall life, Miss Lloyd died practically in harness.

She appeared at the Edmonton Empire, North London, on Monday and Tuesday of last week, but after the first house on Tuesday evening she was so ill that a doctor had to be called in.

He advised Miss Lloyd not to attempt to appear again that evening, but she declared that she could not disappoint the audience, and after taking a tonic went through her performance at the second house.

Miss Lloyd then went home to bed, where she remained until her death. Mr. Bernard Dillen, her husband, and other relatives were present when she died.

SANG TO FAME.

Art that Captured the Hearts of the Public.

This great artist, who sang her way from obscurity to fame, was born in London 52 years ago. She went on the variety stage at the age of sixteen, receiving what she considered the handsome salary of 50s. a week, and before many years had passed was commanding a weekly figure of £400.

"Beloved by the 'gods.'" was a term often applied to Miss Lloyd. And truly she was! Everywhere since her name first rang through the world of vaudeville the "gods"—those keen critics of the music-hall gallery—have received her with rapturous welcome.

And the "gods" knew something! Their affection was not wasted on an unworthy being. "Our Marie," as she was known—and as she will be referred to for many years to come—was a great woman.

Her natural vivacity and charm swept her into the hearts of her audiences right away, and her wonderful, finished art kept her there. Sarah Bernhardt once described Marie Lloyd as the most exquisite artist on the British stage. Praise, indeed!.

Illustrated Sunday Herald 1922

Punch 1922

LOCAL AMUSEMENTS.

KING'S HALL, ACCRINGTON.

To those who delight in stories of Eastern romance and mystery, "The Virgin of Stamboul," presented at the King's Hall, Accrington, during the early part of the week, should prove a fascinating picture. The author is H. H. Van Loan, one of the most successful of writers for the screen, and many of the scenes upon which the picture is constructed form actual happenings in Constantinople, where Mr. Van Loan was stationed for several months as newspaper correspondent. The story is that of a beautiful beggar girl named Sari, who attracts an American officer in command of a legion of troops operating in the desert. This is the foundation of an intensely thrilling story, the climax to which is reached when Sari is betrothed against her wishes to an Arab chief and she and her lover are rescued by the troops of whom the American has been the leader. The settings to the pictures are lavish in the extreme and the whole atmosphere is essentially Eastern. The acting of Priscilla Dean as the beggar girl is one of the features of the production. Though the story is unusually long—seven reels in all—the programme also contains a comedy picture and another instalment of "The Moon Riders" serial. On Thursday Frank Mayo will appear in "The Brute Breaker," an exciting drama set in the wild and impressive region of Northern California.

EMPIRE, OSWALDTWISTLE.

"The Better 'Ole," the war production by Bruce Bairnsfather, pays a return visit to the Empire, Oswaldtwistle, this week. As a play "The Better 'Ole" was acclaimed wherever it was presented because of the intense appeal it made to the emotions. Bairnsfather, with consummate skill, evolved a play which succeeded in demonstrating the heroism of the type of men who made up the British army, and his characterisation of "Old Bill," "Alf," and "Erbert" is wonderfully fine. The story is rich in comedy, and also contains a vein of compelling pathos. The exploits of the three in the trenches and in billets in France provide a succession of irresistible incidents. It typifies the British soldier with his devotion, his undaunted courage, and cheerfulness in a way which touches responsive chords. On and after Thursday the attraction will be "The Family Honour," a melody of life of every day folks, and their joys and sorrows, showing the influence one right-minded person can exert for good.

Accrington Observer 1921

"YES! WE HAVE NO BANANAS."

FRUITIEST CATCH PHRASE FOR 20 YEARS.

WORDS AND MUSIC IN PAGE 4.

"Yes! we have no bananas!"

A week ago this phrase, uttered by a citizen of John Bull's Island, would have suggested nothing less serious than a hefty touch of the sun.

To-day it is familiar throughout the length and breadth of the land as the biggest song hit and the brightest catch phrase since the banana first figured, a generation ago, as a fruity piece of back-chat.

Uncle Sam started it, having picked up the notion from the alien fruit vendors of New York, whose scanty English frequently leads to the invention of strange idiom.

Exported over here in song form, it was readily taken up by "The People," and retailed in poster form to a public thirsty for something new.

Presented to the eye during the week in bold black letters in a cool blue background the poster was irresistible. The public, badly in need of mental stimulus to counteract the heat, snapped it up in a twinkling, bandied it to and fro, and established it in a day as the last word in back-chat.

The phrase has actually crossed the Channel without any loss of verve, and the argot of the boulevards has been enriched by the comment, "Ah, oui! Nous n'avons pas des bananes."

No less success has attended the song to which the expression has given a title, and which has made an equal hit as a music-hall number and as a fox-trot.

Millions of copies have been sold in the States, and the vogue in this country, though only days old, bids to be equally thorough-going.

Jazz-bands and comedians in London and the big holiday resorts have already added the song to their repertoires.

To-morrow it will be rendered by 400 throats at the Hotel Cecil gathering of the Publicity Club of London, when Mr. Robert Thornberry will lead the chorus.

To-morrow night also it will be sung by Lupino Lane in "Brighter London" at the Hippodrome, Mr. Julian Wylie having secured the exclusive rights for the West-End.

By that time it will also be established in the repertoire of hundreds of thousands of amateurs.

In Page 4 of this issue of "The People" the words and music of the song are given in full—and it is a song everybody can learn and sing.

Too often the amateur, asked to charm a social circle has remained the dumb victim of his own diffidence. To-day all that is changed: almost before the request is uttered he will be speeding towards the piano chirping the apt response, "Yes! we have no bananas!"

Rumour goes even further, and alleges that Trotsky recently electrified a meeting of the Bolshie Cabinet by dropping into a discussion with, "Yes comrades! The Soviet has no bananovitch!"

The People 1923

By "The Rake" & "The Rambler"

A Good List

With another season about to get into swing, many will be interested in the changes in teams. With players changing their abode of business and others finishing their University careers, clubs have an influx of very useful new blood. In this respect it is interesting to hear that J. C. Masterman, W. P. Phillips and A. E. R. Gilligan contemplate hockey in the Metropolis. As a natural train of thought, one is led to think of a cricketer-hockey side. Like Mr. "Plum" Warner, we believe in theorising about a game we love. We have no books of reference, but how would this go? C. T. A. Wilkinson, S. H. Saville, G. T. S. Stevens, J. C. Masterman, E. B. Crockford, A. E. R. Gilligan, A. P. F. Chapman, L. P. Collins, R. A. D. Brooks, J. C. W. MacBryan, C. Borthwick, R. W. Crummack, G. K. Chilman, C. Patteson, S. H. Stevens, T. W. Mansergh, P. L. Frith, E. L. Platt, A. F. Leighton, etc.

This list is by no means exhaustive, as one can call to mind the names of Bashford, Lewis, Page, Bennett, and many more still on the active list. It is only written to invite comment, or to stimulate others more capable than us to fix up some such side. Again, keeping to the active list, one could take another good side from schoolmasters or the legal profession. The schoolmasters' side was a topic of correspondence in HOCKEY WORLD last season, but the legal side could start with a useful basis as given : J. H. Bennett, D. O. Light, W. Chitty-Thomas, T. A. Grose, V. R. Price, and many more in North, Midlands and the West, etc. Meanwhile, to come to earth again, things look very promising for England this season. In Hill, Starke-Jones, Rowbotham and Pemberton there are players who will carry on the best traditions of the game.

Hockey World 1923

EVERES
CLIMB
DISASTER.

TWO MEMBERS THE EXPEDITION KILLED.

LAST DASH.

BLOWN DOWN IN T MONSOON.

THE "Daily Express" derstands that Mr. Leigh Mallory and Mr. Irv two members of the Mo Everest expedition, have their lives during the climb.

They were blown down killed by the monsoo nin a

Mr. A. C. Mallory.

race to reach the summit the unconquered mountain.

Mr. Mallory was the lead of the great reconnaissance explore the summit of Mou Everest in 1921. Mr. Irvi was one of the scientists of expedition.

Mr. Mallory was formerly master at Charterhouse. In a tire in London in January 19 he was optimistic about the chance of success providing "they could get the work done before the mo soon set in."

Mr. A. C. Irvine was educated Merton College Oxford. He was member of the boat-race crews 1922 and 1923. He was one of t new members of this year's expedition.

Daily Express 1924

unch 1924

DÎNER DANSANT.

Morning Post 1925

"ALL BLACKS" WIN TEST MATCH.

England Beaten After Brilliant Struggle.

A GREAT GAME.

Visiting Player Ordered Off the Field.

THE PRINCE'S REQUEST.

NEW ZEALAND: Two goals (one penalty), three tries—17 points.
ENGLAND: Two goals (one penalty), one try—11 points.

The Great Rugby Test Match between England and the "All Blacks" at Twickenham on Saturday ended, as anticipated, in victory for the New Zealand team.

From beginning to end the play was of a remarkably high standard. The England XV. surprised their best friends. They started brilliantly, and although they were beaten, the issue remained in doubt until the last few minutes.

Unhappily the game was marred by an unfortunate incident, Cyril Brownlie, the New Zealand forward, being ordered off the field by the referee for kicking one of the England players while he was lying prone on the ground.

A record crowd witnessed the match, among those present being the Prince of Wales and the Prime Minister, Mr. Stanley Baldwin.

A New Zealand correspondent states that the Prince made representations that, if possible, Brownlie should be permitted to resume, a sporting request that has been greatly appreciated by the New Zealanders.

COUNTY LACROSSE.

Surrey 7, Sussex 7, Dec. 12th, Roedean. **Surrey:** Hill, Heinichy, Saynor, Brash (capt.), Du Buisson, Goodall, Stilwell, Morris (1), Tancred (2), Valentine, Abrahams (2), Vincent (2). **Sussex:** Pensotti, L. Powell, Evans, Terry, Harrison, Shepherd, W. Synge, Fryer, Wiggins, Brown (2), D. Powell (capt.) (2), P. Synge (3). The game was played on the Roedean School pitch, and was keenly fought throughout. The pace at the beginning was good, but the general standard of the play was not high. This is probably accounted for by the number of reserves who were playing, clumsy stickwork being the cause of a good deal of roughness. Surrey were the first to score, and pressed strongly for some time, but Sussex pulled themselves together, and by half-time Surrey only lead by 5—4. This was owing largely to the dashing attack of the Sussex 2nd and 3rd Homes. In the second half, Surrey attacked strongly, their 3rd Home worked untiringly, and had it not been for some excellent goal-keeping for Sussex, they would probably have scored more than they did. The play in the mid-field was not good, and this lead to frequent crowding in front of goal. The match on the whole, showed some very good individual play, but neither county showed much sound team work.

Hockey and Field Lacrosse 1925

Monday, June 1

Sir James Barrie spent Bank Holiday in the Cotswolds in the cause of cricket —a game of which he is very fond. He and the Earl of Balfour, members of a Whitsun holiday party at Stanway House, the Cotswold residence of the Earl and Countess of Wemyss, watched the start of a struggle between married and single men at cricket. There were twenty a side. Sir James Barrie's sympathies seemed to lie with the married cricketers. He lay in the long grass with buttercups nearly touching his chin, smoking his pipe and applauding their hits to the boundary. Before the match Sir James opened a new pavilion which he has presented to the club. "I should like the pavilion to be as delectable as Wendy's hut in 'Peter Pan,'" he said. "I have had a lot of pleasure on this cricket ground, and have watched here the greatest of all games played in the best spirit of cricket."

The Prince of Wales has concluded his visit to the Orange Free State, and has crossed into Natal.

British Weekly 1925

H. M. ABRAHAMS WINS

Other British Successes : Weston Suspended for Reckless Riding at Nottingham : Best for To-day: Fierce Hitting Against Surrey Bowling

For the first time in the series of Olympic Games, the 100 metres race has been won by an Englishman. The honour belongs to H. M. Abrahams, who won by two feet in 10 3-5secs.

An American in Scholz was second and a New Zealander in Porritt third. Amongst the defeated men in the final was Paddock the great American sprinter and record breaker, who finished fifth. Americans filled all the first six places except first and third.

At the half-distance Abrahams was lying slightly behind Scholtz and Porritt. He timed his race beautifully, and with a wonderful spurt won by two feet, one foot separating second and third.

All goes well for Great Britain in the 800 metres. H. B. Stallard and D. G. A. Lowe—our two hopes—won their second round heats convincingly in excellent time, while H. Houghton was second to Lowe, with Watters, the American, forced into third place. Thus Great Britain has three candidates in the final, which will be run off to-day.

In the 3,000 metres steeplechase E. A. Montague and S. A. Newey were third in their respective heats. Neither C. E. Blewitt nor D. Cummings ran.

ABRAHAMS' OLYMPIC WIN

H. M. Abrahams won the 100 metres race at Paris yesterday in 10 3-5sec. He finished two feet in front of Scholz (U.S.A.). Abrahams is the first Englishman to win this race in the history of modern Olympiads.

Daily Sketch 1924

THE "ASHES" REGAINED

English cricket has at last arisen, Phœnix-like, from its "ashes." The historic Test Match fought to a finish at the Oval ended on August 18 in a sensational victory for England by 289 runs, the scores being—England, first innings, 280 ; second innings, 436. Australia, 302 and 125. England has thus won the "rubber" for the first time since 1912. The result was largely due to the splendid partnership of Hobbs and Sutcliffe, who made 100 and 161 respectively in the second innings, and to the fine bowling of Rhodes (the forty-nine-year-old Yorkshireman).

Illustrated London News 1926

GAMES.

Competitive Institute Game : Who am I? Each member is asked to write on cards or small pieces of paper the names of six local or world-wide celebrities. Only one name must be written on each card. One member must be appointed mistress of ceremonies. She is placed in charge of box or basket into which the names are dropped. Members line up with their backs to M.C. and she pins a card or slip of paper on every back. When all backs are decorated, the word "Begin" is shouted, whereupon by all sorts of questions to any or every member each player must strive to find out the name of the celebrity she has assumed. When the M.C. determines that a player has guessed aright the name is transferred to the front of her coat or frock. Another name is pinned on her back and she starts afresh. The first player who can show twelve names correctly guessed wins the prize.

General Post up-to-date. This is played just as was the "General Post" of our youth. Each player chooses the name of a town and reports his or her choice to a Postmaster-General. One player is blindfolded, the rest sit round the room.

The Postmaster-General having a written record of all the names chosen will despatch letters, postcards or telegrams from one town to the other or order a general letter, postcard or telegram post.

If letters are despatched the players must walk, if postcards the players must crawl, if telegrams the players must run.

In each case the players representing the towns named when the Postmaster-General says "a letter (or a postcard or a telegram) is sent from X to Y," must change places, walking, crawling or running according to the nature of the missive sent. The object of the blindfolded player is to catch one of the moving players. If a player is caught, he or she is in turn blindfolded. If a general post is ordered, all the players must change places, walking, crawling or running, as ordered and the blindfolded player tries to catch one of them.

Statues. This game can be played by any number. The players are spaced not too near together about the room. A judging committee of, say three, is chosen and a director. The director will then give an order, e.g. : "Represent a girl playing ball, an old gentleman running to catch the train, the statue of Eros at Piccadilly Circus, a fat woman getting into a slip-on overall, a highlander playing the bagpipes," or anything else of which he or she thinks.

The players will then strike the attitude required and remain in it till the committee chooses the best representation. The player chosen becomes director and "makes statues" to his or her will.

County Federation Secretaries are advised to get into touch with the Games Mistresses of training Colleges for women in the counties. Talks and demonstrations on organised games would be welcomed by many Institutes.

Home and Country 1925

Daily
Sketch
1924

LIDDELL WINS 400 METRES

Flying Scot's Amazing Speed : Guy Butler Third : To-day's Test Match Teams : British Golf Victory : Best for Lingfield

Another of the most sought after prizes in the Olympic Games has fallen to a representative of Great Britain.

E. H. Liddell won the 400 metres final, after a wonderful race, in the world's record time of 47 3-5secs.—the third time in the series a record was broken.

Thus to Great Britain has fallen the sprint, the 400 metres and the 800 metres—each of which the American cracks had set their hearts on winning.

It was a wonderful race which Liddell won, and it came at a time when the crowd had sunk into apathy.

Liddell drew the last position, and had to run alone on the outside of the track.

He led all the way at a terrific speed, making the first furlong in 22 1-5secs. Entering the last stretch Liddell was leading by more than four yards from the American, Fitch, the other four men being practically a similar distance behind.

Liddell did not slacken speed for a second, and finished a good four yards ahead of the American. Butler closed up very quickly, and finished by taking third place from Johnson. The Swiss, Imbach, fell at the entrance of the last stretch after he was beaten.

CINEMA NOTES

The Central. Sodom and Gomorrah.

Sodom and Gomorrah ! SODOM AND GOMORRAH ! Is not this the supreme achievement in the art of naming films ? Why even *Twin Beds* seems scarcely " sexy " at all in comparison. (" Sexy " is the technical word in the film industry, I understand).

With characteristic modesty the renters advertise this film as " the mightiest of them all," and indeed it leaves all its distinguished predecessors standing. As a passionate human document it eclipses *The Dancer of the Nile*: as a ruthless exposure of the abandoned depravity of the ungodly heathen it out-matches *Intolerance*: as a sumptuous display of Eastern magnificence and luxury it soars far above even *Chu Chin Chow.*

Nor does *Sodom and Gomorrah* yield to any of its rivals in the sheer literary perfection of its sub-titles. The plot is concerned with a pure young gentleman who is tempted by an impure young lady :—" Youth ! Hot Blood ! The lure of a woman who means to lure ! Intoxication ! " A young lady who " was cruel, but beautiful beyond description. She appealed to the senses." But luckily the young man was actively protected by his guardian and tutor, a Roman Catholic priest, who finally rescued him from the siren's clutches by remonstrating with the lady :—" Back ! Thou art sister to Satan ! Thou art God-forsaken ! "—and with the revellers :—" Stop ! Tipplers ! Sybarites ! Blasphemers ! "—and by inflicting the lady with a couple of shockingly Freudian nightmares. As she remarked, " Twenty minutes, and I have seen sin and its punishment." So all ended happily, without patricide (" Thy Father ! And thou woulds't lift your hand against him ! ")

The Granta 1924

Modern Woman 1926

The capacity for dancing the fox-trot at 76 years of age would seem to render the grafting of the simian gland superfluous for the resuscitation of vitality. It is interesting to learn that Lord Aberconway, who is 76 and has just celebrated his golden wedding, is still capable of the popular dance, though he does not quite manage the Charleston. However, there is another member of the House of Lords, his senior, he states, who does the Charleston. This record does not quite reach that of the gay young spark who took to motor cycling after 80 years of age and won prizes.

Modern Woman 1926

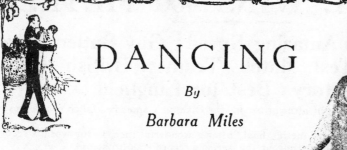

DANCING

By

Barbara Miles

Photo:
Hay Wrightson

Barbara Miles, twice World's Champion of Ballroom Dancing (1924, 1925), who has written an article that will make you a dancer, if you are not one already

WHENEVER I meet women who do not dance, or who speak of dancing reminiscently and rather wistfully as something they used to do "at school" or "before the war," I am sorry—sorry that anyone through diffidence, or just the lack of simple social intercourse, should be deprived of one of the happiest recreations in the world.

* * * * *

Dancing is such a health-giving, beauty-making thing that it should be a part of everyone's life. It is possible, even in little country places now, to find somewhere to dance; and in your home, with a piano or a gramophone and a polished wood floor, it could form a part of any evening's entertainment.

* * * * *

The two essential qualities needed to become a really good dancer are suppleness of body and a sense of rhythm.

* * * * *

Ballroom dancing helps to promote grace of body and an upright carriage, if you *hold your partner correctly*, but not otherwise. (So many girls make the fatal mistake of leaning on their partners.) It also undoubtedly improves the shape of the legs, but ballet dancing over-develops the calves.

* * * * *

The two most common faults of the average dancer are : dancing too much on the toes, and dancing with the feet too wide apart. You should drop on to your heel with each backward step, and the feet should be so close that your ankles almost touch when one foot passes the other.

* * * * *

Other faults which make so many dancers look ridiculous in the ballroom are those of dancing with bent knees, holding each other too far apart, and the woman dragging on her partner's arm instead of having her left hand behind his right shoulder.

* * * * *

Quite the best shoes for dancing are one-bar satin shoes. My personal choice is the nude shade, which matches one's stockings exactly. They look best with almost any colour of day or evening frock.

* * * * *

There can be little doubt that the frock which has a tight-fitting bodice and a flared skirt has beaten every other design. The tight bodice, fitted well round the hips, ensures the frock staying in position when one's arms are raised, and the flared skirt allows the necessary freedom of movement.

* * * * *

Sleeveless frocks are always best for evening wear, but I rather like a sleeve in an afternoon dance frock if it is sufficiently well fitted to allow of raising the arms without pulling the frock up at the sides. I dislike short sleeves—my own choice is always a long sleeve, or none at all.

* * * * *

Georgette, crêpe Romaine or ninon are, to my mind, *the only* materials for dance frocks, because they cling to the figure and move with the dancer. A stiff frock which does not "give" with one's movements detracts terribly from the gracefulness of dancing.

* * * * *

One should avoid wearing one's skirts too short—to show the bend of the knee from behind is so ugly. A dance frock should be a couple of inches *below* the knee, so that it will be just *to* the knee when the shoulders are raised.

Do you want
to play—

GOLF ?

HEATHER THATCHER *was just beginning to shine very brightly as a stage star when she took up golf. She is a member of the Stage Golfing Society, and her advice on the game is well worth having*

IF you are not turning into the brilliant player you expected to be, that day when you made your first round and actually managed to hit the ball on several occasions, it is just for one reason—lack of concentration. For golf, like everything else, you must have patience and confidence and give endless attention to detail. Have you, for instance, learnt yet to keep your head down and your eye on the ball ?

* * * * *

If you are learning with a professional or some friend who is really good at the game, it should not take more than a year for you to become a fine player. But you must play constantly.

* * * * *

It is best, of course, to begin when you are young, but the woman in her thirties can take up golf and soon learn to play an excellent game, provided she is fairly strong. It is less strenuous than tennis,

and for this reason is a game that you can take with you right into middle-age and after.

* * * * *

Golf has this advantage too, it can be played by men and women together without the man having to be heavily handicapped. For, except in length of shots, the woman golfer can compete very well with men.

* * * * *

A short time ago I designed a skirt that I think the perfect one for golf. It is divided in the middle and is worn over a garment that resembles a footballer's shorts —only that they are not very short. This is a most comfortable plan, as it does away with any sort of restriction at the knees, horribly tiring when walking over a rough course. With this skirt I wear a jumper of thin wool, and sometimes a little waistcoat affair like the one in the photograph, over a jumper of washing silk. My hat is of soft felt and has a tiny brim.

* * * * *

Modern Woman 1926

"STARS OF TOURNAMENT" AT WIMBLEDON : NOTABLE MEN PLAYERS.

Illustrated London News 1926

THE FIRST ROYAL COMPETITOR AT WIMBLEDON : THE DUKE OF YORK, WHO IS LEFT-HANDED, TAKING A HIGH "SMASH" IN THE MEN'S DOUBLES, PARTNERED BY WING-COMMANDER LOUIS GREIG (ON LEFT).

The Belper News

FRIDAY, APRIL 29, 1927.

The thousands unable to attend the Cup final at Wembley on Saturday would have the opportunity of enjoying the next best thing, that of listening to the broadcast description of the game. Expectation of a grand contest also ran high on the announcement of the perfect weather prevailing and the ideal condition of the ground, which looked "more like a tennis court than a football field." The preliminary community singing of the popular war songs and the concluding "Abide with Me" were alike memorable items which probably many listeners would enjoy more than the detailed running commentary on the game itself. All must, however, admit that the description by the man at the microphone could not have been bettered. Every movement of the players was duly chronicled without the slightest hesitation of language, and what appeared more marvellous still was the announcer's familiarity with the name of every player on both sides and the readiness with which each name came to his tongue.

—:o:—

Belper News 1927

GEARY MAKES CRICKET HISTORY

Daily Mirror 1929

All Ten Wickets for 18 Runs Against Glamorgan

WONDERFUL FINISH

George Geary, the Leicestershire cricketer, celebrated his recall to the Test team to meet South Africa at the Oval to-morrow in dramatic fashion.

Playing against Glamorgan at Pontypridd, Geary captured all ten wickets in the Welshmen's second innings at the amazingly small cost of 18 runs.

This wonderful performance has no parallel in modern cricket and will secure for the Leicester man a high place in the annals of the game.

The recorded instances of bowlers taking ten wickets prior to 1865 are six in number, but no analyses were kept in these cases. The nearest approach to Geary's feat is A. E. Vogler's ten for 26 in South Africa in 1906-7.

The previous best in England was secured in the first match the Australian, W. P. Howell, ever played here. He took ten for 28 against Surrey at the Oval in 1899. Next in order of merit is Colin Blythe's ten for 30 for Kent against Northampton in 1907.

Geary has never taken all ten wickets in an innings before, although his performances with the ball have been brilliant. His analysis for the second innings reads:

Overs.	Maidens.	Runs.	Wickets.
16.2	8	18	10

In all he took sixteen wickets in the match for 96 runs.

It was a very close call, as when Glamorgan went in to bat a second time they only required 84 to win. They were first nonplussed and then lost in admiration for Geary when the wickets fell so persistently and cheaply.

At one period Glamorgan seemed to have a chance when they wanted 29 runs to win and five wickets in hand, but Geary came along in another deadly spell and captured the last four wickets for 1 run.

Glamorgan were all out for 68 and lost by 15 runs. Score:

George Geary yesterday celebrated his selection for the Test team in place of Maurice Tate by bowling out the whole Glamorgan side for 18 runs.

Bath and Wilts Chronicle 1927

SIR HARRY LAUDER'S SONG.

Couldn't Help Trolling a Wee Bittie.

When he received the Freedom of Edinburgh, his native city, to-day, Sir Harry Lauder broke into a snatch of song beginning, "Sing us a little melody." He did not sing with his usual vigour, but in rather a subdued voice. "No, I could not do it," he said, turning to the Lord Provost. "I was challenged by the Lord Provost not to sing; and I told him I would keep my promise, although I have broken it just a wee bittie (laughter).

Mr VIM PASSES BY

the shop counter, and one can imagine him using the very words spoken by Mr. Pim in the play:

"Oh! we are almost, I might say, old friends, Mrs. Marden."
—*Mr. Pim Passes By.*

Vim is certainly a staunch and loyal friend to all who love brightness. As a friend he is beloved by happy mistresses and maids. He is the friend of every grocer who displays the familiar yellow and black canister on his counter.

Vim makes friends by helping folks to do their cleaning and polishing work more easily, more rapidly, more thoroughly.

Housewives everywhere rely upon Vim to help them in polishing metalwork, cleaning cooking utensils, scrubbing floors, table tops, and all white woodwork, making painted surfaces good to look upon, and adding lustre to china, glassware, enamel and linoleum.

IN SPRINKLER-TOP CANISTERS

Of all Grocers, Stores, Oilmen, Chandlers, etc.

LEVER BROTHERS LIMITED.   PORT SUNLIGHT.

CANON WHO MARRIED AT 91.

Canon John S. Warren, rector of Willoughby, Lincs., who has just reached his 94th year, and who was married at the age of 91, is retiring this month, and will settle at St. Leonards-on-Sea.

The Canon has held the Willoughby living for 48 years. He was previously vicar of Langtoft, near Boston.

He still takes a lively interest in gardening, and prides himself on two servants—a coachman and a gardener—whose services with him average 49 years each.

CANON WARREN.

Illustrated London Herald 1922

Evening Standard 1928

Gramophone Notes

H.M.V.

This firm has produced some good things for February, the most important of which are two sets of complete works with album. The first is the Enigma Variations of Sir Edward Elgar. This composer is interesting in that he is the only great writer of music to-day who has refused to succumb to modern tendencies in composition. His music is as simple and diatonic as was the music of a hundred years ago, and yet it can stand being heard over and over again as well as any of the works of the classical composers. Never do we feel that it is out of date, because throughout it is supremely natural and spontaneous and entirely charming.

Isis 1927

SOME REPRINTS AND CHEAP EDITIONS

* * *

Some love stories at 2s. :—" Love Courageous," by Concordia Merrell (Hodder) ; " To-morrow's Tangle," by Margaret Pedler (Hodder) ; " Mary Beaudesert," by Katherine Tynan (Collins) ; " Unconquerable Girl," by Concordia Merrell (Hodder) ; and some adventure yarns at the same price :—" Cottonwood Gulch," by Clarence Mulford (Hodder) ; " Maid of the Morn," by A. G. Hales (Hutchinson) ; " His Third Master," by Max Brand (Hodder) ; " Man from Morocco," by Edgar Wallace (Long).

NORWEST.

Bookseller
1927

Very Early Music.

It is as rare as it is pleasant to find such enthusiasm for some secluded bywater of art as that possessed by M. Dolmetsch and his family for the music and the musical instruments of the long ago.

The Haslemere musical festival, which he started yesterday, has little of the world-fame of Bayreuth and none of the lusty oratorio singing of Leeds or the Three Choirs, though here is sincerity and, in an intimate way, much charm.

But it is not for the multitude, for Mr. Dolmetsch seems to be convinced that, musically speaking, art stopped short a long time before the cultivated court of the Empress Josephine. For him Bach is almost a modern; the work of Verradosco and other early Italians and of our own composers of the sixteenth century, has a beauty that is not grasped at once, and when grasped, may grow monotonous for all but the dyed-in-the-wool enthusiast.

The lute and the harpsichord have a picturesque air, but the sounds they emit have been compared, irreverently but not inaptly, to the playing of a toastingfork on a gridiron.

The B.B.C. and the Harpsichord.

The B.B.C. have sometimes been criticised, and justly, but those who are of opinion that there is no true art save of the Haslemere school will do well to remember that the harpsichord has been broadcast, in tactfully small doses, and has even attained, through their efforts, some degree of popularity. This is certainly to their artistic credit.

Perhaps one day they will invite Mr. Dolmetsch and one of his associates to broadcast a " duet for two recorders," which has nothing whatever to do with a legal argument between two eminent K.C.'s.

Dropped waists and cloche hats: the fashions of 1928.

SONG WRITER TO WED AT 75.

COMPOSER OF "THORA" & "THE DEATHLESS ARMY."

The engagement was announced yesterday of Mr. Fred E. Weatherly (75), of Bath, the famous song writer, and Mrs. Miriam Bryan, widow of Mr. John Bryan, a popular Welsh singer, of Llanfechan, Montgomeryshire.

Mr. Weatherly is a prominent barrister on the Western circuit, and his songs are familiar to English-speaking people in all parts of the world.

Among his best-known songs are "Darby and Joan," "Nancy Lee," "They All Love Jack," "Nirvana," "We've Come Up from Somerset," "Thora," "Rose of Picardy," "London Bridge," "Tin Soldier," "The Deathless Army," "The Holy City," "Star of Bethlehem," and "To-morrow Will be Friday."

Mr. Weatherly, like his bride-elect, has been previously married.

It is understood that the wedding will take place next week.

The People 1923

Erewhon in Oxford

Oxford is becoming self-conscious, perhaps because of her notoriety in the press. No longer is an affectation of eccentricity *la mode*. The Public School code of uniformity is springing up even in the matter of dress. Our bags are becoming darker again, rude men say with age, but we do not believe that even Oxford, whose dirt surpasses that of London, could have worked so complete a transformation with the lavender and puce of '25. No, it is indicative of a subtle mental change, an exchange of one affectation for another finer, more wholesome Bohemianism that scorns such hollow shams. Rumours of a 'Return to Fig-leaf' movement are in the air. The successor of the aesthete puts on his belt of string and a row of necessary safety-pins and looks hopefully towards the O.U.D.S. for a lead in the matter of woad.

The American invasion is stronger than ever. These tourists are rapidly seizing the positions and prizes that should rightfully belong to British labour. Their peptonised energy paralyses the genial, good-mannered laziness of the natives. 'Oxford for the English' may quite possibly be the slogan of the year.

The morning coffee fiend is less apparent. Lecturers, who fail to see him and Proctors who fail to catch him, hint vaguely of disgusting orgies with a coffee-machine in his own rooms. The case is unproved, however.

The woman question burns more fiercely than before, on the strength of which *The Isis* has engaged a new feminine correspondent, an ardent defender of the unfaithful, to quench the flames.

And this all brings us to the happy conclusion that as usual we are going . . . nowhere.

Isis 1927

Retail Credit World 1928

T. H. SHERRIFFS' STAFF OUTING.

This annual event, which is eagerly looked forward to by the whole of his employees from his four branch establishments in East Ham, Barking, Ilford, and Grays, took place on Thursday the 20th September, when a party of 40 ladies and gentlemen left by saloon coach and private cars for a trip through Essex to the beauty spot at Little Baddow, near Chelmsford. The excitement grew tense when the party reached their destination, the Bracken Hill Tea Rooms, at 2.0 o'clock, when the host and hostess gave them a very hearty welcome.

Preparations were at once proceeded with in marking off the ground with small flags, etc., for the sports. Sixteen events were on the card, and no time was lost in getting the competitors together for the first race. These items included:—"Cigarette Race," "Marriage Lines," "Wheelbarrow," "Three-legged," "Sack," "Threadneedle and Button," "Egg and Spoon," "Bag and Bell," "Flour and Plum," "Land Boat Race," and "Bun and Ginger-beer," likewise a rifle shooting test among the men and youths.

Competition was most keen in each event, especially the "Land Boat Race," where the four branch managers and their staffs opposed each other for special prizes.

A meat tea, in Bohemian style, was partaken of at 4.30 p.m., when 40 persons sat down with good appetites. Mine hosts (Mr. and Mrs. Tunbridge) were most assiduous in their attentions to their guests, and the fare provided was plentiful and of the best quality, that left nothing to be desired.

Mr. and Mrs. James Laird and daughter (Wanstead), Mr. and Mrs. Arthur Halley and daughter (Forest Gate), Mr. Tom Fiskin (Secretary of the London Thistle Football Club), and Miss Agnes Blythe, arrived on the scene soon after 5.0 o'clock, in time to partake of a welcome cup of tea and other sweet dainties, which were all in readiness for their consumption.

At 7.30 the presentation of prizes was made by Mrs. Sherriff, after which sandwiches, cake, and other light refreshments were handed round to the happy party, and a hearty vote of thanks accorded to Mr. and Mrs. Sherriff for all they had done for the party's enjoyment that day, which, needless to say, turned out a glorious one.

Best thanks are due to the following gentlemen:—Mr. Fred Mills, Mr. Harry Price, and Mr. W. J. Gadd, who acted as judges and ably assisted Mr. Sherriff as starter and getting the competitors on the line.

W. J. G.

SIR T. BEECHAM'S LAMENT.

Sir Thomas Beecham, speaking at Leeds to-day, said English orchestras used to rank with the best on the Continent. Now there was not in the whole country an orchestra which could be placed in the front rank, according to the estimate of musical countries.

Instead we had superannuated, obsolete, beastly, disgusting, noisy, horrid methods of making music in superabundance by means of what was known as the brass band.

Evening Standard 1928

W.R. Hammond, Gloucestershire and England Test captain, batting against Surrey in 1928.

Lord Burghley takes the water-jump in the eight leaps steeplechase relay, 1928.

BAN ON WOMAN SPY PLAY.

Story of the Notorious Mata Hari.

FRENCH OBJECTION?

Mr. E. Temple Thurston, the author of the one-act play depicting the shooting of the notorious Mata Hari by the French, which has been banned by the Lord Chamberlain, told an Oxford Mail representative to-day that he was prepared to go to the length of altering the nationality of the central character of his play if this would satisfy the censor.

The play, which was to have been produced at the London Coliseum early in February, with Miss Isobel Elsom as the leading character, has been adapted from the final chapters of Mr. Temple Thurston's novel, " Portrait of a Spy."

The author admits that the chief character in the book, Mata Garass, is based on the woman spy Mata Hari, who was shot in 1916 for espionage.

" I do not know whether the ban was imposed because of any special incident in the play or on grounds of general policy," said Mr. Thurston.

Appeal to the Censor.

" Possibly the Lord Chamberlain fears that the shooting incident will offend the French, but there has never been any objection to the novel, and I cannot believe that the way I have treated the story either in the book or the play would cause the Censor to take any offence.

" In writing the execution scene I was advised by Admiral Sir Reginald Hall, who was at the head of the Naval Intelligence Department at the time, and to whom I dedicated the book.

" If the Censor's objection is due to any special incident in my play, I should be prepared to meet him provided the story is not damaged."

Oxford Mail 1929

MALCOLM SCOTT

Death of Famous Comedian Who Made Queen Alexandra Laugh

Mr. Malcolm Scott, the comedian and "dame" impersonator, died on Saturday at the Pines, Valebridge-road, Burgess Hill, Sussex. He was fifty-seven.

For some months he had suffered from severe throat trouble, due to a growth in the chest. This caused his gradual retirement from the stage.

Mr. Scott, who was a brother of the late Admiral Sir Percy Scott, commenced his career as a Shakespearean actor, but afterwards became a famous comedian. He was given his first big opportunity when Dan Leno was taken ill and he appeared in his place at the London Pavilion. He was a popular wireless performer.

He appeared at a royal command performance during King Edward's reign, and once, while performing as Katherine Parr at a London theatre when Queen Alexandra and the Empress of Russia occupied a box, he greatly amused them by remarking: " Strange that all the Queens should be together."

Mr. Scott was a man of great generosity, and at one time it was his habit to purchase the stocks of coffee stalls on the Embankment and other parts of London and give away refreshments to the poor without disclosing his identity.

NEW WICKET-KEEPING RECORD.

Ames, of Kent, Dismisses 103 Batsmen This Season.

Ames, the Kent wicket-keeper, has created a new record in dismissing 103 men behind the wicket this season.

F. H. Huish, also of Kent, is the only other stumper who has had a bag of 100 in a season. He accomplished the feat twice—102 in 1913, and 100 in 1911.

Evening Standard 1929

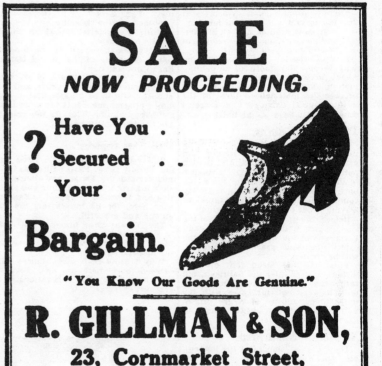
THE ORIGIN AND END OF A STAGE JOKE.

Wigan Pier, an iron structure over the canal at Wigan, is to be dismantled. For fully half a century the pier has been used as a tipping depot for coal conveyed by wagons from the adjacent colliery for transport by waterway, but the colliery having been shut down there is no further use for it. Wigan Pier, which has been the subject of stage jokes for years, was painted by Mr. T. Ramsden, F.R.S.A., in water colours, and coloured prints of the picture had a large sale.

Observer 1929

Daily Mirror 1929

DANCE STEPS OF 1929.
By SANTOS CASANI.

Oxford Mail 1929

MORE graceful steps and far better dancers are what I prophesy for the year 1929 as the greatest changes in the dancing world.

The reason for this is the gradual revolt amongst dancers against the too-Americanised dance steps. Whilst not lacking in appreciation of the many steps that have come from the United States, I have always advocated the need for a departure from the hectic, quick step to one more essentially British in character, portraying the natural grace in slow movements which is a characteristic of our race.

Dancing as Exercise.

There is already ample evidence that dancing in 1929 will be taken far more seriously as education, as well as exercise and pleasure, and the development of graceful bodily movement.

In this especial connection dancing will become far more of a definite social accomplishment. "Poetry of motion," always the poet's dream, will become the materialised ideal of the million; good carriage and graceful dancing will be a social habit.

The Waltz Returns.

Indeed, I confidently expect dancing in 1929 to re-discover the rhythm and grace which used to abound in British ballrooms a few years ago. Evidence of this is not far to seek for the waltz, once the pride of every ball, is slowly coming back and no hostess thinks of leaving it out of a modern programe.

Indeed, the growing popularity of the slow waltz will be maintained and variations of the waltz, with the same captivating and graceful movement, will be created.

This does not mean that the Victorians will re-enter the ballroom, but rather that graceful movement, possible only in very extreme cases with the quick steps, mostly of Negro origin, will again find its traditional home in the modern dance halls.

No More "Stunt Steps."

The "crude" dances of the immediate post-war years are no longer wanted, neither is there a need to be met in supplying the latest "stunt steps" from America.

The fashion in ballroom dancing has definitely changed for the better, and it is a far greater social accomplishment to become a good and graceful dancer than a mere "step hunter." During the reaction days after the war anything in the nature of a "stunt" was considered up-to-date, but now, in dancing anyway, it is viewed out of date.

"Stunt" dances have not lasted, but the graceful waltz has withstood the rather undignified attacks upon it and finally regained its rightful place, by virtue of grace, in dancers' affections. It gives a restful contrast to the Charleston.

Fox-trots "Happy Shuffle."

Of course, all the modern steps will not be eliminated during 1929, as many of them have become just such an institution as the waltz. For instance, the "Fox Trot" will increase in popular esteem because it has an essentially modern appeal in movement and music.

It typifies the spirit of the modern dance, as some of the Round Dances did in pre-war days.

The "Fox Trot" has held its own throughout the post-war years, and can almost claim to be an essential in any dance programme. It is far more than a "happy shuffle," for its movements are fundamentally natural.

Two New Dances.

Likely new dances are the Twist and the Varsity Drag. Paris ballrooms have popularised the Twist, and danced to slow fox-trot time it is simple and effective and is bound to appeal to dancers over here, for its movements are exquisite and graceful.

The Varsity Drag presents little that is new in steps, which being slow will blend with the graceful ideals set in the modern ballroom.

Why I think both these dances will succeed over here is also because they help to lay the foundations of a graceful carriage.

NEW TALKIE STAR

Maurice Chevalier Scores a Success in "Innocents of Paris"

BY OUR FILM CRITIC

Maurice Chevalier, the French music-hall star, has made a great success in his first talkie, "Innocents of Paris," showing at the Plaza. He is good-looking and has a personality like Al Jolson's. Can one say more?

He sings several songs, the best being "Louise," "Valentine" and "It's a Habit of Mine." Sylvia Beecher is good as the heroine, and special praise should be given to little David Durand, who had a "Davey Lee" part.

There is a good scene where he is crying for his mother, who has drowned herself, and Maurice puts on a funny hat and sings rollicking songs to try to make the child laugh.

He finally succeeds, and it is a joy to watch the expression on little David's face change. He is sobbing noisily, and then he begins to look interested in what Maurice is doing and finally laughs heartily.

Daily Mirror 1929

BOATCREW'S MILK.

Oxford Drink This Year.

CANTABS' ALE.

Famous Athletes' Views.

ON the suggestion of Mr. Morphett, the president of the O.U.B.C., it is learned, milk is being drunk by the Oxford crew.

The Cambridge crew, however, are continuing to drink that University's famous ale that is specially sent from Cambridge for their use.

Last Year's Training.

Are the Oxford men going altogether "on the water cart" during their training this year?

Advocates of abstinence from alcohol will be widely excited in that case if the Oxford crew win the race this year. It would be wonderfully good propaganda for the "temperance" cause.

Some indication that this might happen was given last September, when a letter from the secretary of the O.U.B.C. condemning the use of alcoholic beverages in Boat Race training was read by Dr. Courtenay Weeks at the opening conference of the Band of Hope Union at Northampton.

Dr. Weeks then said that just before the 1928 Boat Race he wrote to the secretary of the Oxford crew asking him whether alcohol was obligatory in training, and, if so, what the physical indications were on which the obligation was based.

The answer was that it was not obligatory but was customary.

"Result of Tradition."

"Personally," wrote the secretary, "I am an abstainer, and took no alcohol during training, and No. 7 was also an abstainer. The rest of the crew had half a pint of beer at lunch and a pint at dinner, followed by a glass of port.

"I don't think any physical indications whatever were concerned.

"The training diet of the crew is entirely the result of tradition handed down from previous crews, and I am confident that it is a thoroughly bad one."

Oxford Mail 1929

1930–1939

NORMAN HARTNELL

Harper's Bazaar 1930

THE TECHNIQUE OF LUNCHING OUT

Illustrations by Gilbert Wilkinson

. . . . delightful little places where for quite a little you can enjoy yourself a lot.

IF you happen to be lunching with a *Man Much Older Than Yourself,* dress to look as young as possible, and if you can no longer look " young " then look at least " youthful." Men, for some mysterious reason, when it comes to amusement, enjoyment or relaxation, seldom seem to seek women of their own age, but prefer those who are older or younger, and those who are their superiors or inferiors in some respect seem to them the most worthy of entertainment ! If therefore you are very young, say scarcely twenty, and your escort is quite old, say verging on fifty —then dress colourfully, talk brightly, order him about gaily, but let him order the lunch, and be sure to express your appreciation of his choice of wines. If, on the other hand, you should be nearer thirty than you like to be thought, these last two reminders will be unnecessary. Dress softly, paying particular attention to your neck line, hair line and line of talk.

IF, on the other hand, your host is *Younger than Yourself,* do not by any means endeavour to come down to his level, but raise him, by a few sophisticated gestures of your hands and eyes, to your own.

Dress magnificently, talk with dash, verve, and worldly wisdom ; and if he be very young, you might, if you are the type, suggest a hidden tragedy. But only suggest it—don't mention it ! Your hat would have a double brim—and though he might not know it, he would appreciate it and think it daring. Your conversation might occasionally hold a double meaning also, but your face would belie this and he would think that it was perhaps his quick mind, not yours !

Harper's Bazaar **1931**

Galli Curci : Albert Hall, November 17.

By the courtesy and kindness of a freehold-seat holder I was able to hear this singer again after some years. The faulty methods of production of which I spoke six years ago have had their result and it is a dire one. The voice has all but lost its top notes, which are now uncertain, veiled, and shakily taken, besides showing a pronounced tendency to wobble, and the undoubted facility in *fioritura* of earlier days, although very far from the consummate mastery and brilliance of Melba, Tetrazzini, or dal Monte, even at its best, has all but gone; indeed the decline was startling and shocking when the singer came to the one genuinely searching test in this field, the delicious *Ombra leggiera* from *Dinorah,* in which the runs and *cadenze* were mere slithered-over apologies, and the shakes an exhibition that would have been lamentable from a nobody. In the really great singers, even after their palmy days are long past, there are always *de beaux restes,* a beautiful and polished style, a consummate technical mastery, fine and interesting musicianship, but Mme. Galli Curci, never having had any of these, and but an ordinary voice, has, now the voice has deteriorated so conspicuously, little, if anything, to hold the attention or interest. Her steady vocal decline is all the more terrible and startling in that she is still a comparatively young woman, at an age when she should be approaching the full *effloraison* of her powers; and it is one more awful warning, one more terrible example, of the swift and ruthless Nemesis following on faulty methods.
KAIKHOSRU SORABJI.

New Ag
193

RUGBY UNION AND OFFSIDE LAW

Floodlighting Decision

The Committee of the Rugby Union, after a long meeting in London yesterday, issued a statement setting out, among other points, their decision " that matches by floodlighting shall not be permitted where gate money is charged." The committee expressed the hope that referees and officials, in addition to players, will not supply reports of matches to the press for remuneration. They approved an international blazer for players, which can be obtained through Engineer-Commander S. F. Coopper, secretary of the union.

Referring to the off-side law, the statement continued : " The Committee desire to draw the attention of players and referees to law 17 as to when a player is off-side, and point out that a player on the field of play is off-side in four cases and four cases only—

1. If he enter the scrummage from his opponents' side.
2. If, while the ball is in a scrummage, he, not being in the scrummage, remain in front of the ball.
3. If he stand in front of the line-out, and
4. If the ball has been kicked or touched or is being carried by one of his own side behind him.

" A player is not off-side merely by reason of the fact that he is in front of the ball."

The new date of January 28 for the county championship semi-final match between East Midlands and Lancashire at Northampton was agreed to by the committee.

Manchester Guardian **1933**

SUNDAY CINEMAS.

DURHAM APPLICATION ADJOURNED.

Application was renewed at Durham County Police Court yesterday on behalf of cinema proprietors in the area for permission to open on Sundays, following the passing of the Sunday Cinemas Bill.

Since the last case arising out of the Lord's Day Observance Act earlier in the year, no licence has been allowed for Sunday opening and the magistrates have conformed with the decision of the majority of Benches in the country.

Mr. W. Hateley, of Willington, chairman of the Durham County branch of the Cinematograph Exhibitors' Association, made application for permission to open cinemas in the area on Sundays. He was represented by Mr. H. E. Ferens.

Mr. Ferens said that the application was being renewed following the passing of the Emergency Act through Parliament the previous day. It was bound to receive Royal Assent yesterday, and he asked the Bench to allow them to go back on the old provision subject to the Royal Assent being given.

Brig.-General H. Conyers Surtees: "You will lay yourselves open to objections from other quarters if we give you permission now."

Mr. Ferens agreed to an adjournment for a week and the application will be renewed next Wednesday.

Northern Echo 1931

Halifax Courier and Guardian 1931

Football Lottery.

Fines of £40 at Halifax Court.

Beverley Man Who Was Given Wrong Advice.

At Halifax Borough Court, yesterday morning, William Bloomfield, of 26a, North Bar Without, Beverley, was fined £20, with an alternative of two months' imprisonment, on each of two charges of unlawfully publishing a lottery, to which he pleaded guilty. Mr. H. O. Peters prosecuted and defendant was represented by Mr. Neville Hobson, Beverley.

Mr. H. G. Peters said that a man named Longstaffe, of Clare-road, Halifax, received by post from the Northwold Publishing Company, of Beverley, certain tickets, which he handed to the police. As a result of inquiries, an East Riding constable saw the defendant on March 7. Bloomfield told the constable that he did not know Longstaffe personally, but admitted that football coupons shown to him were published by him. One of the coupons was called the Northwold Credit Tote A ticket, series No. 2 foursomes. These were sold at 6d. each. When the purchaser opened the ticket he found inside a list of football matches to be played on a certain date. The matches were numbered from 1 to 64 and, in a space at the bottom, were four numbers corresponding to four of the matches set out. If the purchaser obtained a ticket on which were the numbers of the four matches at which the highest aggregate scores were made, he won £100. A similar prize was offered for a coupon bearing the number of the four away teams with the highest aggregate scores and there were other prizes on a gradual scale down to 5s. The ticket stated, "You are given an opportunity of exercising your skill. If you don't approve of the four numbers you may cross out one number and one only and write below the one crossed out your own selection." On the other ticket, the Northwold Credit Tote treble and double ticket, there were only three selected teams, of which the purchaser was allowed to alter one.

RACING PIGEON NOTES

A young fancier writes me that his birds have been, for the last few weeks, moulting their down feathers and is rather concerned about it as he thinks they are moulting prematurely.

As a matter of fact this young fancier should rejoice instead of fearing the consequences. This shedding of the down feathers is evidence that his birds are healthy and in good condition. This down forms a warm underlie to protect them from the chill of winter, and with the coming of warmer weather is shed to prepare the way for a new growth for next winter.

The moult of the primaries or long wing feathers is quite another matter. The renewal of these is a provision of nature to repair any damage that may have happened to them and also to ensure that the wing is provided with strong new feathers for the purpose of vigorous flight.

The moult of the primaries starts usually with the rearing of the first nest in the year. Mating the birds late helps to delay this moult, and the idea of delaying the moult is so that the bird may go to the longest race with the moult of the primaries as little advanced as possible.

Once the moult commences, however, it cannot be delayed without endangering the condition of the bird. The young fancier should watch the moult of his birds carefully. Its steady progression is a sign that all is well, and a stoppage is the danger signal that the bird is physically below par. This may be due to the exhaustion of a hard race or to illness.

When the moult stops the wing feather that is in the course of growth may complete itself, but the next feather does not fall as it should do. The result is to the inexperienced eye the wing may appear perfect. But it does not deceive the old fancier.

Perhaps for the benefit of the young fancier it will be as well to explain nature provides that the primaries or long wing flight feathers are moulted consecutively commencing with the first (or tenth if counting from the outermost feather). When the new feather has grown about two thirds of its length, the next feather falls out, consequently once the pigeon has commenced to moult its primaries the complete wing is impossible in a healthy pigeon until the complete moult has taken place. The complete wing is consequently to be viewed with grave suspicion when it occurs in the middle of the racing season.

Halifax Courier and Guardian 1931

ORDER OF RECHABITES.

Local Tent's Success.

The Queensbury Tent of the Independent Order of Rechabites held its annual meeting in the Hall of Freedom on Saturday afternoon, when Bro. W. Jones, Chief Ruler, presided over a record attendance.

Mr. Lewis Jagger, J.P., presented the emblem of the order to Bro. J. McGee, past Chief Ruler. Mr. Jagger, who has a long association with the Queensbury Tent, spoke reminiscently of the period when he first became a member of the Order. Bro. McGee suitably responded.

Bro. B. Priestley, juvenile secretary, presented an encouraging report. During the past year, he said, the juvenile Tent had made 81 new members and had received the Pickard Memorial Shield. He hoped they would long retain the shield and the Tent would go from strength to strength.

Bro. I. Barrett presented the secretary's report and reviewed the outstanding events of the year.

Bros. W. Tomsett, E. Cawthra, J. McGee and G. M. Scarborough, were elected district representatives.

A tea at the Co-operative Assembly Rooms followed the meeting and, in the evening, a concert was held in the Hall of Freedom. The artistes were, Miss L. V. Pickles (soprano), Miss A. Illingworth (contralto), Mr R. Hirst (tenor), Mr. N. Drake (baritone), the Looney Fiddler (entertainer) and Mr. E. A. Moore, Mus.Bac., F.R.C.O. (accompanist).

An old trick to delay the fall of the next feather when birds are sent to a race is to cut about half-inch off the tip. Many fanciers believe this lets air into the quill or shaft of the feather and thus delays its fall. I have not yet been convinced that it does have this effect. In any case my belief is that it is better to let the moult take its course than to attempt to check it.

It is a fairly easy matter by avoiding early breeding to rear a strain of racers that will only be on their third, or at most fourth, primary by the middle of July. With the wing moult no more advanced than this I do not think any fancier need worry that the gap in the wing will affect the flight of his pigeon. In a well feathered pigeon there is enough webbing to allow for the absence of a third or fourth flight without a gap occurring.

It is when two consecutive feathers fall together that a gap becomes a serious matter, or when, as with youngsters, the 7th without a gap occurring.

The nearer the extreme outer margin of the wing a feather is the more important it is and the greater part it plays in flight. One has only to study the greater strength and substance of these outside feathers as compared with the gradually weakening of the inner ones to realise this.

Norfolk Chronicle 1931

Floodlight Football

South London Press
1933

FRIENDS who have played flood-light football tell me it is good sport and ought to prove a financial success if effectively staged.

I should like to try it. It is about the one form of football I have not had a kick at. In my teens I enjoyed two seasons as a wing three-quarter at Rugby; and rather fancied myself as a converter of tries—but that's another story.

Now that Association football has to face the keen competition of several thoroughly up-to-date rivals, no methods likely to tap new followers should be ignored.

Some of the wealthier clubs might profitably experiment in a series of friendly games.

There are unquestionably large numbers of genuine enthusiasts who are unable to attend Saturday afternoon matches and who would jump at the chance to see their favourite pastime in the evening.

Illuminating!

It is not that I tremble for the future of football. But in this age of perpetual change and rapid advancement nothing, not even a game, can afford to remain stationary and allow the wheels to become encrusted with moss.

I am certain the energetic and enterprising men who control the leading clubs will try every new idea in the least likely to bring good results.

Flood lighting might prove illuminating in more senses than one.

Reggie, making a tour of London's Montparnasse, meets leading sculptor's favourite model in the flesh.

Harper's Bazaar 1930

Bournemouth Daily Echo 1932

DANCING AT KING'S HALL.

NEW BAND FOR THIS WINTER SEASON.

Dancers at King's Hall this winter will find a new band installed. During the time that the ballroom has been open the management has pursued a policy of changing bands at reasonably frequent intervals. The present band has had the longest period of service of any so far—four years—and the new one will make its bow to the Bournemouth public next Monday.

It should ably carry on its predecessor's reputation for a perfect dancing rhythm. The individual members have all had long experience of dance bands; in fact, many have played all over the world, while the leader, Mr. Jack Capper, learned the principals of dance rhythm in America, the original home of modern dance music. He comes direct from the dance band of the liner Majestic, and in addition to experience of what may be called lighter music, he has conducted concert orchestras—a fact that should ensure the retention of the popularity of the orchestral concerts given by the King's Hall band in the Bath Hotel every Sunday. In addition to being a capable leader, Mr. Capper is an exceptional solo violinist and trumpeter. He has been provided with good material for the "building" of an outstanding band. Messrs. C. W. and F. N. Black were responsible for engaging this combination of musicians, and as they have extensive business ramifications on both sides of the Atlantic, the band will be able to obtain all the latest numbers without the least delay.

This week there is the usual programme of dancing twice daily—from 4 to 6 in the afternoons, when tea and dancing together cost 1/6, and from 8.30 to midnight each evening. The "after-the-show" suppers entitle patrons to free dancing after half-past 10.

MAKING WIRELESS SIMPLE

ALL-ELECTRIC MURPHY 3-VALVE
SCREENED GRID RECEIVER, A.C. MAINS
ONLY. (Not usable on D.C. Mains.)

1. Single Tuning Control. 2. Illuminated dial
marked in actual wavelengths. 3. Self-contained
moving coil loudspeaker with very high standard of
reproduction. 4. Walnut cabinet of very distinguished appearance, by one of the leading
designers in the cabinet industry.

(As illustrated). CASH PRICE
*Hire Purchase Terms from 39/-
deposit.* **19** GNS.

BATTERY OPERATED MURPHY 4-VALVE
SCREENED GRID PORTABLE.

1. Single Tuning Control. 2. Dial marked in
actual wavelengths. 3. Self-contained loud-speaker
and batteries. 4. Beautiful Walnut cabinet. 5. No
aerial or earth required.

CASH PRICE
*Hire Purchase Terms from 37/-
deposit.* **17** GNS.

★ I have written a book entitled "Making
Wireless Simple," which gives you a simple
explanation of how broadcasting works.
★ It also contains brief particulars of Murphy
sets. I shall be pleased to send you a free
copy on application.
★ In writing for this booklet will you kindly
mention the name of this publication !

WHATEVER people tell you, it is a fact that
sooner or later wireless sets, just like motor
cars, require servicing.

By service, I mean adjustments or replacements to
parts which become worn or lose efficiency with the course
of time. Batteries and valves, for instance, do not last
for ever.

That is why I make it my policy not only to make good
sets but to see that you get first-class service afterwards.
In fact, we will not sell a set to anyone until we know he
can get first-class service from the wireless shop who sold
him the set.

To achieve this we sell only through selected Murphy
dealers whom we know to be capable men, and who hold
their appointment only as long as they serve your
interests. In buying your Murphy set from a Murphy
dealer, therefore, you will be assured of having somebody
at hand should your set ever need servicing in the future.

Frank Murphy

B.Sc., A.M.I.E.E., A.I.Rad. E., Chartered Elect. Engineer.

MURPHY RADIO

MURPHY RADIO LTD., WELWYN GARDEN CITY, HERTS. TELEPHONE: WELWYN GARDEN 800

M.C.81

PHILOSOPHY OF GORDON RICHARDS

"MY CHIEF AIM IS TO RIDE WINNERS"

IMPERTURBABLE Gordon Richards was philosophical as ever when congratulated upon beating Frank Wootton's score of 187 winners at Warwick yesterday.

We quote some of the leading jockey's interesting comments:—

"The statement that I made a bet with a fellow jockey that I would reach 200 winners is all moonshine. I did not even think of it until I had that run of luck a few weeks ago. Then it seemed possible, and if the luck had remained with me I might have managed it. Now it seems out of the question.

"I get more than one offer in many races, and if I had always been able to make the right selection my total would have exceeded 200. As it is, I make it a general rule to take the first mount that is offered me, and it pays well.

"I think Lord Lonsdale's two-year-old Myrobella is—with one possible exception—the speediest horse I have ever ridden. The exception is Tiffin, who was a wonderful filly. I rode her in all her races as a two-year-old.

"It is every jockey's ambition to win one Derby, and naturally I also have that desire, but my chief aim is to ride winners.

RARELY USES THE WHIP

"It might be thought that, because I swing my whip a lot when I am riding that I am using it on my horse. I am not. In fact, I rarely give even the slightest touch to my mount.

"When flat racing is over, at every possible opportunity I go to Wolverhampton to watch the Wolves play.

"I play at right back for the Ogbourne stable team, and during every week in the winter we play home and away games with Manton, Beckhampton, and most of the other stables.

"The great thing for a successful man is to keep his head. When I pick up a newspaper my name may occupy a headline, but what is there in that? I am more interested in the news of the day. It makes no difference whether I am mentioned or not. I just get on with my work. That's all there is to it.

"I have no favourite courses. They all come alike to me.

"If a boy has it in him he will emerge from the ruck. When he's at the top, everything depends on him as to whether he will stay there. That's life in any profession. A level head. That's the only secret.

"If I had my time over again, and the choice of a career, I should still elect to be a jockey. I love every minute of the life."

Sporting Life 1932

Gloucestershire Echo 1932

AMUSEMENTS
FILMS — AND A FINE SHOW BY AMATEURS

SUCCESS IN "YEOMEN OF THE GUARD"

CHELTENHAM Operatic and Dramatic Society add yet another feather to an already well plumed cap by an extremely creditable performance of "Yeomen of the Guard" at the Opera House this week.

At the first night yesterday the audience were evidently charmed with the acting, the delightful singing, the gorgeous costumes, the deft way a company of 70 bore themselves in limited space as though they were half that number, and the general effectiveness of the whole show.

It was a triumph for local amateur acting, to which well timed and ably executed production contributed almost as much as the excellent performance of the principals and the faultless deportment and singing of the rest of the company. Not a prompt was heard, not a misplaced note.

The musical effects were made the most of by a large orchestra under the able direction of Mr. Arthur D. Cole.

Iris James, as Elsie Maynard, the wandering singer, enriches her part with a glorious voice and confidant acting, and W. H. Jones gives a talented display as Jack Point, the strolling jester whose winning sallies and carefree quips disappear when his heart is broken by unrequited love for his fellow troubadour. The pathos of the bruising and breaking of the frolicsome spirit of the Jester, in contrast to the consummation of the happiness of the other characters, with the possible exception of Phœbe Meryll—is brought out with full dramatic effect.

COUNTY THEATRE

TO-DAY (FRIDAY & SATURDAY)

"KING KONG"
"KING KONG"
"KING KONG"

Showing at — 2·30 — 4·35 — 6·40 — 8·35

NO ADVANCE IN PRICES.

Continuous from 2 p.m.

FOR NEXT WEEK'S ATTRACTIONS SEE BILLS

MANCHESTER UNITED'S POOREST GAME

Bad Football on Both Sides, but Southampton Have the Luck

ONLY THE FULL-BACKS PLAY WELL

Manchester United 1, Southampton 2

The match at Old Trafford on Saturday was one of the poorest seen on that ground this season. But for two extraordinary goalkeeping blunders by Moody the United would have won, but they would no more have deserved a reward of two points than did Southampton, who got them. From start to finish the game was an irritating spectacle of incompetent combination, in which three passes out of five went to a player on the other side. Added to this there was some of the most feeble finishing imaginable. In fact, far and away the best shooting was done by two full-backs, for from over forty yards' range Keeping, Southampton's left back, sent the ball sailing inches over the Manchester goal, while Silcock, from even longer range, forced Scriven to make a spectacular save.

Manchester United gained the lead after nine minutes' play when Stewart, unfairly tackled as he was boring his way into the penalty area, placed the free-kick so accurately that McDonald, with a deft flick of the head, easily obtained his first goal for the club. A few minutes later Ridding turned a centre from Spence neatly into goal, but the ball hit the inside surface of a post and in some extraordinary way was scrambled out for a corner. It was in the ninth minute of the second half that Southampton equalised, Moody misjudging a run out to Keeping's long free-kick so that Brewis headed in between the goalkeeper's upstretched arms. Moody's second blunder, four minutes later, left everyone aghast, for Arnold, on the left wing, put in quite a gentle lob which Moody fielded cleanly and then suddenly dropped behind him. It was quickly scrambled away, but this time there was no benefit of the doubt for the defence. Southampton had rarely looked like scoring before this sudden turn in their fortunes, and they rarely appeared likely to add to their lucky lead. On the other hand, Manchester United, although they struggled with more desperation than skill to save the game, rarely looked like getting another goal.

It was the United forward's off day. Chalmers was completely out of form, and the whole line appeared to catch his attack of inaccurate passing. Ridding did fairly well to a point, but he was far too slow in making his shots, even when allowance has been made for the fact that he rarely got the kind of pass he requires. Stewart did some clever things on the left wing, but his effectiveness was greatly reduced by Chalmers's lapses. The half-backs, with Vincent in the centre owing to Frame's attack of influenza, were a sturdy set in defence, but only Manley, the reserve, had really constructive ideas. The most distinguished players were the full-backs. Mellor was sometimes a little impetuous, but Silcock never let us forget that even football can be a graceful game. One sometimes thinks that Silcock might have been a great dancer had he not chosen instead to be a great footballer. There was another first-class full-back on the other side in Keeping. Bradford played well at centre half, and of the forwards the best were the wings. Arnold and Neal.   N. J. N. D.

Manchester Guardian 1933

ANN TALBOT   ELSPETH FOX-PITT   MARION LAMBERT

Harper's Bazaar 1930

CHERRY
Chooses
Clothes
Christmas

CAROUND THE ENTERTAINMENTS

HOLLYWOOD BACK TO LEG THEORY

IS it cricket? as the colonel snarled at the temperance meeting. Hollywood, after all those promises, has gone back to leg theory.

Hostilities in the all-star England-America test match had been fairly quiet of late, with the play slightly favouring the home side, who had been helped by some fine forcing shots from their two opening batsmen, Shepherd's Bush and Elstree.

So this week Hollywood, no doubt thinking that its attack was losing grip on the game, switched back to leg theory in an effort to recapture lost ground.

* * *

A Googly

Leaving aside "Strange Interval," which was a cinematic googly of no mean swerve, we haven't had either leg theory or practice on the films for some time. Even Garbo had been sending down medium-paced stuff of good length and uncertain bite.

Communications from the enemy camp, indeed, suggested that the attack would be mainly confined to mixed slows, some sentiment, a little sob-stuff and an occasional wisecracking leg.

Noted leg theory practitioners, like Lubitsch, had been almost subdued during recent bowling spells, and everything had pointed to a nice polite game.

* * *

But Lewis Milestone, who leads the current attack with "Rain" at the Empire, has the field well placed on the leg side, with Joan Crawford holding some fast ones in the sound track.

An occasional ball bumps rather dangerously, but the censor, who umpired this particular over very strictly, has no-balled some of Milestone's expresses which might have endangered the public.

* * *

Jack Buchanan and Margot Grahame in "Yes, Mr. Brown," a musical comedy at the Tivoli to-morrow.

Sunday Dispatch 1933

THE THIRD TEST MATCH

Paynter Helps in Great English Recovery

AUSTRALIA'S FIGHT FOR RUNS

ADELAIDE, SATURDAY.

A splendid fifth-wicket stand of 96 by Paynter and Verity, backed up by some fine bowling by Larwood and Allen, greatly improved England's chances in the third Test on Saturday. At the close of play Australia had made 109 for four wickets in reply to England's 341. Paynter, in his first Test, made 77 valuable runs in five minutes over three hours. He pulled and drove powerfully and nearly half his runs came from boundary strokes. Verity, though considered only a bowler, stayed in for two hours thirty-seven minutes and scored 45 runs, made up chiefly of leg-glances, although cuts added 10 runs in one over.

When Australia went in Larwood bowled a maiden to Fingleton. Woodfull then faced Allen, and turned the first delivery to leg for a single. Fingleton survived Allen's second ball, but he was out to the next, the ball touching the shoulder of his bat and Ames accepting the chance smartly. The spectators resented Larwood's bumpers, and booed loudly when one delivery got up and struck Woodfull over the heart and made him look shaken and sick. Larwood in his third over had Allen at "silly" leg, Verity at deep fine leg, Jardine at short leg, Sutcliffe at fine leg, and Hammond on the boundary. Bradman fell into the trap. He tried to hook a ball from Larwood, but hit the ball with the bottom of his bat, and Allen had an easy catch. McCabe, who did not look comfortable, skied the last ball of Larwood's seventh over to Jardine at short leg, and so easy was the chance that he began to walk to the pavilion before Jardine had the ball. Larwood had then taken two wickets for eight runs, and when he gave way to Allen at 36 Ponsford snicked Allen's second ball, and Hammond, at first slip, just failed to take a difficult chance. The 50 went up after 80 minutes' batting, and then Voce was forced to retire owing to a recurrence of ankle trouble. F. R. Brown took his place in the field. Allen took his second wicket at 51. Woodfull, who had batted for 89 minutes, played a low ball on to his wicket and was out for 22. Richardson and Ponsford steadily improved Australia's position, and before the close put on 58 runs in sixty-nine minutes.

Manchester Guardian 1933

MISS RAY LITVIN presented her costume characterizations with such charm and delicacy as to win unstinted applause and hold her audience to the end. For nearly two hours some three hundred members listened with rapt attention as she portrayed with skill scenes from works by Dickens, Shakespeare, O. Henry, Chekov and a study of Mistress Pepys with two delightful ballads from Pepys's Diary. Her work was thoroughly enjoyed and those responsible for arranging such a programme are to be congratulated on the form it took. It was instructive as well as entertaining.—Bishop Auckland paper, Durham, November 25, 1933. Touring the Midlands and Northern Counties, October and November. For vacant dates apply—13 Rothwell Street, Regent's Park, N.W.1.

Home and Country 1935

Manchester Guardian
1933

WELSH VICTORY AT TWICKENHAM

Scrambling Game Decided by a Dropped Goal

WOOLLER'S IMPORTANT INTERVENTION

(FROM OUR SPECIAL CORRESPONDENT.)

England 3, Wales 7

LONDON, SATURDAY.

Wales won the first victory they have ever had at Twickenham by a dropped goal and a try to a try, and deserved their success. The result made some of their supporters almost delirious with joy, but the delirious and the sober all joined with the English spectators in describing the play as disappointing. It was a scramble from beginning to end. There was not one bout of really clever passing and running, for when the ball was thrown and caught well the running was never straight for more than a yard or two; there was much poor kicking, "dummies" were accepted freely in the early part of the game, and some of the defensive work was bad; in fact, there was little play of the quality expected in an international game.

Harper's Bazaar
1930

The Bright Young People are busy finding new words for the season which will go with tight waists. Granny is such a help. "Intense" was her favourite word when last she had a waist.

ELECTIONEERING AT FOOTBALL.

COUNCILLOR'S COMPLAINT.

At the Town Council in Committee on Tuesday.

Councillor Austen asked if it was permissible for propaganda asking people to vote for a certain municipal candidate to be on sale on Corporation grounds. He was at the football match on Saturday, and bought a programme, and it advised everyone to vote for a certain candidate. [The Dover Football Club's programme stated:— "Don't forget the election on November 1st. Our Secretary, Mr. E. Bushell, is contesting the Pier Ward, and those of our supporters who live there might do worse than vote for him. Maybe we should get a new grand stand at Crabble and not have to pay so much for the use of the ground."]

The Town Clerk: I should not like to answer that question at such short notice. (Laughter.)

Councillor Austen: I think it was quite out of order.

The Town Clerk said that he could not see any objection at the moment.

Councillor Gore said he thought that there was an objection. If the Football Club had a private ground, it would be different, but this was on the town ground.

Councillor Eckhoff said that he did not know what was referred to, but if he hired the ground, and had programmes printed, was he to come to the Corporation and ask if he could have certain advertisements on them?

Councillor Austen: They are entitled to have it printed and displayed all over the town, but not on Corporation grounds.

Councillor Eckhoff: They hired the ground.

Councillor Austen: Evidently you know who it is.

Dover Express
1935

The world's fastest long-distance race, the
British Racing Drivers' Club 500 Miles event, in
progress at Brooklands, 1932.

Night and Day Hustle

Fifty Men Working To Have World's Biggest Fun House Ready

BEHIND the high walls of the new Fun House, on the Blackpool Pleasure Beach, a gang of 50 men are working night and day in a stern race with time.

Their aim is to have the new amusement house, claimed to be the largest of its kind in the world, ready for the big holiday crowds on Whit-Monday.

Inside the Fun House, which occupies the site of the lake belonging to the old water-chute, the men are preparing sliding, falling and revolving floors, giant slides, and other intricate devices calculated to make holiday-makers laugh with their unexpected movements.

Big electric motors, 30 in number, which are bedded in what was the concrete base of the lake, supply the operating power.

In the construction of the building itself something like 200 tons of steel, 50 tons of stucco, 45,000 square feet of masonry and 6,600 square feet of glass have been employed.

Blackpool Gazette and Herald 1934

Times Literary Supplement 1933

OUR NOBLE ENGLISH

The New Oxford Dictionary is, of course, easily the greatest achievement in lexicography which has ever been accomplished. As a monument of exact scholarship it is unapproached, perhaps unapproachable. The Americans once thought of attempting to rival or even surpassing it. They have, or had, the money and, since their universities are recruited from all the world over, might have found the men. They seem to have thought better of it, however, and are confining their efforts to a dictionary of specifically American uses. In this universal dictionary, a universe indeed in alphabetical order, there is room for all the word-collectors of to-day to roam without ever running up against one another. The tasks of interpretation, which troubled them in the past and caused them to set forth so many fantastic derivations, are here fulfilled, except in the case of an occasional puzzle that has so far baffled all the scholars. But there will always be scope and the scholar's praise for the word-collector who is also a word-collator and can give us essays such as Mr. Pearsall Smith's "Four Romantic Words" ("romantic," "originality," "create," and "genius"), which shows how a lasting-ripe form of literary criticism, linking up English and foreign men of letters and movements, may be securely based on the study of particular words in their historical perspective.

GLYNDEBOURNE FESTIVAL

Music Lover
1934

THE year at the spring, King Sol in his heaven, and Mozart on the doorstep— Pippa boasted nothing better than Glyndebourne can offer during this magic fortnight. Mr. John Christie has worked a miracle. As with all miracle workers, he met with some scepticism when he announced what he was going to do, for it sounded too good to be true! If any sceptics remain they were not among those who travelled back to town on the "opera special" last Monday or Tuesday. Those were two train-loads of enthusiasts. Of course, in all this, I am referring to what John Christie has done, not to the practical support his venture will call forth. That remains to be seen. There is in our public such a percentage of snobs who will travel all the way to Munich and Salzburg for opera, but not the hour's journey to Lewes. It will be of little use to tell them that *Cosi fan tutte* was every bit as good as at Salzburg. Unless that mysterious entity known as Society with a capital S ordains it to be "the thing" to go to Glyndebourne, I much fear that Mr. Christie is fated to experience some disappointment. But he is not a man to be easily discouraged.

Picture then to yourselves a theatre more comfortable than any within your experience, in which you can both see and hear perfectly, in the lovely surroundings of our Southern English parkland, and opera presented with every detail polished to resplendence. There are three hundred seats, raked at a convenient slope, and arranged in alternating rows so that nobody is exposed to that pain in the neck that comes of trying to dodge an enormous head immediately in front.

NIGHT IN CELLS

ALL OVER A GAME OF WHIST

INDIGNANT MEN RELEASED FROM PRISON

Two very indignant men were released from Cardiff Prison to-day. They had spent a night in the cells because of a game of whist—and because the regulations prevent men being released after 10 p.m. They were Albert Rex Berry and Clarence Maidment, and each was fined 10s yesterday for permitting and abetting in a whist drive at May Street Institute and Social Club. Berry is the secretary of the club. In addition, Berry was ordered to pay £15 costs and Maidment £1 costs, and the Recorder ordered that they should be kept in custody until the money was paid. As the banks were closed, and they could not get the ready money, they were driven to Cardiff Jail in a prison van despite a protest by Berry. Before ten o'clock the money was collected among friends, who presented themselves at the prison gates. The chief officer told them, however, that the regulations forbade any release after 10 p.m.

"TREATED AS A CRIMINAL"

When released to-day, Berry said: "I very much feel the indignity I have suffered. I was treated as a criminal and had to undergo the shame and ordeal of prison routine. Immediately on my admission my finger-prints were taken and my own clothes removed from me, and after a bath and a medical inspection I was dressed in prison garb.

"I spent a sleepless night in a dark cell thinking of my two little children who were waiting for me at home. It is an insult to decent citizenship. I am burning with the indignity of it all.

"Where is the justice of it? Whist has been played for years without any action being taken, and actually while I was languishing in my cell whist drives were being held in all parts of the city and even advertised within a few yards of the police headquarters. If I am a criminal because of an innocent game of whist, then God help British justice."

Edinburgh Evening News 1934

PARTIES.

Talking of parties—or were we? Anyway, we should be—last week Miss Eleanor Esdale of St. Hilda's was twenty-one and, with Mr. Graeme Muir, gave a party in St. John's to celebrate the happy event. In animated conversation we saw Miss Edith Shawcross, who is shortly to speak in a debate, the subject of which is 'That men should not be admitted to the University,' and Miss Tania Voronsoff, who is now a member of it. Outstanding among the guests was M. Georges Fisher, whose fur waistcoat drew all eyes, as indeed did the delicate black damask of Mr. W. H. Auden's when he recited his poems on Saturday night to the English Club; which waistcoat we were able to view more closely at the amusing party the Club gave afterwards at the Randolph.

Isis 1934

In this group are included Miss Micheline Patton, Miss Marghanita Laski, Miss Brenda Poole, and Miss Alison Hope. In the centre, seated, is Lady Willert.

A Boat Race Novelty.

Sheffield Daily Telegraph 1933

FLEET STREET, SUNDAY. NIGHT.

EXCEPT for a peppery old man who would insist on talking about the Oxford Union's motion on "King and Country" and kept calling Oxford "a set of vegetarian pacifists," everybody near me at Barnes Bridge yesterday afternoon was sorry not to see Oxford more closely up to Cambridge than a good two lengths. One enterprising spectator had brought a portable wireless set and we were able to follow the early stages of the race through this and knew that Oxford were ahead when the clamour around drowned the broadcast. The owner of the set had a sorry reward. He attracted such a crowd round him that his view of the race was completely spoilt.

Some year loud speakers will be fitted all along the tow path. As it is the people watching the race anywhere except at the finishing post learn the result later than do Brazilian coffee planters.

Bigger Crowd.

People have said in the last few days that interest in the Boat Race had dwindled, but yesterday, although rain threatened, there was a bigger crowd than usual. In the Cambridge Boat Club enclosure at Duke's Meadows undergraduates and Old Blues listened excitedly to the broadcast of the race and stood on chairs when at last the crews came into view. Across on the Surrey bank a dense throng, packed closely up to the water's edge, cheered and counter-cheered as the progress of the race was signalled by the raising of the Light or Dark Blue colours on the club flagpole.

The tide looked unusually slack for a Boat Race, and the water was smooth and unruffled from Chiswick Eyot up to Barnes Bridge. As the crews passed the bridge even Cambridge were tired. A few minutes later an autogyro, which had been hovering like a hawk over the winning post, droned away like an angry bee, and the race was over.

We have been accustomed for twenty years to aeroplanes flying over the course, but not to an autogyro or helicopter poised in the air over it. I wonder whether the judge would like to have one and keep pace with the crews from above?

WIRELESS AND "TALKIES" RIVALLED

First-class Concert at Sidbury

In these days when the talkies and wireless are so well within the reach of most people, it must be a difficult task to stage a village concert that will rise to the expectations of its audience.

This, however, was accomplished on the occasion of the G.F.S. concert at Sidbury, when the Village Hall was packed to its utmost capacity. There were items to suit all tastes, each one in turn being heartily applauded, and in most cases encored. The arrangements were all in the very capable hands of Mrs. Prendergast, who had been fortunate to secure the services of Miss Doris Tutt, a talented contralto. She has a voice of outstanding purity and wide range, and she delighted her listeners with all her songs, particularly in "Softly awakes my heart," "Still as the Night" and "Serenade." This was Miss Tutt's first visit to Sidbury, and her next will be anticipated with much pleasure.

Mr. Huyshe, an old favourite, was given a cordial welcome. The possessor of a fine tenor voice, he sang with his usual perfect artistry and clarity the songs "Mountain Lovers" and "Beauty's Eyes." Two duets, "Merry Month of may," from Merry England, and "Home to our Mountains," by Miss Tutt and Mr. Huyshe were received with well-deserved applause, as their voices blended perfectly.

A great asset to the party was Miss Spencer Jones, who charmed everyone by her natural rendering of the song "Plum Stones," and later in a mime, a feature of entertainment very rare in these days.

A special word of praise must be accorded Mr. D. Finlayson, who "brought down the house" with his song "Buying a postage stamp." In a duet, "Your Girl and my Girl," he and Mr. Langrish both acquitted themselves well.

The soloists were well supported by the G.F.S. concert party, who were particularly smart and effective in the opening chorus, "Whoop-de-oo-dle do," and in "Old Memories." In the latter Mr. E. Smith did remarkably well as the coon and he also showed great ability as an actor in the dialogue (with Miss D. Gant) entitled "Seaside Amusements."

A very enjoyable concert ended with a comedy sketch entitled "Turn him out," in which the artistes were Messrs. C. Finlayson, A. Smith, D. Finlayson, Miss P. Morriah and Miss E. Pinn.

Western Times 1933

GREEK DANCING.

HAPPY HOURS AT A SERVICE CLUB.

Monday evening is a great occasion at the Edwardian Hut, Worcester Street, for it is the one night in the week when Greek dancing is held there. The classes were started last March, originally with the idea of interesting the unemployed girls and young women who were attending the service club. Since then it has become so successful that its popularity is shared only with the Saturday club dances, to which boys and girls are invited.

About 25 girls were dancing there the other evening, and, as most of them had joined at different times, there was, of necessity, a great variation in their ages. Some of the older girls were in their twenties, others were small schoolgirls of 11 or 12, and one tiny girl, who was there for the first time, was only seven years old.

But such discrepancies in both age and accomplishment had no disturbing effect on anybody. When a fresh step was being taught

CASCADE OF FRILLS.

An evening frock in primrose satin with a shoulder trimming of ecru lace. A cascade of frills down the side of the skirt gives a dainty and becoming effect.

the novices sat round the room and watched the more advanced dancers; then, when they, in their turn learnt the elementary steps, the older girls helped them.

What chiefly surprised me, as an interested spectator, was the ease with which the newcomers picked up the different movements; their greatest difficulty was the slowness of each action, but by the end of the lesson they were all—more or less—falling into the correct rhythm.

Enthusiastic Learners.

During a pause in the music several of the dancers came and stood by me.

I asked them how long they had been doing Greek dancing.

"I came the first night," said one girl, "and I haven't missed once."

"Neither have I," and a chorus of enthusiasm rose from the little group around me. Most of them were wearing the blue tunics which denote a stage of proficiency. The beginners were still wearing their ordinary clothes, but they were nearly all bare-legged.

A pleasing feature of these classes is the friendly way in which the older girls help the younger ones. Previously there has been a very marked barrier between the different ages. Older girls have kept to themselves, refusing to be drawn into club activities which are shared by the smaller children. Now a common appreciation of Greek dancing has banded them into one large, happy class.

"Do you like it?" I asked one child. "No, Miss, I don't," she replied; "I love it."

D. M. H.

Birmingham Mail 1934

Vocalists

One does not hear much of **Adelaide Hall** these days. She was, I believe, one of the "Blackbirds" of 1928 and though she has recorded both for Brunswick and H.M.V. before, I do not remember a record so quaintly humorous as the present one (H.M.V. B8849). *I can't give you anything but love* is almost a sentimental ballad the way she sings it, until **Fats Waller** who accompanies her on the organ butts in with vocal interruptions. Much the same thing happens in *That Old Feeling* on the reverse. Incidentally, Waller's manipulation of the organ is cleverly done.

Simple and Sweet well describes **Connie Boswell's** singing of the song on Brunswick 02689. Even so I have a slight preference for *Summer Souvenirs* on the reverse. I like the resonance in her voice in this number. **Vera Lynn** sounds thin and hard by comparison; in *Cindrella* and *Is that the way to treat a Sweetheart?* she is ably assisted by the **Six Singing Debutantes** who make all the difference so far as the entertainment value of Decca F6903 is concerned.

The Gramophone 1939

FILM CENSORSHIP.

CRITICISM BY G. B. SHAW.

VIEWS ON SEX APPEAL.

Mr. George Bernard Shaw and Miss Madeleine Carroll figured in a surprise item on the wireless on Sunday night, when they gave their views on film censorship.

Licensing, in Mr. Shaw's opinion, had been the most expedient so far for keeping decent order, and censorship he condemned as silly.

Mr. Shaw said—" Sex appeal is a perfectly legitimate element in all the fine arts that deal directly with humanity. The Archbishop speaks of undesirable films. There are no undesirable films. No film studio in the world would spend £50,000 in making a film unless it was a very desirable film, indeed—possibly not desirable by an Archbishop but certainly desirable by that very large section of the human race who are not archbishops. Still as archbishops are very like other respectable gentlemen, except that they wear gaiters instead of trousers, any film corporation which devoted itself to displeasing archbishops would soon be bankrupt. Therefore, let us stop talking about desirable and undesirable, and consider whether he can weed out from the great mass of desirable films those which are detrimental to public morals.

" The censorship method, which is that of handing the job over to some frail and erring mortal man and making him omnipotent on the assumption that his official status will make him infallible and omniscient, is so silly that it has produced the existing agitation, and yet some of the agitators are actually clamouring for more of it."

Others were obsessed with sex appeal. Sex appeal's treatment under the censorship was often vulgar—yet he believed that on balance the good that had been done by the films in associating sex appeal with beauty and cleanliness, with poetry and music, was incalculable.

It was in quite other directions that the pictures were often mischievous, and if a new public inquiry was set on foot its business must be to ascertain whether on the whole going to the films made worse or better citizens of us. So far licensing had proved the most effective expedient for keeping decent order pending the time when theatres and picture houses would be public institutions under the control of a Ministry of Education and the Fine Arts.

Miss Carroll said—" The average Englishman quite rightly hates having his liberty curtailed. I sincerely believe he is his own best censor, and would much prefer to remain so."

Londonderry Sentinel **1935**

Things to Come.

In the Wellsian future, I am pleased to report, there will be no more colds, no more pestilences of any kind. The world will have been made fit for middle-aged dreamers, like Mr. Wells, and for young sybarites, like Mr. Sayers. There will be gadgets galore, all the fun of the fair and no cheating, free rides on merry-go-rounds and turnabouts, perpetual masquerade, and the Big Thrill of the Space Gun which will blow you, if you care for such things, to the Moon. Well, well . . . Wells, in short.

But first there's going to be a real nasty WAR—poison gas and all that. You'll just wake up one night about midnight and find yourself coughing out your guts. Mr. Wells seems to think that this will be inevitable. In fact, he seems to think that it will be desirable, or at least necessary, and that the sooner it comes the better, because, until it does come and the entire swarm of modern citizens are extirpated, we —that is, Mr. Wells and myself and all the other nice people—can't set about fixing up our nice new merry-go-round world of the future. To put it flatly, Mr. Wells thinks that we cannot have the nice Future until the nasty Present wipes itself out of existence.

New English Weekly **1936**

THE MASTER

JACK HOBBS has played his last innings in first-class cricket. He announced his retirement on February 25 in a letter to the President of the Surrey C.C.C., and one of the greatest cricketers the world has ever seen passes from the stage. His record stands alone—both in aggregate of runs and in the number of centuries—and his performances in Test Matches are wonderful. I use the word advisedly, for on more than one occasion he made big scores in Test Matches—notably at the Oval in 1926—on wickets which were giving the bowlers every possible assistance. He was undoubtedly the best batsman in the world between 1910 and 1928, and in any discussion as to who is the best batsman cricket has so far produced, his name inevitably occurs. In his *prime* he was, I think, the greatest batsman, *on all wickets,* I have ever seen. He was equally fine against every type of bowling. On sticky, difficult wickets, he always struck me as more at home than anyone else—V. Trumper and J. T. Tyldesley not excepted, and he was a masterly player of the googlie both on matting and on grass. The Australian fast bowlers, A. Cotter, J. M. Gregory and E. A. McDonald also suffered heavily at his hands, as did our own fast bowlers. Like " W. G." in his prime, " he didn't care who bowled," but he was a far finer player of slow bowling than The Champion.

D. G. Bradman, on a fast, true wicket must be accounted his superior, but we have not seen enough of Bradman on sticky wickets to be able to compare him with Hobbs.

Hobbs has been called The Master, and that's exactly what he was.

And his fielding was almost on a par with his batting. He was, indeed, one of the greatest cover-points in history—a dead sure catch, very quick on his feet, and with a lightning-like and invariably accurate return. On the M.C.C. tour in Australia in 1911-12, he ran out *fifteen men,* and he did not play in every match.

Everything Hobbs did was graceful to a degree. His style of batting was perfect—easy, well-balanced, sound, and he was master of every stroke. He, like Woolley, stands out as a model for the young cricketer.

And what a delightful man ! Success never spoilt him in the least. He was always the same—modest, kind, and appreciative of others. His gentle manner endeared him to people, and he had plenty of character behind all his gentleness, as so many gentle people have.

On a tour long since gone by he was a great prop to me in time of trouble, and I am happy to think that I played much of my cricket at a time when he was at his zenith.

He exercised a great influence, and he was immensely and deservedly popular. The Australians, one and all, from the member in the pavilion to the man on The Hill at Sydney, or in the " Outer " at Melbourne and Adelaide, almost worshipped him.

He was equally admired in South Africa, where they still talk of the manner in which he dealt with Faulkner and Vogler.

J. B. Hobbs was a cricketer whose peer the world has seldom seen, who played the game in a great and generous spirit.

The Cricketer **1935**

Humour and Hill Billies

Sandy Powell bursts into song this month. His version of *Hear all, see all, say now't* should serve as a shining example to others who sing this song. Invariably one hears Yorkshire (and Lancashire) dialect hopelessly distorted by both radio and recording artists. Dance band vocalists are the worst offenders. *I'm getting on nicely, thank you* is another song which suits Powell's style to a nicety. Hear them both on Rex 9467. As usual " big-hearted " **Arthur Askey** is as effervescent in the recording studio as over the air. In both *Woof! Yap! Bow-Bow-Wow* and *Have a bit of pity on a Crooner* on H.M.V. BD650 his personality and his really funny asides come over exceptionally well. **George Formby,** on the other hand, is comparatively tame in *Kiss your Mansy Pansy* on Regal-Zonophone MR2947. The reverse side, *Sitting pretty with my fingers crossed* is definitely more entertaining and just a shade suggestive.

The Gramophone **1939**

Laurence Olivier as
Hamlet at the Old Vic,
1937.

Theatre Worl
193

PORTRAITS by ANTHONY

DONALD WOLFIT
as
Hamlet

● Donald Wolfit is earning an excellent
name as a Shakespearean actor, and is
already (despite the fact that he is still
in his early thirties) well to the fore in
the eyes of the public and the critics.
Last year was his first at Stratford-on-
Avon, where he came with an excellent
reputation as a romantic actor, a
reputation which he has since enhanced
with magnificent performances as
Hamlet and Petruchio, both last season.
His Hamlet is repeated this year, and
amongst other parts he appears as
Autolycus in *The Winter's Tale*,
Iachimo in *Cymbeline*, Touchstone in
As You Like It, Kent in *King Lear*,
Ford in *The Merry Wives of Windsor*
and Chorus in *King Henry the Fifth*.

BRITAIN'S STRONGEST OLYMPIC TEAM SO FAR

Encouragement For Field Events Men; Two Great Veterans Included

By E. A. Montague

High Jump

R. K. I. Kennedy (Cambridge University an l Achilles), J. L. Newman (London A.C.), S. R. West (Polytechnic H.)

Hop, Step, and Jump

E. Boyce (North Belfast H.).

Throwing the Discus

B. L. Prendergast (St. Mary's Hospital), L. R. Carter (London A.C.).

Throwing the Hammer

N. H. Drake (Sutton-in-Ashfield H.).

The team is a good one, and the selectors are to be particularly congratulated on picking nine field-events men, none of whom has any appreciable chance of scoring a single point. The experience should be invaluable to these men, and the fact that their promise has been thus recognised will be a tremendous encouragement both to them and to the rest of the unfortunate jumpers and throwers who are for ever being told how useless and incompetent they are. N. H. Drake, for instance, though he is unlikely to get a place in Berlin, is yet the only Englishman since the war except M. C. Nokes who has thrown the hammer 150 feet. F. R. Webster has beaten the English native pole-vault record three times this season, the last of them yesterday. S. R. West is the most stylish high jumper that we have produced so far, and E. Boyce, of Northern Ireland, is the only British long-jumper since H. M. Abrahams who has beaten 24 feet. Both B. L. Prendergast, a Jamaican, and L. Reavell-Carter yesterday threw the discus more than 140 feet, a distance which seemed unattainable by any British discus-thrower half a dozen years ago.

Manchester Guardian 1936

FITNESS

DURING the next three years the Government has budgeted to spend more than £2,000,000 on the deal of making Britain a fitter nation. A White Paper sketching the Government's proposals to fulfil one of this country's most pressing needs was published yesterday.

National Advisory Councils, one for England and Wales, the other for Scotland, will be established to discover the best roads along which to lead our people towards health. A national College of Physical Training is to be founded, and local authorities empowered to organise community centres for those who are "getting fit." Two grants committees to disburse the necessary money complete the main machinery. The first year will largely be spent in shaping the programme. Four months have already gone since Mr. Chamberlain spoke of the urgent need to make British citizens more robust, yet we are still at the preliminaries.

"alien to the national temper and tradition," any hint of compulsion has been rejected. To what extent the voluntary advance towards better health succeeds will depend on the enthusiasm of local authorities and of the many existing organisations. Happily, in recent years there has been a new and strong impulse towards "keeping fit," and it is to be hoped that whatever opportunities are made available will be seized. Other nations have stolen a march on Britain in this primary matter of pursuing health. If our town-bred population begin to realise as the old Greeks that body and mind are interdependent, this nation will gain new happiness and poise.

Daily Mail 1937

"NOT AN I.R.A. TERRORIST"

A J.P. Court was held in Thurso on Tuesday. Ex-Provost Asher and Mr David Begg on the bench.

Hugh Bradley, vagrant, of no fixed residence, was charged with being drunk and disorderly and committing a breach of the peace at Scrabster Pier on Monday afternoon.

The Procurator-Fiscal (Mr D. Keith Murray) stated that accused was seen by the police and was cursing and swearing and using filthy language, causing a large crowd to collect. He then attempted to enter the Pentland Hotel 'bus but was refused, whereupon he threw the bag he was carrying at the 'bus and said "It is a pity it is not a bomb as I would blow the whole place up."

The accused said he had no connection with the I.R.A. terrorists as he was a native of Hamilton and of Scottish parents.

The Bench said that, owing to the seriousness of the times such conduct could not be tolerated, and sentenced accused to ten days' imprisonment without the option of a fine.

Caithness Courier 1939

Lawn Tennis

Manchester Guardian
1936

PERRY WINS AT WIMBLEDON

LONDON, FRIDAY.

The final of the men's singles at Wimbledon was played to-day between F. J. Perry (Great Britain), the holder, and G. von Cramm (Germany). Perry won, and won as he liked, for Cramm sprained a muscle in his thigh on the first service of the match.

The two men both wore white jackets when they appeared, and neither carried the many rackets usually associated with the first-class player. Instead, a servitor, also in a short white coat, appeared in their rear, carrying rackets and towels for the two combatants. Perry was nervously looking behind him in order to be quite sure that the servitor was in due attendance.

The first game promised a grand fight; the first game in Perry's match with Budge yielded ten deuces and this one nine. It was Perry's service, and he was serving well. Each had two net cords, and Perry won it after all on a net cord of his own. He had made mistakes and had even double-faulted, but he was also making great shots and playing confidently. One game all was called, Cramm winning his service to thirty on a great back-hand. Perry led 2—1, having served finely, and after that there was no fight at all. Perry never relaxed, which was as well, served finely, and was obviously in form, for his famous forehand worked smoothly. One sympathised with both men on an unsatisfactory and unhappy final. When all was over Perry went off with Cramm, giving the latter's hair a tug, presumably for sympathy. Thus Perry became champion for the third successive year, and all in forty minutes.

Sunday Referee
1936

—He's Got Rhythm—

Mr. D. M. de R. Winser, scholar of Corpus Christi College, stroke of the (unsuccessful) 1936 Oxford crew, has won the Newdigate prize at the University with a poem on "Rain."

He won the King's Gold Medal for verse while at Winchester.

Yesterday he said that half a year's work had gone into this year's prizewinning entry. "I did most of it in railway trains while travelling abroad, and some of it at the end of boat-race training, when I was so bored I did not know what else to do.

"I am afraid it is not very good. It does not rhyme, and I am not sure in what metre it is written."

110 MILES IN A GLIDER

New British Record

What is stated to be a new British gliding record was set up yesterday by a young London shipping merchant, Mr. Philip Aubrey Wills of Chapel Street, E.C.

He started from Dunstable at noon and came down on the rifle range at Pakefield, Suffolk, at 3.30 p.m., having covered a distance approximately of 110 miles. He was flying one of the first British high performance gliders to be designed and constructed in this country.

A record was not anticipated when Mr. Wills took off, but conditions improved, and he decided to make an effort for a record. When near Whipsnade he was able to rise to 3,800 feet, but owing to low-lying clouds he was on one occasion forced down 800 feet.

Mr. Wills told a reporter at the end of his flight: "The limiting factors for British gliders are physical endurance and the smallness of the British Isles compared with countries like Germany, where the gliding record is 310 miles."

The previous distance record for a British-made glider was set up on April 19 by Mr. A. L. Slater, of Matlock, with a flight of 75 miles, during which he reached a height of 4,800 feet and attained a speed at times of 60 miles an hour. A previous flight of 96 miles was made in England by Mr. G. E. Collins, of the London Gliding Club, in August, 1934, but the machine he used was of German construction. Mr. Collins met with a tragic death last July, when he crashed in a glider at an air display in Huntingdonshire.

Manchester Guardian 1936

A "Vic" First Night

The long-standing wish of Ralph Richardson and Laurence Olivier to appear together in "Othello" will be realised next Tuesday when the play is presented at the Old Vic with Mr. Richardson as the Moor and Mr. Olivier as Iago. Mr. Richardson appeared at the "Vic" a few seasons ago as Iago, but both actors come fresh to their present rôles. Curigwen Lewis will be the Desdemona, and Martita Hunt, who was John Gielgud's leading lady during his memorable Old Vic season of 1929-30, will be welcomed back as Emilia to the theatre where she did some of the most interesting work of her career. Other important rôles will be taken by Anthony Quayle, Cassio; Stephen Murray, Roderigo; Tristan Rawson, the Duke; Frederick Bennett, Gratiano; and Andrew Cruikshanks, Lodovico. Tyrone Guthrie is the producer.

Curigwen Lewis

This Evening's Star

Jessie Matthews, star of stage and screen, will sing many of the songs that she has made popular in her broadcast this evening at 6.30.

Radio Times
1936

Sunday Times 1938

" Giselle "

Margot Fonteyn and Robert Helpmann in the Sadler's Wells Revival

Bystander 1937

The Prince and the Vintner's Daughter

This Gothic two-act ballet to Adam's pleasant music is of some antiquity, having been first performed in Paris (with Grisi as Giselle) in 1841 and making its English debut at Sadler's Wells next year, with Mrs. Honner as Giselle and Dibdin's notorious tank stage for the water effects in the second act. In the revival of *Giselle* at the Wells—Sergeeff's 1934 production, modelled on Coralli's choregraphy — seventeen-year-old Margot Fonteyn has stepped gracefully into the impressive tradition set by Andreyanova, Pavlova, Karssavina and Markova. Her Giselle, cleverly supported by Robert Helpmann's Prince, is a performance which reaches an exquisite climax in the mad scene at the end of the first act ; the pas de deux is attractively executed by Harold Turner and Mary Honer and Pamela May is an efficient Queen of the Willis in the nebulous second act. With small alterations, William Chappell's 1934 decor and costumes are used

Profit from Ogee THEATRICAL Supplies

Comparatively few Hairdressers realise how much business awaits them in Theatrical and Carnival supplies. In every town and almost every village there are Dramatic and Operatic Societies who need costumes, grease paints and various other make-up requirements. Then, of course, practically every family captures the festive spirit with masks, hats and humorous novelties that are invariably difficult to buy locally. This is the Hairdresser's legitimate business ! This is where **you** can make extra profit, not only at Christmas but all through the Winter Season ! Take, for instance, the time-honoured Santa Claus Masks literally bought in thousands at this time of the year: we have them in paper at 4/- doz. or linen at 9/- doz.; with cloth hood 12/- and 24/- doz. The popular Comic Mouse Mask costs 10/- doz. or larger at 15/- doz. The rather fearsome face on the right is one of many assorted designs in Comic Linen Masks at the low price of 7/- doz. You can fix your own profit of course! Then we have hundreds of comic noses, bald heads, whiskers, animal heads, etc., etc., that sell on sight by hundreds. Our Gipsy Dancer represents a very large variety of material fancy costumes. This one, with black sateen bodice, white sateen skirt, trimmed gay colours, and gold sateen sash and headdress costs 16/6. We have them in paper also at 8/4. Hawaiian or Policeman, we have the costumes your customers want. Why not come and see them all !

OSBORNE, GARRETT & CO., LTD.,
51-54, FRITH STREET, LONDON, W.1.
Also at Birmingham, Glasgow and Manchester.

Gipsy Dancer

Time and Tide 1938

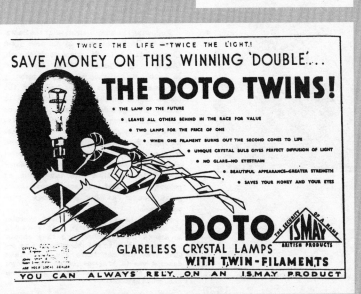
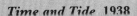

ART

Germans and Englishmen

PLATO discussed the advisability of showing artists the door, and in historical practice a good many poets, painters and creators of imaginative works have had it slammed behind them by their native town or state. The modern Germans—not all still alive—whose pictures are to be seen at the Burlington Galleries are for one reason or another not looked upon by the German authorities to-day as patriotic enough. However some of them are very good painters.

Liebermann, who died in exile, knew so well how to express the quintessence of the good earth, that he would probably not have come under official displeasure if he had not been a Jew. But Kandinsky and Klee, for instance, are obviously no more the Nazi cup of tea than compatible with Victorian ideals of naturalism : they are surrealist, they might be Frenchmen, and no sort of a moral could possibly be read into their pictorial fancies Corinth would seem strong enough and German enough for anyone, and a grand sense of beauty could not, I should have thought, be denied him ; the same seems to me to apply to Kathe Kollwitz. This is an important exhibition, the first of its kind to be held in London for many years.

POOL BETTING

The second resolution, also formally moved by the President, was on Pool Betting :—

"That this Annual Meeting of ministers and delegates of the General Assembly of Unitarian and Free Christian Churches, believing that the widespread and increasing growth of pool betting is a danger to the moral health of the country—

(a) Urges the churches to undertake an educational campaign on the subject, and to encourage in every way the provision of alternative outlets for the instincts which at present find expression in gambling ;

(b) Requests the Government to press forward with effective legislation for the purpose of curbing the evils inherent in the Pool Betting system."

The REV. F. COTTIER (Gorton) had been summoned home and his speech was read by the REV. S. MOSSOP (Manchester). He demonstrated the extraordinarily rapid increase of pool betting within the last four years. The promotors kept their accounts secret, but it was estimated that they handled £34,000,000 a year, with no risk of loss to themselves and no legal supervision, other than the elementary laws governing credit betting. A vested interest had been created, and had reached such a point of expansion that it was a real menace. He urged that we should educate our young people to a true sense of values, and that we should ask the Government to put the pool-promoting companies under control, limiting their profits and ordering the publication and audit of their accounts.

Inquirer 1938

Daily Record 1939

THE "PUB" DARTS FANS ARE PEEVED

TO dart or not to dart. That was the question in 200 Glasgow public houses last night. Nobody knew the answer. Nobody knows the answer now.

Glasgow Licensing Court yesterday delivered itself of the commandment: "Thou shalt not dart nor domino nor play any game whatever that is in a public house "—or words to that effect. Similar rulings were given by the courts in Paisley and Peebles.

Trouble is no one knows when the order assumes all the majesty of the law.

Glasgow has about 1100 public-houses. There are 100 or thereby in the darts league. There are at least 200 which feature darts officially or outwith the league.

A round of many of these last night did not produce one with a dart board in evidence.

Two facts emerged:—

Darts are immensely popular in pubs, as elsewhere.

Darts reduce drinking instead of encouraging it.

Talk last night was of a petition to the Magistrates. Rough-and-ready estimates guaranteed 5000 signatures.

THE RECORD BREAKER
ENGLAND v. AUSTRALIA AT THE OVAL, 1938.
L. HUTTON, c HASSETT, b O'REILLY, 364

The Cricketer
1938

All Night Dances

R.C. Bishop's Warning

Will Clogher Follow Kilmore ?

IN the Diocese of Kilmore by order of the Roman Catholic Bishop all night dances are forbidden and such functions must close at 11 p.m. The order is being faithfully observed.

Will a like order be made for the Roman Catholic Diocese of Clogher ?

Following the administration of the Sacrament of Confirmation to 33 children from Clogher parish in St. Macarten's church, Clogher, on Tuesday, Most Rev. Dr. M'Kenna, R.C. Bishop of Clogher, strongly denounced all night dances and said the people should put their heads together to see if these all night dances could not be done away with. From 6 till 11 o'clock p.m. was quite long enough for a dance. After these all night dances those who attended them were not able to work next day. Young people now-a-days after leaving school seemed to get filled with the notion of getting amusement, exposed themselves to grave danger as far as morals were concerned.

Parents, he suggested, should exercise vigilance over their children if they wanted to attend these dances, and they should accompany them to the dance halls and see that they did not leave the hall while dancing was in progress, or go into motor cars, or expose themselves to any other dangerous associations.

Impartial Reporter
1938

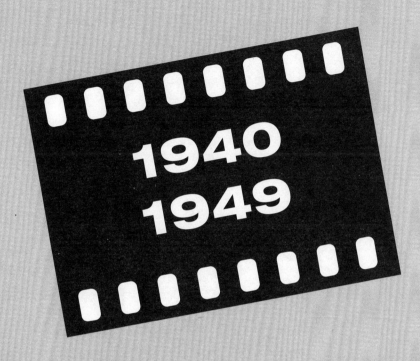

1940
1949

OUR MUSEUMS

THE problem offered by our public museums in war time is inevitably one of the very greatest complexity; and for obvious reasons it is a subject which at the present moment it would be inadvisable to discuss in all its implications. We venture, however, to prophesy, that when all reasons for reticence will have vanished and the full story of our museums during the war can be told, the manner in which this particular problem has been handled will call forth the unreserved commendation of those sections of the community to whom the museums represent a most important part of the structure of present-day civilization.

Obviously, " safety first " must be the guiding principle in the matter of museum administration during the existing emergency: but the very concept of " safety " is one which is none too easily defined and among the prized possessions of our museums there must be many, precisely for whose safety the process of removal itself offers risks the gravity of which can scarcely be exaggerated. Again, though it is an imperative necessity to ring down the curtain on normal museum activities in times such as those through which we are passing, yet it is an indisputable fact that the public call for the instruction and, indeed, entertainment derivable from museums and art galleries will never wholly cease to make itself felt. More particularly does this hold good of present-day Great Britain, where the concourse of young and active arrivals from overseas is so great. The museum curator who in this country just now endeavours to cater for such a demand, finds himself faced with a grave dilemma: for, on the one hand the exhibits which are going to be placed on view, must be of sufficient interest and representative quality to attract and hold attention; and, on the other hand, nothing of irreplaceable value can be shown, in view of the imminent risks of complete destruction.

Burlington Magazine
1940

JOE DAVIS CALLING

Now that my fractured wrist is completely normal again, I have been playing a few exhibition games for various charities. When staying at the Queens Hotel, Manchester, recently, I walked into the Billiard Room and was challenged by Mr. D. MacKay and a few of his friends to play a game of snooker. I agreed to do so if they would make a collection for my fund. The result is indicated in the list below. I will be happy to play anyone at any game if they will guarantee a similar result. Many thanks, Mr. MacKay.

While in that area, I also had the pleasure of giving an exhibition of billiards and snooker at the Victoria Social Club, Holmes Chapel, which is the Recreation Club attached to Wall Paper Manufacturers Ltd., and succeeded in raising £60 for the "Aid to Russia Fund." I am much indebted to Mr. Chesney, the Managing Director; Mr. Jackson, another Director of the Company; and to Mr. Blease for their support.

Billiard Player **1942**

BOOS FOR NOEL COWARD

When Noel Coward appeared last night on the stage of the Piccadilly Theatre at the end of his new play, "Blithe Spirit," there was a little booing from the gallery and a shrill voice called out: "Rubbish!" several times.

A sceptical author arranges for a seance to study medium mystic methods. To his consternation a spirit is materialised and proves to be his first wife. This ghost-wife comes to live in the house and carries on a duel with his real wife.

Fay Compton, Kay Hammond, Margaret Rutherford and Cecil Parker play the principal parts.

B. B.

Daily Mirror **1941**

SECRETS OF A ROAD IN WAR-TIME

By B. MYFANWY HAYCOCK

THERE are no more sign-posts at the cross-roads, no more milestones along the white road. Pillar-boxes have shed their identity discs and all places are named Somewhere.

Walking is an adventure these days!

How tame those pre-war hikes seem now. Then we always knew where we were and what village came next. But now our walks hold a large element of the unex-pected. Cross-roads can be the in-struments of Destiny. We waver when we reach them and our in-different sense of direction fails to come to our aid. Finally we decide to "toss-up" and let Fate choose our road.

Country miles can be long, long miles when there are no milestones to hold them apart. The road hops over a stream and runs teasingly up and around the hill. It has a secret now—the secret of where it is going and how far it is.

Gas-masks keep company with haversacks on our backs. We clutch our identity cards closely in case anyone should decide that we have a fifth (or even sixth!) columnish look.

Our way is marked and measured by landmarks which used to pass unnoticed. A green gate, a few Scotch pines, an old tin can in the hedge—we note them and remem-ber.

FILM: Scarlett O'Hara Comes to Town Next Week

Western Mail 1940

Sphere 1940

VIVIEN LEIGH AS SCAR-LETT O'HARA PRESENTED IN LONDON NEXT WEEK

The long-awaited film from *Gone with the Wind*, the enormously popular novel of the American War, appears on April 18. Miss Leigh is partly Irish

"MRS. CHARLES HAMILTON—ONE HUNDRED AND FIFTY DOLLARS—IN GOLD": Then she was on the floor and Rhett Butler was advancing towards her through the aisle of the crowd, that nasty mocking smile on his face. She was going to dance again—A dramatic incident at Atlanta

Sphere 1940

The World of Music
VERDI AND HIS OPERAS

MR. HUSSEY'S STUDY

MR. DYNELEY HUSSEY'S ex-cellent study of Verdi (the Master Musicians Series; J. M. Dent) might seem to come at an inopportune moment. As a matter of fact, it is good to be reminded that the great Italian composer was a man of the Risorgimento, of the Italy of Garibaldi and Mazzini, which Mussolini has betrayed.

Verdi was not only a man of honour but a man of vision, who felt it a shame that Italy should remain inactive when France was invaded by the Germans, and who again and again warned his countrymen against the blind worship of Teutonic art and ideals.

The present rulers of Italy have derided the liberal ideals that gave us Verdi—what have they given us instead? There has never been a period as sterile in the history of either Germany or Italy as the years that saw the creation of the totali-tarian state.

Daily Telegraph 1940

BOLSOVER RINGERS' LOSS.
DEATH AFTER AN ACCIDENT.

We regret to announce the death of Mr. Charles Mason, of Bol-sover, Derbyshire, who died in Chesterfield Hospital on Saturday, March 28th, after an accident the same day in the local colliery.

Mr. Mason had been connected with Bolsover belfry for over 30 years and has been steeplekeeper for the whole of that time. In addition, he had been a chorister for 35 years and had served the church he loved so well in many other ways. He will be a great loss to the Bolsover band.

He had rung about 95 peals, made up of Bob Major 4, Double Norwich Major 22, Kent Treble Bob 11, Superlative Surprise 20, Nor-folk Surprise 12, Rutland Surprise 2, Pudsey Surprise 4, Belgrave Surprise 1, Yorkshire Surprise 12, Cambridge Surprise 4, New Cam-bridge Surprise 3.

The deceased served in the last war for four years in France as a farrier and rose to be staff-sergeant.

He was laid to rest on April 1st and was borne to his resting place by members of the Ambulance Brigade, in which he had served for 36 years.

Ringing World 1942

Country Diary
TRAVELLING CIRCUS
by Suffolk Farmer

THE countryside dull? In the month of May? Ask young Bill from Barking.

In the wood there's a rippling azure sea of bluebells. In the corner of the paddock the grass is studded with gems, the bright orange cowslips, the paler yellow oxlips.

Even nearer to his heart's desire are the frisky foals, keeping close to their mothers, on the meadow. And the moorhen's nest on the half-submerged trunk of a fallen tree in the pond.

Birds nesting, too. The village boys laugh at Bill when he makes a nest, puts it in the hedge, and hopes that an obliging bird will lay an egg in it.

And then, once a year, the travelling circus!

*   *   *

WHAT thrills! Performing bears. Bejewelled ladies in silver and blue costumes skipping on horseback as their snow-white steeds canter round the ring.

A pony that nods yes and no, walks upright, pretends to lie down dead. A little dog that dances and jumps over hurdles. An elephant that never forgets.

These and many more at Ginetta's Great Circus and Jungle, on Cherry Meadow.

Nearly all the village boys and girls are there. They sit in tense excitement under the big billowing yellow and green canopy. With them are their pals for the duration, from Lambeth and Ilford and elsewhere.

*   *   *

Daily Herald 1941

Noel Coward in the tremendously popular 1942 film *In Which We Serve*.

HAMPDEN ROAR FOR STAN MATTHEWS

SCOTLAND 0   ENGLAND 4

A RECORD football wartime crowd of 105,000 people saw England give a grand exhibition at Hampden Park, Glasgow. The famous Hampden roar usually reserved for Scotland, was heard on this occasion acknowledging the brilliance of Stanley Matthews.

Horace Carter, his partner, soon placed England on top by scoring two goals in 40 minutes. The first came when Carter met a fine pass from Denis Compton and beat Dawson all the way with a terrific 15-yards drive. Next Matthews, by dazzling footwork, had the Scottish defence guessing, and Carter easily found the net again from short range.

Early in the second half Denis Compton slammed home the third goal, and a few minutes later Hagan worked an opening for Westcott to make the margin 4—0.

The closing stages were marred by some vigorous tactics, and Cullis, the England captain, had to leave the field temporarily following an incident which occurred while the game was held up.

The Scots were particularly poor in their finishing, and Wallace, as leader of the forward line, found that he could never get the better of Cullis.

England, with eight Army players, were as well together as Scotland, who fielded three newcomers and were disjointed.

The Compton brothers and Swift also played a prominent part, and altogether the winners reached a high standard of excellence.

Young made a praiseworthy debut for Scotland, but Buchan and Kean were far from successful on their first appearance.

This was England's fifth victory in the nine games played during the war, and the team played up to peace-time standards.

The People
1943

LISTEN TO BERLIN, B.B.C. SAYS

THE B.B.O. European Service last night invited its listeners in the oppressed countries to tune in to German radio stations.

Why? Because the Nazi network was broadcasting a concert by the Berlin Philharmonic Orchestra, conducted by Furtwangler, in *which Beethoven's Fifth Symphony —the V symphony—was included.*

The symphony starts with the three short notes and one long (. . . ———) which is morse code for V, the Victory sign to Britain's millions of fifth columnists all over Europe.

Germany appears to be so alarmed over the spread of the V campaign that last night the Nazi-controlled Dutch radio station at Hilversum started its programme with the V in morse, the announcer saying it was "the V for *German* victory."

Daily Herald
1941

THE THEATRE

"Blithe Spirit." By Noel Coward. At the Piccadilly.

IT is not unfair to say that without Thorne Smith and the "Topper" films Mr. Coward's new play would never have been written. Invisible ghosts who fling vases on the floor, a blonde and mischievous *revenant* in the style of Miss Constance Bennett, and a motor-smash, all bear the marks of their origin. What Mr. Coward has added to the Thorne Smith theme is crammed into an admirable and witty first act: the rest is all words and repetition and a bad taste of which Thorne Smith was never guilty. For death is a tricky subject; nobody remembering *The Wrong Box* or *A Slight Case of Murder* will deny that death may be an admirable subject for fooling, but the fooling has to be on an impersonal level—we mustn't be allowed to take the corpse seriously. One cannot draw a picture of a normally happy marriage and try to chill the blood at the idea of the harmless, aggravating wife driving to her death in a car with which her ghostly predecessor has tampered, and then a moment after the catastrophe dissolve an audience into laughter as the new ghost sets about her rival, pulling hair and hacking shins. The sudden transitions are not only maladroit; they show a taste-lessness with which Mr. Cecil Parker, Miss Fay Compton and Miss Kay Hammond were powerless to cope. No wonder that they were acted off the stage by the character who had the fewest words to betray the author with—Miss Ruth Reeves as Edith (a Maid).

The first act is magnificent with its portrait of Madame Arcati (Margaret Rutherford), the hearty healthy medium with her bicycle and her schoolgirl slang and her powerful Thurber jaw, who brings disaster on the Condoman household by materialising (to Condoman's eyes alone) the ghost of his first wife, Elvira. The lovely silly charming little creature, with her pale grey face and her blonde hair, dried and dusted with the chalk of a grave-yard, is matched against the large living woman—Ruth the second wife, with her efficiency, her clarity and her will to manage-ment, and between these two the agreeable badgered novelist, *homme moyen sensuel*, tired out as the curtain falls with mis-understanding and oddly happy with the ghostly breeze playing in his hair.

GRAHAM GREENE.

The Spectator 1941

The World of Music
THE "PROMS" SUSPENDED

REMARKABLE SEASON

THE 1940 Promenade Concerts season has had to be suspended after running half its course. But in those four weeks the "Proms" made history.

When theatrical or musical ventures close down before the appointed time the reason is usually want of public support. The "Proms" had to be cancelled for the opposite reason. They appealed to a vast public at a time when it was unwise for people to mass together.

Even last Saturday, with a concert that began after the sirens had given one warning and ended with another alarm, the audience was estimated at well over 1,200. There was no questioning the very sincere pleasure derived from the performances of the soloists and orchestra, performances often of the highest quality.

Sir Henry Wood has conducted Beethoven's C minor symphony on countless occasions, but he never gave a more inspiring and polished performance than that of last Friday, when Ida Handel also contributed a reading of Beethoven's violin concerto that was both warm and pure. Moiseiwitsch, Clifford Curzon, Joan Cross, Eva Turner and many others have given performances that will not be forgotten.

Novelties Postponed

There will be disappointment at the delay now inevitable before some of the promised novelties can be heard, such as the new work by Frank Bridge and the Edmund Rubbra symphony, which, in view of the composers' reputations, aroused great expectations. Vaughan Williams's Choral Songs may not be sung in public yet awhile, but they have been published by the Oxford University Press and all who care may read them.

The Shelleyan text voices with Shelleyan art and with a prophet's vision thoughts that are now in the minds of all concerning both war and peace. The full effect of the musical settings will only be apparent after the performance, but a reading suffices to show that the text was very much after the composer's own heart; his music possesses in an eminent degree the qualities of sincerity, strength and gentleness.

No review of the past four weeks' doings can ignore the wonderful Promenade audience which packed Queen's Hall night after night, in spite of heavy handicaps. Ours is said to be an unmusical nation; what other city in Europe could provide so shining an example of devotion to music?

The National Gallery concerts are being continued as usual, but will now be given in the air-raid shelter instead of under the glass dome.

Daily Telegraph 1940

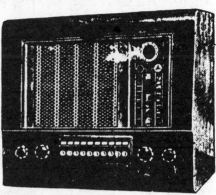
SIR HENRY WOOD
The Times 1944

A GREAT CONDUCTOR

Sir Henry Wood, C.H., the conductor of 50 consecutive seasons of promenade concerts, died in hospital at Hitchin on Saturday, after a short illness. He will be remembered as a great teacher of music in the fullest sense of the word—as one who had not only trained generations of students at the R.A.M., created choirs and orchestras, and always lent the helping hand to young composers and instrumentalists, but had raised the whole musical taste of his country by bringing great music to the people.

Over a period of more than half a century he also conducted, besides the "Proms," a large number of symphony concerts at Queen's Hall, and in the provinces famous choral festivals, concerts in America, ranging from Boston to the Hollywood Bowl, and Continental concerts too numerous to be summarized. It was he who first made orchestral conducting a whole-time occupation for a British-born musician, and by concentrating on that art paved the way for others to distinguish themselves in it, which they have not been slow to do. He may safely be described as the most popular musical figure of his time.

British Captives Give Jerry A Soccer Lesson

News Chronicle
1941

Frank Thorogood's SPORTS DIARY

ONE touch of sport makes the whole world kin even in war-time, and friend as well as foe will smile the smile that has no cruelty at the festive note which reaches England from a prison camp in Eastern Germany.

In that camp, so the story runs, a German Guard regiment, who have not apparently forgotten the good old days when England and Germany met in Soccer internationals, challenged a group of British prisoners to a game of football.

Halted at 27—0

WITH unconcealed delight our Tommies took up the challenge and when the game was halted—was it an armistice?—the score read 27—0 in favour of the British team.

Then the Nazis learned that their opponents were members of a well-known English League club who enlisted in a body and who were taken prisoners at Dunkirk.

The result does not matter, but it does matter that men who belong to nations with daggers drawn can quench all discord with the aid of a Soccer ball.

The incident reminds one of another when Charles Fry dined in Berlin with Hitler and Ribbentrop and suggested that Germany should play Test cricket as a means of a better understanding with Britain.

WHEN A GIRL EATS A BANANA ON THE EMBANKMENT

—well, it's news. Satisfied consumer in picture below is 23-year-old Miss Lee Ray, of the Fox Photographic Agency staff. Where did she get the banana? It was brought carefully from Algiers by two R.A.F. boys. Note public reaction.

Sunday Exp

Paris Expels Wodehouse

IT is expected that P. G. Wodehouse, arrested by the Paris police as an alleged collaborator, will be released conditionally this morning.

He and his wife will be required to live 60 miles outside Paris at a place chosen by himself but approved by the police.

The charge against Wodehouse of aiding the Germans, by his broadcasts from Berlin in 1941 appears to have been dropped.

Daily Herald
1944

"Luckily, George managed to get a box . . ."

Woman's Own 1948

Close-up view of banana—refresh your memory.

SHERLOCK HOLMES'S IDENTITY

CONAN DOYLE HIMSELF

Mr. Adrian Conan Doyle writes from the Berkeley Hotel, Berkeley Street, W.1:—

Since the death of my father, the late Sir Arthur Conan Doyle, there has been much speculation on the origin of his celebrated creation Sherlock Holmes. These conjectures have been revived in lively form by the recent publication of a biography by Mr. Hesketh Pearson. In his book Mr. Pearson tells us, and the newspapers have given some prominence to his words, that my father was in fact very unobservant man, and this, not unnaturally, has led to a renewal of the old discussion as to whether the remarkable characteristics of Holmes were based on Dr. Bell, of Edinburgh University, or on the strange Dr. Budd, or merely rooted in the influence of Edgar Allen Poe.

In view of the public interest, my family and I consider that it is high time that the truth, in sharp contrast to the above-mentioned conjectures, be placed on record. The fact is that my father himself was Sherlock Holmes.

Mr. Pearson gives us a few instances in which my father was slow to pick up a perfectly obvious fact. I accept those instances, and can indeed recall many more amusing ones, such as the occasion when my father arrived at a large banquet in London wearing full evening dress but with a black waistcoat, the situation being saved only by the fact that the guest of the evening—a world-famous scientist—turned up in the same attire ! When engaged upon the mental processes of some highly speculative problem, I have known him absent-mindedly to put on a brown shoe with a black one.

But what do these things prove ? In short, that my father had a mind with all the characteristics of a microscope. The obvious passed unnoticed because the obvious was entirely unimportant compared with the fact that his brain was focused upon the problem to hand, dissecting, exploring, and weighing the evidence that his extraordinary powers of perception could unearth from some detail that would yield nothing whatever to a brain less keen than his own. Many cases that had baffled the police were brought to him, and though none of them were of the homicidal order, I can recall no single instance in which my father failed to solve the problem.

Dr. Joseph Bell did indeed help to develop my father's immense power of observation and conclusions, but it must be placed on record that those powers were indubitably innate, and for the mental prototype of Sherlock Holmes we need search no farther than his creator.

The Times 1943

2 MILLION ON STOLEN AIR
BBC Lose £1,000,000

Britain's biggest "pirate" hunt is on. The hunted are the thousands of people with wireless sets for which they have no licence.

In Britain's 12,000,000 homes there are approximately 9,000,000 who regularly take out wireless licences. Approximately 1,000,000 homes have no wireless sets, leaving 2,000,000 owners of sets who are dodging payment—a loss to the revenue of £1,000,000 a year.

Daily Mail 1944

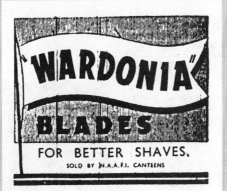

"WARDONIA" BLADES

FOR BETTER SHAVES.

SOLD BY N.A.A.F.I. CANTEENS

B.B.C. AS A FORUM FOR DISCUSSION

Mr. Bracken's Advice

Mr. Brendan Bracken, Minister of Information, yesterday told the B.B.C. to be more controversial and not to be afraid of politicians. He was speaking at a luncheon given by the B.B.C in honour of Sir Henry Wood to mark his seventy-fifth birthday and the fiftieth year of the Promenade Concerts which he created.

The B.B.C. had done miraculous work in this war, said Mr. Bracken, and the heads of broadcasting institutions in other parts of the world looked upon it as the world's greatest broadcasting system. "Never truckle to the politician," he said. "It would be a very good thing if the B.B.C. were to become more controversial, to be a public forum, and not be intimidated by Parliamentary questions or by being a constant target of political publicity hounds—I will take care of them.

"In any educated democracy every side should have its say. Bring the B.B.C. above all party levels. I am absolutely certain that the future of the B.B.C. is in being a real forum for great public discussions."

Sir Henry Wood, replying to speeches by Sir Allan Powell, chairman of the governors of the B.B.C., Sir Adrian Boult, and Mr. Bracken, invited the B.B.C. to become "curator" of the "Proms" and to accept the right to carry them on for as long as they thought fit. "I hope with all my heart that the B.B.C. will carry on my concerts as a permanent annual institution for all time."

He said he hoped that enough money would be subscribed to his jubilee fund to build a concert hall acoustically perfect and conveniently situated for everyone and seating 4,000.

Sir Adrian Boult said he had great pleasure in accepting Sir Henry Wood's gesture on behalf of the B.B.C.

Sir Arnold Bax, Solomon, Frank Dobson, Mr. C. E. M. Joad, James Agate, and Sacheverell Sitwell are among the contributors to a book which the B.B.C. has produced as a tribute to Sir Henry, and copies of which, though it is not yet on sale, were on the table.

Manchester Guardian 1944

B.B.C. BAN ON CROONERS
MORE VIRILE MUSIC

THE B.B.C. has decided to ban crooners of both sexes, slushy, over-sentimental songs, and dance band versions of the classics.

In a letter to music publishers and dance band leaders, the Corporation says that its many contacts with the public, the Services and the factories show that there is a desire for more virile and robust music in its programmes, and it asks for the co-operation of publishers, band leaders, and artists in seeing that this demand is met.

To this end the B.B.C. defines its policy as follows:—

To exclude any form of anæmic or debilitated vocal performance by male singers.

To exclude an insincere and over-sentimental style of performance by women singers.

To exclude numbers which are slushy in sentiment or contain innuendo or other matter considered to be offensive from the point of view of good taste and of religious or Allied susceptibilities.

To exclude numbers, with or without lyrics, which are based on tunes borrowed from the classics.

Sentiment must be Sincere

The B.B.C. is inviting music publishers to submit in advance of publication any doubtful numbers. It hopes for the closest co-operation with publishers, leaders and artists in a policy which should help to improve the standard of dance music in Britain.

The B.B.C. emphasises its intention not to exclude from the programmes sentiment which can be assessed as sincere.

The decisions will be made by a committee consisting of representatives of the variety, and music departments of the B.B.C. They will be final.

Yorkshire Post 1942

NOW THE 'GIN AND—' RACKET

AMERICAN and Allied troops are being "soxed" by unscrupulous publicans who sell "gin and limes" which contain 75 per cent. lime-juice.

The so-called "gin and limes" are ready mixed for sale in a bottle behind the bar. Three bottles of lime-juice cordial—costing 2s. 6d. each—are added to one bottle of gin.

The cost of four bottles of this concoction to the publican is 33s. 3d. From each bottle he can obtain 32 small glasses, which he sells for 1s. 9d. each.

On an outlay of 33s. 3d. he makes a profit of £9 10s. 9d.—550 per cent.

DROWNED

A licensee told the *Sunday Dispatch* last night that there is apparently nothing illegal in the practice of "drowning the gin with lime." He added that a reasonable percentage of lime was considered to be about 33⅓ per cent.

A variation of the racket is for the licensee to state that gin cannot be sold "neat" but must be ordered with some addition such as lime. The drink is then served already mixed—with no certainty that a full measure of gin is in the glass.

Sunday Dispatch 1944

ACTORS BY THE THOUSAND

From *Actors by the Thousand*, Longmans, 1944.

The passion for acting is an instinct. It is displayed by the followers of the witch-doctors of primitive tribes, in intercessions for rain, in war-dances after a victory. It is closely associated with the instinct to express emotions by dancing. The love which all children have for "dressing-up," the spirit of "Let's pretend," is the essence of drama.

But among the civilized peoples of to-day the widespread passion for acting is much more than this. It is based on a creative desire to put life into the written word, to bring one's own interpretation into the characters which an author has created (much as the instrumentalist can put his own interpretation into a musical score), to lift ideas out of the printed page and re-present them in action.

The production of a play, moreover, does not require only acting: it also provides an outlet for the creative energies of people who can paint scenery, design costumes, and arrange effective lighting. It provides the means by which a great many people can make use of their artistic ability—and by doing so give emotional and æsthetic pleasure to others.

The passion for acting has a firm hold on the people of the British Isles. In normal times, it is rare to find even the tiniest village without its group of players; it is impossible to name a town which has not at least one dramatic society, whilst most towns have several. These societies demand—and certainly receive—enthusiasm from their members. The people who belong to dramatic societies are nearly all fully occupied with a hard day's work; but you can see them learning their parts while they eat their lunches in crowded restaurants—you can notice them rehearsing gestures as they stand in packed trains. When overalls and office clothes have been put off, even now in war-time when the claims of Home Guard and Civil Defence have to be met, these enthusiasts still somehow find time to devote themselves to drama.

A scene from "The Barretts of Wimpole Street"

"Twelfth Night"

"The Tempest"

The Most Amazing Document of the War!

HOW THE NAZIS TRIED TO CRUSH JAZZ

ONE OF THE MOST AMAZING DOCUMENTS OF THE WAR HAS FALLEN INTO THE HANDS OF THE "MELODY MAKER"!

It exposes in black-and-white the humiliation of Continental dance-musicians playing under the Nazi yoke, but, more than that, it shows how the Germans ruthlessly tried to stamp out, with a thoroughness worthy of a better cause, any non-Aryanisation of dance music.

The document comes from Holland and was issued by the Nazi "Department of Popular Education and Art."

This high-sounding body published it in the form of a long-winded four-page pamphlet meticulously forbidding dance bands to play anything that savoured of "Negroid and Negrito factors in dance music," and even forbidding them to use, in print or verbally, the common musicians' phrases for various effects.

It seems unbelievable that a nation even so humourless as Germany should be so undignified and carping as to forbid, by ordinance, "the effects known as 'dinge,' 'smear,' and 'whip'"; "scat"-singing, "boogie-woogie," "honky-tonk" or "barrel-house," the use of certain specified brass-mutes, and "the long-drawn-out 'off-beat' effect" among other incredible decrees.

NEGRO GRAND-PARENTS!

Even more extraordinary is the forbidding of "'licks' and 'riffs' *repeated more than three times in succession by a soloist or more than sixteen times for one section or for two or more sections.*"

But the final absurdity is surely the statement that an exception may be permitted to these decrees "*where such music is interpreted by persons having two or more Negroid or Negritic grand-parents*"!

Well, here is the document, translated from the Dutch, and the MELODY MAKER can only say that, when Germany wastes so much time and trouble drawing up such a footling and ridiculous set of restrictions—no wonder it has lost the war!

The following explanation is appended as a footnote, regarding the meaning of the words "Negroid" and "Negrito":—

NEGROID=belonging to a Negro race. This includes the African Negroes (and also those living outside of Africa), also Pygmies, Bushmen and Hottentots.
NEGRITO=in the wider sense of the term, the short-statured, curly or frizzy-haired, dark-skinned inhabitants of South-Eastern Asia, Melanesia and Central Africa.

The pamphlet reads:—

DEPARTMENT OF POPULAR EDUCATION AND ART
Conditions
GOVERNING THE GRANT OF LICENCES FOR DANCE MUSIC AND ENTERTAINMENT MUSIC

The embargo on Negroid and Negrito factors in dance music and music for entertainments.

INTRODUCTION

The following regulations are intended to indicate the revival of the European spirit in the music played in this country for dances and amusements, by freeing the latter from the elements of that primitive negroid and/or negrito music, which may be justly regarded as being in flagrant conflict with the European conception of music.

These regulations constitute a transitory measure born of practical considerations and which must of necessity precede a general revival.

PROHIBITION
CLAUSE 1

It is forbidden to play in public music which possesses to a marked degree characteristic features of the methods of improvisation, execution, composition and arrangement adopted by Negroes and coloured people.

CLAUSE 2

It is forbidden in publications, reports, programmes, printed or verbal announcements, etc:—
(a) Wrongly to describe music played or to be played with the words "jazz" or "jazz music."
(b) To use the technical jargon described below, except in reference to or as a description of the instrumental and vocal dance music of the North American Negroes.

In relation to Clause 1, the Secretary-General may permit exceptions—
1. Where such music is intended for a strictly scientific or strictly educational purpose:
2. Where such music is interpreted by persons having two or more Negroid or Negritic grand-parents.

Melody Maker 1944

UNKNOWNS' 'CAMBRIDGE' TRIUMPH

First Win for Esquire and His Boy Rider

Esquire, a three-year-old, who had run 12 times previously without success, caused a big surprise when he won the Cambridgeshire, the last big race of the season, at Newmarket yesterday. Carrying bottom weight, he started at 40 to 1.

He was ridden by an almost unknown apprentice, Guy Packer, whose first winner this was. The boy has been with R. J. Colling for two years and comes from Cambridge. He is not yet 16. His parents were present and were besides themselves with excitement.

Bob Colling, who ran Hunsingore as well as the winner said "The boy rode a fine race. I had thought Esquire would run well but cannot say I expected him to win."

Esquire was bred by the Aga Khan and changed hands twice as a yearling, the second time for 100 guineas. He was then bought as an unbroken two-year-old for his present owner Mr. J. C. Bueno, a South American.

Northern Echo
1945

BBC Broadcast New Soviet Anthem

The new Soviet Anthem was broadcast for the first time by the B.B.C. last night.

An orchestrated version by Augustus Franzel was played by the B.B.C. Symphony Orchestra, conducted by Sir Adrian Boult.

At the special request of the Prime Minister, Marshal Stalin has sent him a personal copy of the music.

Daily Worker
1944

BY THE WAY

DEVOTEES of steam-roller racing will greet with enthusiasm the splendid news that, due entirely to my efforts, there is every possibility of this sport getting under way again soon, and for the first time since 1939.

Already Esher (Surrey) Council, whose enterprise cannot be too highly praised, are putting in running order their notable trio of steam-rollers, Spring-Heeled Jack, Dorando II, and Little Pegasus; the last named as polished a performer over the classic distance of "Fifty yards and back again" as any I have driven since breaking the sprint record with the redoubtable Flying Wallaby in 1932.

Now there, girls, *there* was a steam-roller for you!

Daily Express
1945

VIVE LE CRICKET

CRICKET is the game they are trying to popularise in France. This is what a handbook, published in Paris for the guidance of schoolboys, says about our national sport: "Cricket is a national game *par excellence* and an exercise of the most violent, as well as being extremely complicated. To become a successful performer one must have solid shoulders, robust arms and agile legs, and possess, at the same time, great patience, sang froid and judgment." The book goes on : "A game of cricket, once begun, may go on for days—a communique being issued at the end of each day. It is a beautiful spectacle, but demands more patience of the spectator than of the performer."

The Leader 1946

"Henry V"

Laurence Olivier Embodies the Fighting Spirit of our Ancestors

● The world premiere of *Henry V* took place at the Carlton Theatre, Haymarket, on Monday last in aid of the Airborne Forces and the Commandos Benevolent Funds. The film has a tremendous cast which includes Robert Newton as Ancient Pistol, Leslie Banks as Chorus, Renee Asherson as Princess Katharine, Esmond Knight as Fluellen, Harcourt Williams, Francis Lister, Nicholas Hannen, Felix Aylmer and so on and on. More pictures of the film itself and of its brilliant cast will be published in our issue next week

" *We few, we happy few, we band of brothers* "

Henry exhorts his troops before Agincourt. " Gentlemen in England, now abed, shall think themselves accursed, they were not here "

Tatler 1944

THE L.S.D. OF FOOTBALL

A FEW weeks ago we foretold of the trouble that was brewing in the ranks of footballers, playing for first-class clubs, over the lack of reward for their efforts in comparison with their gate pulling power. We claimed then that the twenty-two men who skilfully kicked the ball around to the delight of tens of thousands of fans on a winter's Saturday afternoon in every town in these isles were not getting a fair deal. My plea to club directors to see that their players were given " a strong energising transfusion of £.s.d." was ignored.

With the commencement of what appears to be the greatest ever football season, the players, realising their own strength and encouraged by a few sports writers who are not afraid to speak their mind, have decreed that they will no longer tolerate the poor return for their efforts and seek to gain an increase on their paltry maximum salary of ten pounds a week.

With most clubs this would represent an extra £80 per week on the wage bill—about £2,500 per season. The vast majority of first-class clubs pay a lot more than this to the Exchequer in profit tax.

Last season, under anything but ideal conditions, clubs enjoyed a bumper season. This year gate and profit records will be topped —that is certain! Yet there are still many first-class footballers who do not, even now, get the agreed £10 a week—nor did they get the maximum when it was only £8.

It would be tragic for the sport if the players were forced to carry out their threat, and strike. Not that I think they would—they are, generally speaking, too good a band of sportsmen to do that. It must not be thought, however, that they will not do so, and under no circumstances should their club directors or the ruling body permit the matter to rest until the players are forced to do something drastic before their fully justified demands for increased pay are agreed to.

I suggest, too, that instead of a maximum wage being agreed, it should be a minimum wage that is settled. This would then enable the wealthier clubs with the big " stars " of the sport on their books to pay their players a salary that really does represent their gate pulling power. If this was done there would be less squabbling over the fantastic transfer fees that are paid by clubs without any financial benefit to the player himself. If a club wanted a player so badly that they were prepared to pay thousands of pounds for him, he would then be able to agree to his transfer, knowing that he was to get an increase in salary.

The life of a first-class club professional footballer is short enough as it is and it is only right—as is the case with every other profession—that he should be permitted to reap the full reward of his short-lived brilliance.

Sports Pictorial 1946

DECLINE AND FALL

TOLL the bell slowly. This is a lament for London's legendary West End. Everything that went to make up that legend—the tradition, the sober elegance, the musty grandeur, the unpretentious standards of perfection, the aloof courtesy and that unassailable air of surety, have vanished as completely as if pulverised by high explosives.

To me, after five years away, the West End seems a wilderness, a dismal, shoddy waste, peopled by a new race —the great uncouth. Snob talk? Maybe. But the decay of standards, whether their outward form is a white tie or good manners, the wearing of a hat or the grilling of a chop, is a sad state of affairs.

Eight o'clock used to be the magic hour: the sleek cars nosed up Piccadilly, making for the theatres; Eros presided over the Circus—and now he's back again, whatever else has gone. The women, some of them magnificently formal in their diamonds and their classic décolletages, were matched by the men, impeccable in their tails and opera hats. (After the war, in 1918, it was said that evening dress had gone for good; but the officer then commanding the Brigade of Guards thought otherwise. He decreed that any officer escorting a lady to the theatre must wear evening dress, and so, all the splendours returned for another lease.) But who, now, among the younger of us has thirty-two coupons and as many pounds for a tail suit, and all its trappings? Even the carnation buttonhole has gone along with the flower-women. Who has the heart for such junketing when, after 10 p.m., taxis vanish, and expensive cars must be hired?

Harper's Bazaar
1947

GENERAL RELEASES

The Prime Minister *(John Gielgud).—Disraeli postponing war with Diana Wynyard's help and a whiskery Cabinet.*

The Ghost Train *(Arthur Askey).—Fertile antics and excitement on a Cornish station by night.*

Daily Herald
1941

Australia crews still favourites for Henley

By HYLTON CLEAVER

There are no surprises among the Henley entries, except, perhaps in the sculls.

W. E. C. Horwood was beaten in the Diamonds of 1939... and he holds the N.A.R.A. championship. R. Flux, of City Police, has been sculling for ten years. The rest are new to me, but they include an American and a sailor.

We must commend the courage of some crews in the Open Eights: but I wish more had amalgamated. It would make for better racing.

Three Oxford colleges (New, Queen's, and St Edmund Hall) have combined to call themselves Oxford Triads.

No Leander, no London

Missing are the names of Leander and London.

London's clubhouse was occupied by the N.F.S. in 1939, and still is. But there must be a few oarsmen here, who could have made up a London-Leander eight.

Thames and Kingston have entered individually. Neither looks strong; they, too, might have linked up. But I know the difficulty. Would such a crew row from Putney or Kingston?

So it comes back to the fact that Australia still look the most likely winners.

Hospitals' men

Guy's Hospital looked an interesting possibility until the Hospitals' Race at the week-end. Not only did they then celebrate their centenary by losing to St Bartholomew's in a heat; but in the final Middlesex took a length and a half off Bart's!

Middlesex have no university oarsmen; they were rowing in a portable boat borrowed for the occasion. They will be at Henley.

It does not mean that in a level race Guy's may not yet prove the faster crew.

As Guy's won the fours and their stroke won the sculls, the eight are probably still kicking themselves, or each other.

Evening Standard 1945

meet some of the SPEEDWAY stars...

"SPLIT" WATERMAN TOMMY PRICE of WEMBLEY GEOFF PYMAR of NEW CROSS BILL KITCHEN, Captain of WEMBLEY

Sporting Pictorial 1947

ENGLAND GET TEST LEAD

Evening Standard
1945

SCORE IS:

ENGLAND

L Hutton, c Cheetham, b Williams		11
C Washbrook, c Carmody, b Pepper		63
J D Robertson, c Whitington, b Ellis		26
W R Hammond, c Hassett, b Cheetham		100
E R T Holmes, b Ellis		6
W J Edrich, lbw, b Pepper		1
G H Pope, c Ellis, b Cheetham		35
S C Griffith, c Hassett, b Cheetham		2
R Pollard, b Pepper		11
W B Roberts, b Williams		4
D V P Wright, not out		7
Extras		20
Total		**286**

Bowling: Williams 16-4-31-2; Cheetham 15-2-47-3; Ellis 33-9-66-2; Pepper 30.5-6-86-3; Miller 13-3-19-0; Price 3-0-17-0.

Second Innings

L Hutton, not out		4
C Washbrook, not out		3
Extras		2
Total (no wkt)		**9**

AUSTRALIA

R S Whitington, c Wright b Pope		17
J A Workman, c Pollard b Pope		6
A L Hassett, b Pollard		5
K R Miller, run out		17
D K Carmody, c Hammond, b Wright		42
C Pepper, c Hammond, b Wright		21
A G Cheetham, b Pope		10
S G Sismey, c Pollard, b Pope		5
C F Price, c Pollard b Pope		0
R G Williams, not out		5
R S Ellis, run out		1
Extras		23
Total		**147**

Bowling: Pope 21.5-4-58-5; Pollard 17-5-41-1; Wright 9-3-14-2; Edrich 5-0-10-0.

Cambridge Daily News
1945

BRILLIANT PIANIST'S RETURN

Myra Hess at Guildhall

DAME MYRA HESS was given an enthusiastic reception at the Guildhall, Cambridge, on Friday, when a huge audience in paying tribute to her brilliant playing of Bach, Schubert, Brahms and Schumann, took full advantage of its first peace-time opportunity of acknowledging her magnificent services to music during the war years.

It may now be recalled, incidentally, that on the last occasion that Dame Myra played in Cambridge, under the auspices of the Thursday concerts series, the building was shaken by the explosion of a nearby V-bomb, yet, apart from pausing a few moments in deference to an unmusical siren, she played imperturbably on.

Last evening she played works of mainly classico-romantic school, which on this occasion seemed to symbolise the pianist's relaxation in the opening of a new era.

Bach alone represented the classical period, but there is an exhuberance of spirit in his French Suite (No. 5 in G), which, in its seven movements all in dance form, fits—at least in sentiment, if the label may be stretched—into the romantic group. Dame Myra illustrated her matchless gift of perfection of phrasing, touch and control, from the range of the Allemande to the Sarabande, and terminating with the Loure—one of the best-known examples of its kind—and the well-known and popular Gigue.

PEOPLE WHO ARE IN THE PUBLIC EYE.

MR. ALASTAIR SIM.

Elected to the office of Rector of Edinburgh University on November 2. A well-known stage and screen actor, he was at one time a lecturer in phonetics at New College, Edinburgh. The polling figures were: Mr. Sim. 2078; Mr. Harold Macmillan, M.P., 802. Mr. Sim is appearing in a revival of *The Anatomist*.

Radio

The "Third" Hits Out

By W. E. WILLIAMS

WHAT strikes me most about the Third Programme is its self-confidence. Instead of playing itself in, like a cautious opening batsman on an unfamiliar wicket, it went for boundaries from the start. Stephen Potter, for example, on the first night, took liberties of comment and impersonation which he has to deny himself (and us) in his usual "How" programmes. The opening discussion in "Living Opinion" was equally bold. It displayed no deference to maiden aunts of either sex, but assumed on our part a willingness to accept robust and plain-spoken opinion. The standard wireless discussion too often resembles a Paul Jones danced on hot bricks, but in "Living Opinion" there was no such evasive footwork. The performers seemed to be going somewhere, and made their differences seem the real stuff of our current dilemmas.

Observer 1946

Illustrated London News
1948

Scottish Rugby Triumph

England ... 11 Scotland ... 18

AFTER four successive defeats in Service internationals, Scotland beat England at Leicester by three goals and a try, to a goal, a penalty goal, and a try on Saturday. No one among the crowd of 20,000 could have doubted the justice of the result.

The almost new Scotland team had to make late changes, which included the playing of J. B. Nicholls, normally a forward, on the wing, but the whole side worked together much better than England.

Youthful as they were, the Scottish pack held their own in the tight with the infinitely more-experienced English eight, and were the better in the open.

D. D. Mackenzie and Black, the halves, created a fine impression, and Maclennan and Henderson, the centres, not only displayed solidity in defence, but a dash and pace that often disconcerted their opponents.

Good Kicking

Geddes at full back, too, committed few errors, and, like Ward at the other end, kicked an admirable length.

While the English three-quarters were none too well together, and consequently had to rely upon kicking to make progress, the New Zealander Goddard brought off some capital runs in the centre, and Weston, late in the game bore a hand in both tries for his side.

McClure, Hastie, and the Dominion second row forward R. M. McKenzie and Wilhelm were the pick of the Scottish forwards, with Doherty and Weighill perhaps the best for England.

R. M. McKenzie put Scotland ahead in eight minutes with a try that Geddes converted, and, though Ward responded with a penalty goal, Grant increased the advantage before the interval, Geddes placing another goal.

In the second half, Maclennan added a try for Scotland. Ward dashed in with one in reply, then, in the last few minutes Orr crossed for Scotland, Geddes converting, and Goddard raced in for England's second try, Kilthorpe kicking a goal.

Too Many Are Playing, Too Few Listen

By A Staff Reporter

WHAT has all the appearance of a first-class economic crisis has developed in the field of orchestral concert-giving. Audiences have sharply dwindled in recent months, promoters in the happiest of cases are finding it anything but easy to make ends meet, and, in certain instances, guarantors and artistic "backers" are being called upon to meet substantial losses.

The financial situation of the Royal Philharmonic Society is such that it was unable to comply when Nikolai Malko, the eminent Soviet conductor, sought an extra rehearsal for Shostakovitch's Ninth Symphony, which was to have been given at their orchestral concert in the Albert Hall last week-end.

In consequence, the Shostakovitch had to be withdrawn from the programme, together with a second symphonic novelty by a U.S. composer named McDonald. Tchaikovsky's familiar Fifth Symphony was substituted. The Society has weathered several economic storms during its 134 years' history. The present position is described as very disquieting, none the less.

£1,000 Loss

It is announced that the current series of concerts at Chelsea by the Boyd Neel Orchestra, which specialises in rare classics and modern works, is being cut from nine, as originally planned, to five. Since December there has been a further marked decline in support. A year ago up to 200 were being turned away from the doors at every concert. Latterly, the hall on occasion has been only a quarter full. It is understood that the loss on the September-to-Christmas series alone came to about £1,000. The decision to curtail activities was therefore unavoidable.

THE STARS DIRECTS THE PLAY SCENE IN "HAMLET"
Sir Laurence Olivier in his Hamlet costume. He holds his director's megaphone, sits on the end of the crane and discusses a moving shot with the cameraman

OLIVIER'S HAMLET

SIR LAURENCE OLIVIER'S film of "Hamlet," which is to run for two and a half hours, is of momentous importance for British films. It has absorbed a good deal of time and money, as well as the energies of our leading star. But the film should increase the world prestige of British films as much as *Henry V* did.

A feature of the décor is the 13th-century European murals and frescoes painted in sepia tones on the walls and corridors of Elsinore Castle. There is no exact period in the costumes. In order to take in the tremendous number of incidents, and players, the lighting has been arranged so that the camera has an unusual depth of focus. The famous speeches are said in movement, and this, while adding enormously to the technical difficulties of filming, tightens and speeds up the story.

Included in the cast are Eileen Herlie as Gertrude, Basil Sydney as Claudius, Jean Simmons as Ophelia, Felix Aylmer as Polonius, and Harcourt Williams as First Player.

The film will be in black and white. Olivier's explanation "I see it as an engraving rather than as a painting."

The quotations published with the pictures on these two pages we have taken from the Oxford University Press edition.

Greyhound Racing

Harringay

FIFTY-FIFTY

I have been going out with a very nice boy, and we had good times together and got on well. I know he likes me a lot and looks forward to our outings together, because he has often said so.

Just lately he has been making excuses though, when I suggest an evening at the pictures or at a dance hall, and our friendship looks like fading out.

I feel certain that he is just as keen on me as before, and no other girl has come between us. But he isn't earning a great deal—not as much as I am, in fact—and I don't think he can afford to go on taking me about.

So far I have always let him pay for us both, because I have been brought up to think the boy should pay. But now I would willingly do my share, if I only knew how to suggest this without hurting his pride. Do tell me what I could say, as I should be so disappointed if our good times ended for such a small reason as this

2.30 (525 yds).—BERKELEY TENANT (1) 1, 11-2; Kronstadt (2) 2, 5-1; Jean's Fancy (6), Ballygan Seal (4), Chancery's Taner (3) (13-8 F), Kopperfield (5). T. 14/9; pl. 10/-, 4/9. F. £3/14/0. 3½l. 31.15.

2.45 (525).—JUBILEE FORM (4) 1, 6-4 F; Whistling Numba (6) 9, 7-1; First Gamble (6), Handsome Russell (3), Our Little Girl (1), Libellous Letter (5). T. 5/6; pl. 3/3, 6/6. F. £1/12/9. Sht hd. 31.37.

3.1 (525).—MODEL GRACIE (2) 1, 11-3; Carolina Fame (4) 2, 7-1; Griffinstown Lad (6), Antic Mary (1), Talon's Step (5) (6-4 F), Black Gambler (3). T. 12/3; pl. 8/-, 18/3. F. £7/6/9. 2½l. 30.61.

3.17 (700).—Q.R. BALMORAL (4) 1, 7-2; Albanian Chief (6) 2, 5r2 co-F; Loch Lomond (5) (5-2), Faithless Gillian (1), Lido Lad (3), Admiral's Cook (2). T. 10/9; pl. 5/-, 4/9. F. £2/13/9. 1½l. 43.23.

3.34 (525).—RETARD (3) 1, 5-2 co-F; Lady Like (6) 2, 7-2; Dark Ration (2), Kanaris (1), Brindled Jubilee (4), Retainer (5) (5-2). T. 7/-; pl. 4/-. 4/6 F. £1/18/3. 3l. 30.82.

3.51 (700).—BLACK RAIL (1) 1, 5-4 F; Unwin Beauty (6) 2, 2-1; Ryan's Rose (2), Chittering Handyboy (4), Don Bend (3), Wood's Leu (5). T. 5/-; pl. 3/3. 3/6. F. 9/6. 2½l. 41.10.

4.8 (525).—QUEEN OF CYPRUS (2) 1, 7-2; Legal Argument (4) 2, 6-4 F; Walkern Bebe (1), Amiable Counsel (6), Carnagh Blonde (5), Ballycannon Beauty (3). T. 10/-; pl. 4/6. 3/3. F. 1½l. 30.97.

4.25 (525).—CONNIE LARRY (5) 1, 4-1; Fort Grant (2) 2, 9-4 F; Bark Time (3), Curracloe Flutter (6), Admiral Oxy (4), Dickason (1). T. 11/9; pl. 7/3, 4/3. F. £1/10/6. 2l. 31.04.

David Niven—a Scot who went to a very English public school—looks exactly the same in real life as he does on the films

Woman's Journal
1947

Woman and Beauty
1946

Allen Lane—the man who has changed the meaning of the word 'penguin' from a bird into a book.

A MEAN TRICK

Here's a coin trick to start off with—a mean trick, a dirty trick! Still, it's fun, and it's Christmas, and it takes all kinds of ornaments to make a Christmas-tree—so why not?

Take six matching coins, any coins—pennies will be fine. Arrange them in the shape of a cross—four coins in the upright, three across. Can anyone present, by picking up one penny and changing its position, so change the entire cross that there will be four coins both in the upright *and* the crosspiece?

Great minds will worry over this, and give up. Then you (you dog) simply pick up the penny at the bottom of the upright, and place it on top of the middle penny of the crosspiece. See? Now there are four pennies in both upright and crosspiece. (Oh, how I hate this trick!) But, even so, hate's a good strong emotion for stirring up stagnation, isn't it?

Woman and Beauty
1946

ALLEN LANE

THE newspaper quiz asks, 'What is a Penguin?' Once the Englishman scratched his head and answered, 'A bird,' or, remembering he had seen it only at the zoo, 'A rare bird.' Nowadays he is as likely to answer, 'A book,' and if he belongs to the vast, often-frustrated Penguin public, may add wryly 'A rare book,' for nearly all the million Penguin books which are published monthly are sold to the canny early customer, before the first dust settles on them. The tricks and stratagems of the legions foiled in their pursuit of the Penguin, Heaven alone can number or describe, but it is a commonplace that the owner of a new Penguin faces grave risks and, if wise, will guard it well.

This is very cheerful knowledge to Allen Lane, who, with his brothers, founded Penguin despite pessimism and cautioning from the entire book trade, which declared that cheap books had never caught the public in this country and never would. Lane heeded his own inner voice and he has had no regrets. He knows that he could sell millions more Penguin books if he could produce them. Already Penguin publishes in the United States and Australia, and it is only a matter of time and the maturing of plans before the same thing happens in other parts of the world.

Allen Lane is brisk, bright-eyed, full of mirth. He laughs as though he could not stop himself—his pink cheeks grow pinker, his blue eyes well with merriment—you behold the taking picture not only of a man enjoying a good joke, but of a man enjoying a good life.

Lane won't listen to any handsome words about what he has done. 'It's all nonsense, you know,' he says, characteristically direct and staccato—Lane never wastes breath—' it's easy, like publishing for myself.' That gives a clue to the peculiarly Lane gift—a phenomenally sensitive intuition about the direction and breadth of public taste. He moves to meet it in all its variations, always at a high level, never pandering to its weaknesses. Ten years ago Allen Lane staked instinct against experience and won. He believed in the universality of excellence, and millions of English people, many of whom had never before owned a good book, or perhaps any book at all, proved his case for him. Straight away Penguin went into partnership with the English public at large, and they have been advancing together very successfully ever since.

Benjamin Britten

Varsity 1948

Punch 1949

Though Britten had shown a genius for song-cycle and incidental music, the beauty and emotional power of "Peter Grimes" came as a surprise to the sceptical, and a joyful justification to the faithful. Success was immediate and acclamation lavish. The opera was produced all over Europe and in New York. Britten, from then on, saw opera as the chief part of his musical vocation, and many other British composers were encouraged by his success to begin opera-writing—among them Arthur Bliss and Constant Lambert.

Observer 1946

SOLD OUT: REPRINTING

Daphne Du Maurier's new novel **THE KING'S GENERAL**, which was published on April 1st, is sold out & is reprinting. The new edition will be on the market in about six weeks.

"The Prospect Before Us?"

Mr. Orwell's nightmare *Nineteen Eighty-Four* is not just another inverted Utopia. The horrors of his totalitarian future are developed logically from those of the present, and he does not allow his effervescent ingenuity to disrupt his best novel into unrelated bright ideas. It is a good story, written in the prose that has sometimes seemed his chief claim to greatness and with character-drawing that at last fulfils the promise of Verrall in "Burmese Days." Influenced, or rather fertilized, by Arthur Koestler he has fused his interest in politics and his love of people and their surroundings into real political fiction. He imagines the world divided into three Empires, with Britain as an outpost of the American "Oceania." The form of government is "Oligarchical Collectivism," rule by a Party which desires only power and maintains itself by constant war, by the control of thought and language and by destroying the past. The hero, whose job is rewriting back numbers of *The Times* to fit in with the shifts in "Big Brother's" Policy, is first tricked into mental rebellion and then crushed not only into submission but into love for his executioners. It is all horribly credible—but fortunately not inevitable.   R. G. G. P.

Moira Shearer and Marius Goring in *The Red Shoes*

Your Film GUIDE

The Red Shoes Hans Andersen's story of how a pair of red shoes took charge of their owner and danced her to her death is certainly the cruellest of our fairy tales—and yet, for all its cruelty, one of the most enchanting. Its modern film version by Messrs. Powell and Pressburger faithfully reflects the spirit of the original.

This is a cruel and enchanting picture: cruel, because it ends tragically; enchanting, because its course runs beautifully.

The new story tells of a ballerina, Moira Shearer, torn between the conflicting claims of her love for a musician, Marius Goring, and her career with a cold-blooded impresario, Anton Walbrook.

Its central and most important section is devoted to the particular ballet which brings her fame. This dance of the Red Shoes is a major contribution to the arts, alike, of ballet and cinema.

The colour is vivid, violent and superb; the dancing by Massine, Helpmann,

Moira Shearer

Shearer and corps de ballet, flawless.

Here is a wedding between the Film and the Dance which makes all similar efforts by Hollywood, in the lesser realm of musical comedy, look pale, pasty and anaemic.

If I describe a single detail, I shall rob you of some of its enchantment.

A fairy tale for children has become a fairy tale for grown-ups. Go to it!

The Woman in White This is a leisurely but good and faithful film transcription of Wilkie Collins' classic Victorian melodrama about a lunatic lady, a villainous Italian count, a murderous British nobleman and a doddering art dealer.

Its horrors come not so much thick and fast as thick and slow; but with Alexis Smith, Eleanor Parker and the gargantuan Sydney Greenstreet all at the top of their melodramatic form, I found it vastly entertaining.

BY DAVID RAGLAN

Woman's Own 1948

CHAPTER I

WHY CAMP?

From Ministry of Education Pamphlet No. 11, *Organised Camping*, 1948.

FOR many young people, the initial appeal of camping may well be that it is a very inexpensive way of getting a holiday in the country or by the seaside. But there is far more in it than that.

Camping provides a quality of enjoyment that no other form of holiday can give. It improves bodily health and physique and is an antidote to some of the more harmful effects of urban life. It can inspire new and lasting interests. It can promote both self-reliance and unselfishness. The spirit of fellowship which it can create will extend into the organisation to which the young campers belong. Indeed it is difficult to over-state the beneficial effect that camp life at its best can have upon the happiness, health, character and tastes of young people.

To-day the word " camp " has come to have many meanings, but this pamphlet is concerned only with the kind of camps which are so organised that each boy or girl has a part to play and a contribution to make in the common adventure. Such camps may be large or small, under canvas or in hutments, but they should always offer a new way of life in which the individual feels his significance and responsibility ; and the way of life must be attuned to the surroundings of the camp.

As a summer activity for school and youth service organisations camping can be expected to become even more general during the next few years. Written primarily for leaders of youth service camps, most of this pamphlet should prove valuable also to teachers organising camps for schoolchildren.* It does not set out to be a comprehensive manual of instruction in campcraft, but rather to serve as a guide to those responsible for introducing young people to camp life, and to give some idea of what constitutes " good camping." And since it is important that anyone who undertakes camp leadership should do so not as a job or a duty but as an adventure, an opportunity and a privilege, it is hoped that these pages may convey also something of the spirit which is needed to make camping yield its finest fruits.

But camping cannot be learnt from a book. The authentic flavour of a camping holiday can be tasted only through personal experience. Before taking on camp leadership for the first time, it is advisable to attend, perhaps as a helper, a camp run by an experienced leader, or to spend a week at a practical training course for camp leaders run by the Ministry of Education, a local authority or a national voluntary organisation.

---

* It will, however, be understood that in the case of camps for schoolchildren different considerations may apply, particularly in regard to such matters as finance, administration and camp routine.

A SAMPLE MENU — SIX-DAY CAMP

So long as rationing continues and ration and points values fluctuate no specimen menu can do more than offer an indication.

	BREAKFAST	LUNCH	EVENING MEAL
Saturday			Corned Beef, Potatoes, Salad ; Fruit and Custard
Sunday	Porridge, Scrambled Dried Egg and Tomatoes	Roast Meat, Potatoes, Greens ; Rhubarb and Custard	Chunky Vegetable Soup ; Bread and Cheese
Monday	Porridge, Bacon and Fried Bread	Cold Meat, Potatoes, Salad ; Steamed Pudding	Rabbit-and-vegetable Stew ; Semolina Mould
Tuesday	Porridge, Haddock	Brawn in Batter, Potatoes, Pease-pudding ; Coffee Junket	Meat Pies, Vegetables ; Chocolate Semolina
Wednesday	Porridge, Tinned Sausages and Tomatoes	Rabbit or Liver or Tripe, Potatoes, Greens with Cheese Sauce ; Fruit Whip	Fish and Vegetables ; Coffee Custard
Thursday	Porridge, Kippers	Roast Meat, Greens and Potatoes ; Chocolate Semolina	Vegetable Hot-pot with Cheese Sauce ; Fruit and Custard
Friday	Porridge, Cheese-and-potato Cakes	Meat-and-vegetable Stew and Dumplings ; Vanilla Junket	Fish and Salad ; Bread and Jam
Saturday	Porridge, Boiled Eggs (shell)		

Cocoa served every night before bed.
Tea or coffee served with breakfast, lunch and supper.
Cereal in place of porridge as desired.
Bread and marmalade or jam at all breakfasts.
Tea and buns in the afternoon according to programme.

LAYOUT FOR MIXED CAMP (about 2 acres)
For a single-sex camp sleeping tents might be differently arranged, and only one set of latrines and wash-houses provided.

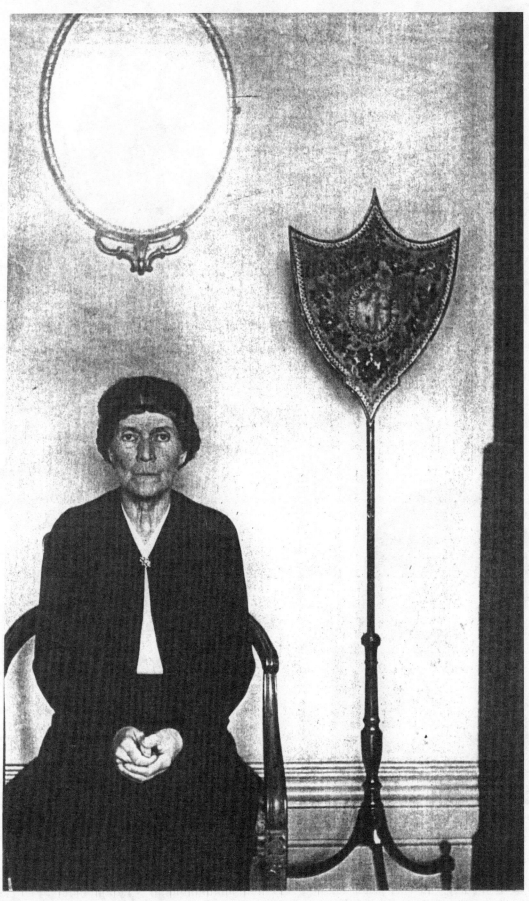

Ivy Compton-Burnett, whose new novel, *Two Worlds and Their Ways*, was published this summer, is one of our most remarkable contemporary novelists. Her ten earlier novels are all marked by an uncanny perception of overtones in family life, a sardonic, muted wit that kicks like a whip, a talent for creating a devilish atmosphere out of streams of apparently innocuous dialogue

HANS WILD

Mai Zetterling and Paul Scofield as Nina and Constantin in a production of Tchekov's *The Seagull*, with Isabel Jeans and Ian Hunter. This first London performance since 1936 lacks integration, is yet a welcome revival

Vogue 1949

Mr. Tommy Handley, the radio comedian, who died suddenly on January 9. Mr. Handley was well known to listeners for nearly twenty-five years; it is, however, as the presiding genius of 'Itma', which celebrated its three-hundredth performance last October, that he will always be remembered. In the course of a broadcast tribute, Mr. Ted Kavanagh, the 'Itma' scriptwriter, said of Mr. Handley: 'He loved people, and from a deep well of human sympathy and kindliness he drew his inspiration. It was this innate kindliness that was the keynote of his character, the secret of his success. . . . My own sense of personal loss will be felt by many millions'

The Listener 1949

Winter Sports 1949/50

Once again, memories of Winter Sports Holidays are recaptured as the 1949/50 season draws ever nearer. Lillywhites cater for the experienced ski-runner and skater, for those not quite so expert, and for the complete beginner going out for the first time. If you cannot pay a personal visit to Piccadilly Circus please write for our illustrated catalogue in colour showing all the latest clothing and equipment for Winter Sports.

The charming Grenfell cloth windjacket above is shown with its fur trimmed hood turned down to make an attractive collar. Colours are gold, scarlet, turquoise, grey, royal and ice blue. Sizes 34-40. £10.10.0. *Lillywhites popular Vorlage trousers complete the outfit.*
Prices range from £7.10.0 *to* 13 *gns.*

Lillywhites LTD

TELEPHONE:
WHITEHALL 3181   OF PICCADILLY CIRCUS

Lawn Tennis

HARD MATCHES AT WIMBLEDON

Sixty-Game Set in Men's Double

From our Lawn Tennis Correspondent

Manchester
Guardian
1950

LONDON, THURSDAY.

Miss A. L. Brough will defend her women's singles title against her partner and rival, a former holder, Mrs. M. O. Dupont in the Wimbledon lawn tennis championships on Saturday. Miss D. Hart, whose challenge this year seemed so strong after her victories in the French and London championships, faded out badly after gaining a 3-1 first-set lead until finally Miss Brough won 6-4, 6-3, and had nothing to beat. Mrs Dupont, on the other hand, was hunted home by Mrs. P. C. Todd, who was at her most determined, and played splendidly against a better server and volleyer, who, however, is not so quick at the net as she was. Mrs. Dupont was caught at 5-all in the final set after leading 5-3 but won 8-6, 4-6, 8-6.

Play did not begin until three o'clock owing to a strong drizzling rain. The singles match between Miss Hart and Miss Brough took little time, but the match between Mrs. Dupont and Mrs. Todd was not finished until well after five. Meantime, however, there was in progress on court number one the longest set ever played in these championships and one of the longest in the history of the game. In it B. Patty and T. Trabert (United States) having taken the first set off F. A. Sedgman and K. McGregor (Australia) by 6-4 won the second by the remarkable score of 31-29. This set lasted two and a half hours, longer than many five-set matches and in consequence the day's programme was disrupted seriously.

Bowls News
1950

Grasshoppers.

The club held their 32nd annual dinner and dance at the New Harmonic Hall, East Ham, President Arthur Davies presiding over a company of 128, including the deputy president, immediate past president, hon. secretary, and past hon. secretary (R. Wadsworth) of the Essex Association, Mrs. Wainwright (I.P.P. Essex Woman's B.A.) and H. Wainwright (president Valentines Park) etc. Hon. Sec. Ray Davies was the efficient toastmaster and officiated at the dance. The various toasts from the chair were accompanied by the singing of suitable ditties and caused considerable fun. A feature of the evening was the presentation of a bedside rug to that "grand old man" of the club, Jimmie Whadcoat and a handbag to Mrs. Whadcoat. The absence of Charlie Gray, who had sprained his ankle as a result of a slight accident, was regretted. Speeches indicated the virility of the club in spite of its small membership, their loyalty to the county association and the hope that President Arthur would in the near future receive higher honours in the county. Mrs. Davies made the prize presentation. Carmen Hare entertained musically and the Harvey Nicholls Ballroom Orchestra supplied melody for the dancing.

Edmundo Ros and his Rumba Band have two more new Deccas to their credit; F9542 is a tuneful bolero sung in Spanish by Ros, *Maria Dolores*, backed by a more ordinary *Gimpel Baynish Rumba*, this being the name of a street flautist. Decca F9555 gives us *Mambo*, which I found monotonous, as often these ultra-modern Latin things are, but its coupling, *Samba Polka*, is both tuneful and lively.

As with Joe Loss, it is surely unnecessary to recommend Roberto Inglez to my readers? Nevertheless, I will do so. If you have wanted a superbly lush, but not saccharine, dance record of *Autumn Leaves*, without vocal, as I have done, and have held your fire, you should be thrilled with Inglez's beguine treatment of this lovely haunting melody (Parlo. R3349). The other side, *All My Love*, is a simple, pleasing tune, beautifully done.

The Gramophone 1951

England Reach Rock Bottom In World Cup Soccer

From John Graydon

Before one of the most one-sided crowds ever English football took its mightiest blow when beaten 1-0 by American part-timers in the World Cup at Bello Horizonte yesterday. It was pathetic to watch English football losing to a side most amateur elevens would beat at home, and there was no fluke about it.

TRUE the ground was bumpy, but it was the same for both sides. The Americans were on top because they were prepared to take chances and appeared not only faster but possessed greater stamina. The crowd, pro-American from the first, were delighted at the smoothness of the U.S. machine.

The England side never got going. Even allowing for great shots by Finney and Mannion hitting uprights and a Mortensen drive rebounding from the bar the U.S. were on top most of the game.

Recall Matthews

England were thoroughly beaten and the American side thoroughly deserved the wonderful ovation backed by brilliant fireworks.

Billy Wright and company looked dejected, as well they might, when walking from the field. It was a shocker. As for England many changes are certain for the game against Spain. The recall of Matthews seems certain. How he was missed!

Newcastle
Evening
Chronicle
1950

Daily Mirror
1951

Let's go —on time!

WHO likes to see the end of a picture before they've seen the beginning?

I know what the answer to this question would be if put to the vast majority of cinemagoers.

"What else can we do when our turn comes in the queue—we've got to go in no matter what part of the programme is on," is the retort I can hear. Then I think it is time that more cinema proprietors considered replacing the continuous programme with the fixed performances system.

says REG WHITLEY

two-feature programme. For some time British producers have claimed that their films suffer by word of mouth comments from customers who have come into the cinema in the middle of the picture.

Susan Noel's Tennis Course

LORNA CORNELL, present Junior Champion, and MARGARET EMERSON, winner of Hampshire Open Championship and Junior Champion of Lincolnshire are demonstrating LESSON SIX

The Lob and Drop

LORNA CORNELL (left) has brought her opponent up to the net. This is the time for the "lob." She prepares to come underneath the ball so that it will be hit up to land just inside the back line. Right foot takes the weight

She has now moved forward, bringing the weight on to the left foot. Following the flight of the ball, the racket finishes in an upward movement, and Lorna's left arm is raised to keep balance

MARGARET EMERSON (right) prepares for the drop shot which will send the ball close to the net in the opposite court, putting her opponent in a defensive position. As always, weight is on the right foot, in preparation

Since the ball is to travel such a short distance there is scarcely any follow-through. Margaret's left foot now takes the weight at the close of a useful "surprise" shot in tennis

NEXT WEEK, with the same champions to demonstrate, SUSAN NOEL explains SINGLES TACTICS

Woman 1950

Tit-Bits 1951

DANCE HALL DRUG SCANDAL

Chemist-Shop Dope Boom Among Teen-Age Jive Fans

HAVE you ever heard your teen-age son or daughter speak of " Muggles," " Gee Tees," " Benzy " or a " Lift " ? If so you've cause to worry : for these are the jargon of the rapidly increasing numbers of youthful dope addicts in this country.

They are all newly discovered drugs of the jive, bop and jazz fans, available to all and within the range of every pocket. How would a youngster get them ? Simply by walking into the nearest chemist's, paying two shillings or so for certain proprietary articles (which for obvious reasons we are not naming), taking them home, preparing them . . . and creating enough poison not only to cause slap-happiness and hallucinations, but also violence and even death !

The effects of these drugs are eminently suitable for inducing the abandoned state necessary to jiving, jitterbugging, playing or listening to hot jazz. They give a feeling of boost, unlimited energy and well-being, a general " letting down of hair." While under their influence a normally mild and well-balanced youth or girl can become assertive and over-aggressive, devil-may-care and violent : with no stimulus other than jazz music he or she can attain a state of semi-hypnotized exaltation.

BBC WILL BAN ARTISTS WHO WON'T 'SING BRITISH'

THE B.B.C. will ban variety artists and dance bands who persistently feature all U.S. tunes instead of British ones, writes Clifford Davis.

This follows protests by British music publishers and the Song Writers Guild of Great Britain against the un-British attitude of some bands and performers.

Variety chief Michael Standing has sent a circular letter to performers and band leaders telling them it is his " positive intention " to secure a fairer hearing for Britain's popular composers.

His letter confirms that the B.B.C. will " tend to favour those who play British tunes."

Daily Mirror 1951

Johnny Dankworth Seven
- ●●●*Excerpts From The Conway Suite—Lament, Wild Dance* (Dankworth) (Esquire M-7-120)
- ●*Don't Blame Me* (Fields, McHugh) (V by **Frank Holder**) (Esquire M-7-121) (Esquire 5-010—5s. 9d.)
- ●●●*Get Happy* (Arlen Koehler) (Esquire M-7-119)
- ●●●*Perhaps* (Charlie Parker) (Esquire M-7-118) (Esquire 10-103—6s.)

Dankworth (*alto*); **Don Rendell** (*ten*); **Jimmie Deuchar** (*tpt*); **Eddie Harvey** (*tmb*); **Bill Le Sage** (*pno*); **Eric Dawson** (*bass*); **Tony Kinsey** (*dms*). October 14th, 1950.

To-day the word Suite can mean almost any set of more or less related compositions in light vein. But even so, I doubt whether Johnny Dankworth's *Conway Suite* can fairly be called a Suite. It consists of only two movements, and they are so brief (the first runs to less than a minute) that they can hardly be described as more than short themes.

The explanation of this is that Dankworth wrote them for a concert in which he took part at the Conway Hall, London. He had intended that there should be five movements which would be worthy of the term Suite. But he found himself so pressed for time that he was unable to write more than these very sketchy two.

(Subsequently he wrote a third, but that has no bearing on the matter in hand, because he used it as a separate item—*Seven Not Out*, which we have already had on Esquire 10-093, reviewed last October.)

Admittedly, as far as they go both *Lament* and *Wild Dance* are fascinating morsels. The former is an Ellingtonish fragment adequately described by its title. The latter, with its riding character, is in quality, if not in quantity, the equal of most worthwhile compositions conceived in the name of jazz. Also the performances are well up to the Dankworth standard. But I cannot help feeling that Dankworth would have been better advised to wait until he could find time to extend the pieces to the length they deserve before committing them to wax.

The Gramophone 1951

Dick Barton faces a fight for survival

By CLIFFORD DAVIS

DICK BARTON is facing the greatest struggle of his career—for survival. Talks now going on at Broadcasting House may mean the end of radio's blood-and-thunder hero when the present winter series closes in March. Some B.B.C. chiefs feel that Dick Barton has had his day.

In September, when the four-year-old serial returned to the air, the broadcasting time was moved to 6.15 instead of 6.45 after complaints that it kept children up too late. But since the change the number of listeners has dropped from 5,000,000 to about 2,000,000.

The new time, so close to Children's Hour, has also brought fresh criticism from some officials of this programme who have always been against Dick's adventures—so utterly opposed to the policy of all other children's programmes.

Authors Edward J. Mason and Geoffrey Webb—who provide 80 per cent. of his adventures—are now busy scripting the new daily serial " The Archers."

Daily Mirror 1951

Relaxing at the Festival of Britain site, on the south bank of the Thames in London, 1951.

Dog gets drunk

JULIANA, the dog that went to a wedding reception and got roaring drunk, was still trying to shake off a two-day hangover yesterday.

She refused breakfast with a weary gesture. She sighed and uttered low moaning noises. Her legs gave an occasional twitch.

Down her bird-cage throat Juliana gulped bowl after bowl of water. But she yearned, oh, how she yearned for a hair of the man that bit her.

The wedding guest, a blood-shot-eyed, wobbly-limbed Airedale, was found on Saturday night staggering around among shoppers in a large store in Southend High-street.

"Poor creature," sympathised the shoppers, "she's been run over." Juliana hiccuped, gazed owlishly at the crowds, and sat down limply.

The police were called. The dog was still having trouble with her hind legs and drooled gently into a sergeant's hand.

Then came Mr. Ken Adams, of Our Dumb Friends' League. He felt Juliana's legs and peered down her throat. Then he reeled back, coughing.

"The dog's full of whisky," he said in an awed voice.

At that, Juliana lurched to her feet, shook herself and scattered a shower of confetti before lying down again and waving a nerveless paw.

Her secret was out. She had clearly been to a wedding—and gone on to the reception.

"And it must have been quite a reception," said Mr. Adams yesterday. "All she wanted was to be left alone to sleep it off."

The Airedale was carried to an ambulance and spent the night in the police-station. She blinked into dazed consciousness next morning in the unfamiliar surroundings of the Southend Corporation Dog Pound.

"She has drunk an awful lot of water," said the dog-keeper. "Poor thing, she's got a mouth like a tramdriver's glove."

Mrs. C. Summerfield, of Eastwood-road, Rayleigh, Essex—seven miles from Southend—claimed Juliana last night. She says she sits up and begs for tea.

One theory is that the dog made friends with strangers going to a wedding party, and sat up and begged—for whisky.

Daily Mirror 1951

Sporting News

THE BOAT RACE

OXFORD SINK

FROM OUR ROWING CORRESPONDENT

Race to be re-rowed to-day at 2.30 p.m.

Not since 1925 has a Boat Race crew suffered the fate that overtook Oxford on Saturday. The wind had veered from the south-west to almost due west. Rough water was certainly expected, but few, at least until the crews got afloat, can have realized quite how bad it was.

Oxford won the toss and chose Surrey, a decision which, in retrospect, one can see was wrong. But at the time it seemed right enough. For the wind was almost dead ahead in the Putney Reach, and, with the stake boats moored well over towards the Surrey shore, there was no reason to suppose that either station would have any particular advantage off the start. And between the Mile and Hammersmith there would have been shelter under the Surrey bank which would have more than compensated for the first Middlesex bend.

The crews had some difficulty in getting straight on their stake boats, but the umpire got them away to a level start at almost exactly 1.45 p.m. Even in the few minutes they were waiting for the word to go it seemed that the wind was increasing, or perhaps it was that, with the attention focused on the two eights, one realized for the first time just what was in store for them.

By some freak of chance, or perhaps because they were a little less in the tide, Cambridge seemed to have much better water. But let credit be given where it is due; the water in which they started was still extremely rough and they went through it wonderfully. But Oxford were struck by a major disaster almost on the first stroke. From the Press launch, which was ahead and to a flank of the crews at the time, the Oxford bow and two were hardly visible for the first three strokes. It is pointless to argue whether or not Oxford were as clever in the rough water as Cambridge; the spray that obscured their bows in the first few strokes came not from their blades, but from water breaking clean over their cut-water and over bow's and two's riggers.

To all intents and purposes that is all there is to report of the race itself. The Oxford boat was more than half waterlogged in the first minute, and it was all too plain that they must sink. Cambridge steered straight for the Middlesex shore, where the water was rather better, and being well clear of Oxford in less than a minute were able to let their rating down. Oxford actually sank after two and a half minutes, just short of Beverly Brook, and off the Fulham Football Ground the umpire came up with the Cambridge crew and told them that the race was off.

The Times 1951

DENIS COMPTON got his hundredth 100 at Lord's, at exactly 6 p.m. yesterday. He cracked a ball from Freddie Brown, former England captain, to the Tavern rails—and there it was. You see Compton pictured just at that moment. Freddie Brown began to clap. Applause swept round the field.

In the stands and pavilion the crowd stood and clapped (writes Crawford White), and the game stopped for a moment while Compton waved his bat.

Then on with the game.

Nobody leapt the rails in the excitement of the occasion. Nobody ran up to shake hands. Not at Lord's.

News Chronicle 1952

THE JOKE THAT THE LISTENERS DIDN'T HEAR

MILLIONS of listeners settled down by their radios last night to listen to a broadcast of Tommy Trinder from the first night of the Prince of Wales Theatre show, "Fancy Free."

They heard Tommy begin to tell a joke about a nude girl. Then suddenly there was silence. The programme had been cut off the air.

The silence lasted for five seconds. Then the programme came through the speakers again. And the theatre audience was roaring with laughter. But the listeners did not know what the joke was.

The five seconds' black-out was no "technical hitch." The B.B.C. admitted that engineers cut the broadcast on instructions because it had been decided that the material was unsuitable for broadcasting.

And what was the joke the B.B.C. cut out? It was this: Trinder mentioned the growing number of nude girls appearing in London shows. "Soon," he quipped, "there will be 500 nude girls on London stages—that would be a thousand pities." Then he paused, and added. "For the ladies don't like it."

'Supreme Test'

After the show Trinder told the *Daily Mirror*:

"The B.B.C. heard this joke three times—once this morning at the final rehearsal and twice on Monday. No one took any exception to it.

"I wrote the joke and the build up for it myself, and I put it to my supreme test I use for any new routine—is it fit for my mother to hear? I decided it was."

While the show was being broadcast engineers followed Trinder's script, word for word, through their earphones. When Tommy started his nude joke an engineer's hand shot to the control panel.

Daily Mirror 1951

Woman's World
1952

The policeman is obviously having a difficult task—he was one of many who struggled to control a huge crowd, mainly teen-agers, at the premiere of the film "Rio Grande" in London last night.
Stars Tyrone Power and Forest Tucker had to be "lifted up by police and thrown into the cinema," said a cinema official. It took police five minutes to open the door of Tucker's car, so great was the pressure of the crowd round it. The police then decided that it was hopeless to try to get film star John Wayne in by the main door, and decided to smuggle him in at the rear of the building.

HE LOST HIS TROUSERS AT 50 m.p.h.

ROLLER-SKATING star Johnny Ravio was swinging round at 50 m.p.h. a volunteer from the audience at a Luton theatre last night when there was suddenly a white flash . . . the man's trousers had shot over his knees.

The audience rocked with laughter as variety stars carried out face-saving moves. Ventriloquist Peter Brough shouted for the curtains to be drawn, and mouth-organist Ronald Chesney took off his dressing-gown ready to wrap it round the man.

The man hobbled into the wings, with Chesney's dressing gown round him. Then he went back to his seat.

Johnny Ravic said afterwards: "He was a youngster wearing grey flannels. When I was spinning him at top speed, I noticed a blur of white. Then with a whoosh, his trousers shot past his knees.

In future I shall have to ask only for volunteers wearing braces."

Daily Mirror
1951

Going to the Pictures

OUR WEEKLY FILM NEWS.

"PAT AND MIKE" is a new MGM film release you must not miss seeing. It stars SPENCER TRACY and KATHARINE HEPBURN in characters ideally suited to their respective personalities.

He is a pugnacious but lovable sports promoter who sees in Katharine the makings of an all-round woman athletic star. Katharine knows she could be good but she suffers with a "jinx," in the shape of her blustering fiance, WILLIAM CHING, whose presence at any sporting event gives her such an inferiority complex that she invariably loses the game, whether it be golf or tennis. Spencer quickly spots this and persuades her to sign a contract with him. Under his guidance she becomes queen of the athletic realm and finally rids herself of her "jinx" in a very original way.

Besides the stars you will have the thrill of watching such top-line sports stars as Gussie Moran, Don Budge, Alice Marble, Frank Parker, and many others in action—and it may interest you to know that Katharine Hepburn really is a first-class amateur tennis and golf player and she gives some very fine examples of her talents in the film against the professional stars.

Even if you are not a sports fan you will find this film wonderful entertainment.

NO one can accuse BINNIE BARNES, whom we do not see often enough in films these days, of being a conceited woman. She is the wife of Mike Frankovich, who is filming "Decameron Nights."

"I am playing a part in my husband's film—only because he couldn't get anyone else suitable. I wouldn't mind if I never acted again, and I don't think anyone else would."

I don't agree with Miss Barnes and I am sure those who have enjoyed her films in the past will look forward to seeing her again on the screen.

Besides playing a part, she is production assistant on the film which is being made in Spain.

YOU'LL be surprised when you see LAURENCE OLIVIER (he drops the "sir" professionally) in "Carrie" the new Paramount film release in which he is co-starred with JENNIFER JONES.

In this rather sombre film set in 1900 he appears as a middle-aged manager of a luxury restaurant who goes downhill because of his association with Jennifer—not that it is her fault; she loves him deeply and he gives up everything he has for her, too. But he has a cold, calculating wife in MIRIAM HOPKINS, who had cleverly arranged matters so that everything he has is in her name. The theme of the "eternal-triangle" is not unusual but the clever working out of the story is, and both the stars and Miriam Hopkins play out this drama in grand style.

This film is adapted from Theodore Dreiser's classic novel "Sister Carrie," and is worth seeing if you don't mind a depressing subject, beautifully produced and acted.

FASHION FLASH

THOSE of you who play tennis will find the sports clothes worn in "Pat and Mike" particularly interesting.

In one scene, Katharine Hepburn wears a new style tennis two-piece which could be copied quite easily for your own wardrobe. The shorts are attached to a sleeveless top similar to that of a pinafore, and under it Katharine wears a high-necked, short-sleeved sports shirt. This is an excellent idea for the "all-weather" player, for the shirt can be exchanged for a sweater should the day be cool.

(Above)
Spencer Tracy puts Katharine Hepburn through some physical training exercises in "Pat and Mike."

(Left)
Laurence Olivier and Jennifer Jones play out their tragic romance in "Carrie."

Screen Girl

TRUEMAN THE TORNADO :

High-speed camera slows the high-speed man who routed the Indians . . . See now the secret too fast for the eye

STROBOSCOPIC
That is the word for this super high-speed study specially photographed for the Daily Express by ZOLTAN GLASS.

By PAT MARSHALL

THE 21-year-old Yorkshire lad called Fred Trueman—who took nine Indian wickets in the third Test on Saturday—bowls *fast*, faster than any Englishman playing cricket.

Now, in this new-style action picture, you can see just how he does it.

The secret is co-ordination—of mind and muscle, movement and intention.

The process starts with a 30-yard-long, smooth-actioned run to the wicket at gradually increasing pace.

Here you see Trueman completing the final two strides of his run. All the power he has gathered on the way to the wicket is now concentrated and co-ordinated as his left arm goes up, his right arm down, and his torso inclines backwards.

Without any break in the rhythmic movement the climax is reached. Over comes that right arm. The massively muscled back straightens and all the pent-up power is released as the Trueman right arm whistles past the Trueman right ear and goes on to complete a near-circle.

SERVICE NOTE: A.C.2. Trueman got five days' leave for the Test. Thanks to him, it finished in three days. So, today —back to his R.A.F. station.

Daily Express
1952

Why, Sir Thomas, did you not start with this?

By CECIL SMITH

FORGIVE me, Sir Thomas Beecham, for harping on a tortured subject, but the concert Eduard Van Beinum and the Amsterdam Concert Orchestra gave in Usher Hall last night was the one that should have opened the Edinburgh Festival, instead of your insular little Sibelius programme.

First came a tribute to the region the orchestra is visiting —Mendelssohn's "Hebrides" Overture, then one of the sublime masterpieces of all music, Beethoven's Pastoral Symphony played with deep spiritual penetration.

Finally came the most important single piece written in our time— Stravinsky's "The Rite of Spring," the revolutionary work which paved the way for much of the most progressive music of the past 40 years. This, Sir Thomas, was a programme of international festival stature.

The Beethoven performance was wonderful. The discipline of the players was absolute, their interpretative instinct unanimous.

It was an exciting evening.

Daily Express
1952

MR. R. S. CLARK'S NEVER SAY DIE, RIDDEN BY L. PIGGOTT AND TRAINED BY J. LAWSON, WINNING THE DERBY BY TWO LENGTHS FROM ARABIAN NIGHT (left), WHO TOOK SECOND PLACE FROM DARIUS BY A NECK

Country Life
1954

NO-LICENCE LISTENER LOSES RADIO

The Post Office will sell it

By Daily Mail Reporter

MR. William John Daniels lost his radio set yesterday. The Post Office will sell it, and give to the Chancellor of the Exchequer whatever price they get.

When Mr. Daniels, of Ambassador-close, Hounslow, Middlesex, was fined £2, with 10s. costs, at Brentford yesterday for operating his sound radio without a licence, the magistrates made the third "confiscate the set" order in 15 years.

"Only in flagrant cases is application made for confiscation of an unlicensed radio," a Post Office official said.

Daily Mail 1954

The Stage 1952

This girl knew she could not drown . . .

Miss Jean Manchester, of Morecambe, was thrown into the Thames at Battersea, S.W., her hands tied behind her and her ankles lashed—and knew she could never drown.

The secret was in her smart black bathing costume, a new, unsinkable swimsuit, invented by Mr. Mark Shaw, aged 47, of Morecambe. "The principle of the suit," he says, "is a panel of trapped air worked into the material." Yesterday's demonstration was arranged by the Infantile Paralysis Fellowship. The suit has helped in water treatment of polio victims.

Another demonstration will be given on Friday before officials of the Admiralty, the Royal National Lifeboat Institution and health and school services.

Daily Graphic 1952

York Minster concert

By ERNEST BRADBURY

Last night's concert in York Minster, though an enjoyable event in itself, was also an experiment of the York Festival Society, in preparation for another York Festival next year. This time the music came from the north transept, with orchestra and singers placed under the famous Five Sisters window, instead of the west end of the Minster.

But alas, the echo pursues us still! From this point it is not, indeed, a 10-second echo, at least to those listeners immediately in front of the orchestra. Yet the shorter echo rolled around at the end of movements and pealed like thunder in Haydn's drum passages, and very naturally blurred many an outline in the Suite in D of Bach, and in the symphonic music.

Different impressions

How different—and how perfect in sound—was the tiny Latin evening hymn which the Minster choir sang before the concert! Every listener would have a different impression of last night's music, according to his listening position, and in the second part, when for Haydn's Third Mass I sat as far from the performers as possible, by the door in the south transept, even Haydn's more boisterous movements were reduced to a smooth, impersonal sound, though giving a general, pleasing effect.

The choir were a section of the Leeds Philharmonic Society under Mr. Allan Wicks, who was not blind to details in the score, as he showed, for example, in the sforzando-crescendo opening chords of the *Sanctus*, which carried most effectively. The solo singers — Ilse Wolf, Janet Baker, Arthur Millington and Tom Moore—blended well as a quartet, as in these circumstances they were bound to do. [Incidentally, why was one singer's name printed in larger type than the others? A printer's error, or sheer bad taste?]

Yorkshire Post 1953

PIANIST BOOED AT WIGMORE HALL

Express Staff Reporter

DAVID SECOMBE, who calls himself Vladimir Levinski, who calls himself the Paganini of the Piano—and the Reincarnation of Liszt—was booed at Wigmore Hall last night. Many of the 500, who had paid 3s. to 9s. for seats, walked out and demanded their money back. They did not get it.

WIGMORE HALL

MONDAY JANUARY 21st at 7.30

VLADIMIR **LEVINSKI**

● *The handbill that drew 500 to Secombe's recital.*

First surprise came when Mr. Levinski - born - Secombe stopped to talk about Liszt, whose picture stood on the piano.

Some people left before the interval, others followed the pianist to the dressing-room to ask if he felt ill.

Then his first few bars set people whispering. A few more bars and they were up and making for the doors.

Some paused in the aisles to protest. The pianist paused in his playing to protest, too: "I cannot concentrate with all this noise."

His was not, in the opinion of the man who let the hall to him—about £90, including advertising and printing—"a performance up to concert standard."

'Inspired . . .'

And what about Mr. Levinski ("please don't call me Secombe, please, please")?

"I feel the concert was a tremendous success," he said.

"I paid no attention to the scurrilous students—the minor few—who tried to interrupt my work. I went straight on right through the whole programme, and a bit more.

"I played furiously. I was inspired.

"After it was over there wasn't enough room in my dressing-room to hold those who came to congratulate me. Many had to be turned out."

Mr. Levinski—"*great men must have great names*"—is 21 and lives at Cheltenham. About music lessons, now. Mr. Secombe, pardon, Levinski, laughed. "I have no time for them.

"I have a technique of my own. I started playing the piano when I was three and a half. Since then, I taught myself. I developed my own style.

"Later I went to a couple of teachers, and what do you think they tried to do? They tried to teach me to play the piano. Of all things."

Daily Express 1952

A TWO-DAY ULSTER G.P.

Geoff Duke (Norton) Wins the 350 c.c. and 500 c.c. Races and in Doing so Becomes World Champion for Both Classes

Reported by CYRIL QUANTRILL

He thus becomes the first-ever double world champion and as this is the first occasion on which the 350 c.c. and 500 c.c. races have been run separately in the "Ulster," Duke also becomes the first man ever to win both classes in this meeting. He has also ensured a "double" for Norton in the manufacturers' championships.

Motor Cycling 1951

By CLIFFORD DAVIS

THE Television Toppers, the B.B.C.'s own dancing team, have been dropped from Saturday night variety this winter.

The twelve girls, who are under contract to the B.B.C. at £12 a week, are at present on a month's holiday. When they return they will be told that their services are no longer required at week-ends.

Instead, the girls will appear in a variety programme on alternate Thursday evenings—TV's repeat night, when only a handful of viewers switch on their sets. The girls' salaries are not affected.

The Toppers' departure from Saturday night variety, when there is a peak audience of nearly 10,000,000—biggest of the week—follows criticism that the girls' routines have become hackneyed and their dancing ragged.

This criticism, in my view, is unfair, and the B.B.C. denies that it has affected its decision.

Daily Mirror 1953

CUP FINAL IN FULL WILL BE ON TV

THE Football Association Cup Final at Wembley on Saturday, May 2, is to be televised and broadcast in full.

The BBC is to pay the FA £1,000 for the TV rights, it was announced last night.

The broadcasting chiefs originally made an offer of £750, but the FA suggested £1,000—the figure finally settled on.

All the most up-to-date TV equipment, including new "zoom" lenses, will be used.

"We are confident that we can even show viewers the seams on the ball," said officials last night.

Daily Herald 1953

And they estimated that about 15,000,000 people all over the country will "look-in" at the match.

Viewers will see and hear all the Wembley "trimmings"—the community singing and marching before the kick-off, and, afterwards, the Queen presenting the Cup and the medals to the two teams.

The FA decision to allow TV is a great triumph for the television chiefs.

An historic moment. Geoff Duke (Norton) adds the 500 c.c. Individual World's Championship to his 350 c.c. Championship as he crosses the line to win the Senior race.

Motor Cycling 1951

Brighter Sundays move rejected by 224 vote majority

THE Sunday Observance Bill, to allow theatres to be opened and games to be played on Sundays, was rejected by the House of Commons yesterday when, by 281 votes to 57, a majority of 224, a second reading to the Bill was refused.

Western Mail 1953

The House also defeated by 172 to 164, a majority of eight, an amendment moved by Mr. Eric Fletcher, Soc., Islington East, to appoint a Commission to inquire into what respects the national welfare called for a revision of the existing Sunday Observance laws in England ad Wales.

The Bill was a private measure brought by Mr. John Parker, Socialist M.P. for Dagenham.

NEWS CHRONICLE REPORTER

ENGLAND waits tiptoe on the edge of expectancy this morning to hear that 94 runs have been scored—and 10,000,000 TV viewers expect to see the Ashes return, at last, to the home of cricket.

Only 30,000 could watch Percy Chapman's men 27 years ago—the last occasion when Australia were beaten in a series in England.

Today, TV will begin at 11.25 and stay with the play until the end. This decision came after the M.C.C. had first "regretfully refused" permission for it to start any earlier than the customary 1 p.m.

County cricket gates, it was explained, must be protected.

Once in a lifetime

For three hours after that announcement, the telephone of M.C.C. secretary, Mr. R. Aird, never ceased ringing. Nor did that of Mr. S. J. de Lotbiniere, the B.B.C.'s head of television outside broadcasts.

Viewers all over the country desperately wanted to see an event that, as one TV commentator put it, "may happen only once in our lifetimes."

The B.B.C. repeated their request, but the M.C.C. could not grant it until the county clubs had been consulted.

Then—late last night—the counties gallantly agreed to waive their rights under the standing agreement.

So the biggest audience ever to see cricket played will now watch run by run as the total creeps up to—victory.

A film will also be made of the closing scenes, and will be televised later in the day.

Millions not watching will listen. The Light Programme has cancelled all its morning features. It will begin the Test commentary at 11.30 a.m. and continue to the finish.

Yesterday all Light programmes were abandoned from 3 p.m. until the close of play, and "Mrs. Dale's Diary" was squeezed into the tea interval.

TV also held on while Australian wickets fell, and the children's feature was put back 31 minutes.

From India

In the Overseas broadcast services the B.B.C. scrapped programmes to Persia, Iraq, Persian Gulf, India, Pakistan, Malaya, Burma, New Zealand and the Fiji Islands.

Millions in these places heard instead the ball-by-ball description of England's climb back to cricket supremacy.

News Chronicle 1953

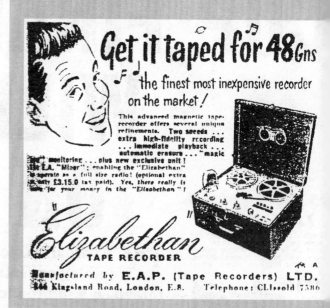

Get it taped for 48 Gns

the finest most inexpensive recorder on the market!

This advanced magnetic tape-recorder offers several unique refinements. Two speeds ... extra high-fidelity recording ... immediate playback ... automatic erasure ... "magic" monitoring ... plus new exclusive unit! The E.A. "Mixer"; enabling the "Elizabethan" to operate as a full size radio! (optional extra only £3.15.0 tax paid). Yes, there really is for your money in the "Elizabethan"!

Elizabethan TAPE RECORDER

Manufactured by E.A.P. (Tape Recorders) LTD. 344 Kingsland Road, London, E.8. Telephone: CLissold 7586.

A head for fashion

Enough to make your hair stand on end? A pipe-smoking man having a perm.

Mr. Robert Fryer, of Streatham, S.W., is unconcerned by conventional scorn. To him a hair-do is the tops on top.

★

As he sat yesterday in the West End salon of his choice, he could regard himself as a pioneer—if the experts are right. They say one man in ten is a potential perm client.

And they are now offering the clients a new perm process. It takes about an hour, costs 25s. — and produces wavy locks guaranteed for two months.

Daily Graphic 1952

THIS IS ART, BUT IT MYSTIFIES

HENRY MOORE'S latest work, "The Seated Woman," mystifies Miss Julie Lawson, a visitor to the Institute of Contemporary Arts Gallery in London, where an exhibition of Moore's works is being held. The figure is in terra-cotta and is the largest he has ever done in this medium.

Daily Herald
1953

Daily Mirror 1953

THE MAN AND HIS FRIENDS

ZOO MAN CANSDALE LOSES HIS JOB

THE Zoological Society yesterday sacked Mr. George Cansdale, superintendent of London Zoo—by abolishing his post.

The council of the society announced that the post has been abolished for "greater economy and efficiency."

Mr. Cansdale's duties, it said, would be re-allocated among the existing staff.

Mr. Cansdale, aged 43, has been superintendent of the Zoo since 1948. He is well known for his animal programmes on television.

Last night, he said: "What I feel about this I dare not let myself say. The only dignified thing to say is 'no comment.'"

He said that he hoped his television series would go on and that he planned to do some lecturing and writing in future.

Under the terms of the council's decision, Mr. Cansdale will be paid one year's salary (between £1,500 and £1,600) and will continue to live in the superintendent's house in the Zoo grounds for six months. But he will cease his duties at the Zoo immediately.

George Cansdale as televiewers know him—at ease with his animal friends. Here he shows a baby chimp how to bottle-feed a fawn.

Daily Herald 1953

THE ENGLAND TEAM WHICH WON THE FIFTH AND LAST TEST MATCH OF 1953 AND THUS REGAINED THE ASHES, AND (RIGHT) THE ENGLAND AND AUSTRALIAN CAPTAINS, LEN HUTTON AND LINDSAY HASSETT (ON THE RIGHT).
Our group shows the England team which on August 19 won the fifth and last Test Match of 1953 at the Oval by 8 wickets, and thus regained the Ashes. They are (l. to r., back row) T. Bailey, P. May, T. Graveney, J. Laker, G. A. R. Lock, J. Wardle and F. Trueman; and (in front) W. Edrich, A. Bedser, L. Hutton (captain), D. Compton and T. G. Evans. After the match both Len Hutton and Lindsay Hassett spoke on a microphone in the Pavilion, and both teams stayed on for an informal reception, at which a handsome iced cake was cut.

Illustrated London News 1953

Winifred Atwell plays a jungle rhapsody as the lioness roars.

WINIFRED IN A LION'S DEN

Daily Mirror
1953

WITH perspiration glistening on her forehead, Winifred Atwell sat in a circus cage yesterday and played the grand piano to a two-year-old African lioness—for twenty-three tense minutes.

The queen of the jungle sat at the back of the piano, just one jump away from the queen of boogie-woogie, who was completely unprotected. Her only comfort was that the lioness's trainer, Frenchman Gilbert Houcke, was also in the cage.

Winifred had promised to play in the lion's cage at Jack Hylton's Earls Court Circus, London, if another cage were built round the piano. But the organisers of a charity show for ex-Servicemen and needy children said that the second cage would take away the thrill for the crowd. In the end, Winifred agreed to risk it.

Yesterday was rehearsal day for the show, which goes on tonight. Winifred played a number composed specially for the occasion called "Boogamba," a jungle rhapsody. But the lioness, Royal, just sat and, every now and then, gave a roar. In the next cage, a lion, Pluto, roared, too.

'Call me Isabel' says TV's Lady Barnett

1d more for some seats at the cinemas

Big cinema circuits announced yesterday by notices in their foyers that the price of most seats will go up by a penny next week.

The lowest prices (1s 6d) and the highest (4s) will not be affected. But prices of the 2s 3d, 2s 8d, and 3s 1d seats will go up.

The chains operating the increase are Gaumont, Odeon, A.B.C., and Granada.

One cinema manager said that higher operating costs were the cause.

"Installation of wide-screens and other technical steps forward, we take it, are causing some higher operating costs."

Many independent cinemas are expected to follow the price rises.

Dundee Courier and Advertiser
1954

By CLIFFORD DAVIS

TWO newcomers to television parlour games—Lady Barnett, wife of a Leicester solicitor, and actor Michael Denison—join the panel of "What's My Line?" when it returns on Sunday week.

Lady Barnett, 33, said last night: "It's all rather fun, and I'm terribly pleased. I do hope they'll call me Isabel—that's my Christian name. I know that Eamonn Andrews, the chairman, runs the show on a Christian name basis.

"I don't want any of this 'Lady Barnett' business on TV. I just want to be one of the crowd like everybody else."

Lady Barnett, who owes her inclusion in TV's most popular programme to her wit, charm and speedy answers in a "Town Forum" relay from the Midlands last August, added: "I thought they only wanted film stars—I didn't think they would ever want me. It's going to be a bit of a problem finding different clothes every week — most of my outfits are for the country

"But I can change around the tops and that should keep me going for six weeks at least.

"One thing—I'll be able to wear some of the clothes I wore last year when my husband was Lord Mayor of Leicester. I thought I wouldn't have another opportunity."

She chuckled as she added: "Leicester may have seen them, but they'll be new to the rest of you."

Daily Mirror
1953

Daily Mirror
195

ROBERTS
WEYMOUTH

FINE BOILED SUGARS

Sweet Comfort
HERBAL TABLETS
8d. per quarter

Something you'll be looking at tonight

By CLIFFORD DAVIS

HERE in the picture on the right is what you will see on your TV screen tonight in place of the B.B.C.'s Coat of Arms, which opens up programmes at present.

Thirty-nine-year-old Abram Games, who designed it—he designed the Festival of Britain emblem —says it will be a bit frightening at first.

"But when you get used to it I'm sure it'll be quite all right," he told me last night.

The whole thing moves—in three different directions. What viewers will

It looks like this.

see is a film of a brass model in movement.

It seems to twist and turn. Eyelids and an eyeball in the middle mean VISION; the flashes of lightning at the sides mean electrical FORCE.

The sign has been speci-

ally prepared so that it can also be used when colour TV arrives—in two or three years—and it will sometimes be seen during intervals.

'Prestige Job'

Mr. Games said: "The fee wasn't very much. It's really a prestige job and I'd charge a lot more if I were asked to do it for commercial television.

"It's the most advanced job I've done and it took me over two months."

Mr. Games has no TV set. "But I shall go round and see it at a friend's," he said.

"The Dark is Light Enough"

EDITH EVANS as the Countess Rosmarin Ostenburg.

CHRISTOPHER FRY'S latest play—a winter story—was written for Edith Evans, who gives an exquisite performance as the Countess who loves all mankind. The play was reviewed fully in our last issue and the pictures in the following pages will give some idea of the great beauty of this production at the Aldwych Theatre, which is directed by Peter Brook, with décor by Oliver Messel.

Theatre World 1954

Davis's snooker record may not be equalled
—Mr. George Nelson

Joe Davis

By a Yorkshire Post reporter

Commenting last night on Joe Davis's world record snooker break, made at Leicester Square Hall, London, on Saturday, when he scored the maximum of 147, Mr. George Nelson 78-year-old former Yorkshire champion, said: "It is a wonderful feat and has been expected for some time, but I do not think anybody will ever do it again.

"He had everything in his favour, because he has been playing on the table all season and as it was an exhibition game he could afford to take chances. It certainly crowns his career and crowns the career of the hall.

"Joe is a marvellous position player. His success is due to the fact that he cannons his red balls into position for his next shot every time. To carry on a break like that he must have looked forward 30 or 40 shots from the beginning. That would need a lot of skill and concentration."

Davis, for 20 years the undefeated world professional champion, cleared the table, potting 15 reds, 15 blacks and all the colours. His previous world's best was 146 which he compiled at Manchester in 1950 and equalled last month at Leicester Square Hall.

Davis said: "That just about crowns everything. I feel now I have done everything that can be expected. I am particularly pleased at accomplishing the break before the hall closes at the end of this month."

Davis, who is 53 has held practically every snooker record during his illustrious career. He was playing Willie Smith at billiards and snooker, the two matches resulting:—

Billiards—Smith (rec 3,000 points) 6,988, Davis 6,036. Snooker—Davis 23 frames, Smith 13 frames.

Yorkshire Post 1955

DANCING ON TABLE IN WAITING ROOM

A BRISTOL youth who stood before Bath magistrates this morning charged with wilful damage of a table at Bath Spa railway station on May 14, was stated by Bristol police, said Chief Inspector Leslie Priddle, to be "one of the Bristol Teddy Boy gang."

The youth, who, the Chief Inspector stated, was convicted at Bristol on March 18, of being in possession of an offensive weapon and fined £25 was Brian Michael Hurley (18), of 428, Long Cross, Lawrence Weston, Bristol.

Mr. R Blackmore (chairman) said: "I understand you belong to this Teddy Boy gang, and I suppose you think you belong to a smart set.

"BREAKING UP"

"I can tell you that the magistrates and the general public will be very glad indeed to see the breaking up of these gangs, not only in Bristol, but here and in other parts of the country.

"You could do a lot of good, but instead you go about the countryside doing all sorts of damage to persons and property. We just don't understand you."

Bath and Wiltshire Chronicle 1955

CENSORS HAVE DATE WITH 4 SAUCY MERMAIDS

HERALD REPORTER

Daily Herald
1954

A DEPUTATION of councillors will troop down to the seafront at Cleethorpes, Lincs, tonight to take a close look at four scantily-clad mermaids.

They want to see them at night because it is then that the mermaids are supposed to look most " rude."

If the councillors agree that they are " rude " they will be censored. How? That has not yet been disclosed.

IN SEAWEED

But the mermaids—part of the seafront illuminations — have brought protests from holiday-makers that " they are rude and unsuitable for children to see."

They are painted in vivid colours, clothed only in " seaweed " and are grouped round a fountain and lily pond on the Promenade.

At night they are floodlit by coloured lights which make the fluorescent paint on them stand out.

So the council has decided to examine them.

NEAR THE MARK

Commented the Deputy Mayor, Councillor A. Baden Winters, who has already had a look: " I can't see anything disgusting about them. I think they are just naughty."

And one holidaymaker, 61-year-old miner Joss Willey, of Greasbro, near Rotherham, Yorks, agreed.

" They are no worse than some of the girls I have seen on the beach in bikinis," he said.

But Mrs. Lucy Cuskey, of Bradford, on holiday with her two children, declared: " The mermaids are a bit near the mark, you must admit. I think they should wear a bra."

THE DRESS THAT SHOCKED VAL PARNELL

Sabrina planned to wear the dress for her first ITV appearance — in the Jack Jackson show tomorrow night. She will present her first recording, a song called " I want a man."

'Precaution'

Mr. Parnell, chief executive of Associated TeleVision, told me last night :

" As a precaution I thought I'd better inquire what Sabrina was going to wear.

" Peter Glover, the producer of the show, brought along a picture.

" I saw at once we couldn't have anything like that on TV."

Showman Val paused and chuckled. " What was wrong with it ?

" Well, er . . . er . . . THERE WAS JUST TOO MUCH OF SABRINA."

Daily Mirror
1957

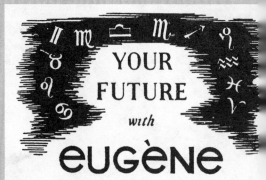

By PETER BLACK

Daily Mail
1954

TELEVISION'S new family series, "The Grove Family," will begin on April 9.

Yesterday the actors were chosen from 250 applications to represent the lower middle-class London suburban family who will be seen each Friday evening for 13 weeks.

Here, with characteristics as supplied by John Warrington, the producer, is the cast:

Father Grove, a jobbing builder earning around £16 a week (Edward Evans); "*a pleasant bloke with a dry sense of humour.*"

Problem child

Mother Grove, a North Country woman, warm and independent (Ruth Dunning); "*the type who always jumps up first to put the kettle on in a TV interval.*"

Jack Grove, 23-year-old son, in the Army (Peter Bryant); "*one of the boys, thinks he's very sharp and clever.*"

Pat Grove, 21-year-old daughter, assistant librarian (Sheila Sweet); "*very pretty, lots of boy friends, gay, but proper.*"

Daphne Grove, 13 - year - old schoolgirl daughter (Mary Downs); "*a bit of a problem child who has trouble under the Education Act—she can't pass exams.*"

Chris Grove, 11-year-old schoolboy son (Christopher Beeny); "*very bright, passes exams without effort.*"

Frank Turner, neighbour (John Salew); "*lugubrious, always giving advice, most of it bad.*"

And, finally, Grandmama Grove (Nancy Roberts); "*99 years old and going strong, crotchety, dis-agreeable, but with something lovable about her.*"

The series has been written by Michael Pertwee and edited by his father, dramatist Roland Pertwee. Mr. Michael Pertwee said: "The idea is to show, slightly exaggerated, the small ordinary things which happen in family life—and some of the sad ones too.

"We're trying to condense into the 13 weeks most of the things which could happen in a lifetime, but the characters will stay the same age throughout.

"We shall keep it topical—there will be references to things like Easter, the Boat Race, and the Queen's return.

"I've kept the characters mostly from the south, because the south is my own area. But other people from other parts of the country will be brought in from time to time."

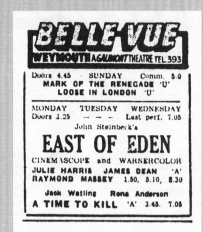

BELLE-VUE
WEYMOUTH GAUMONT THEATRE TEL. 393

Doors 4.45 - SUNDAY Comm. 5.0
MARK OF THE RENEGADE 'U'
LOOSE IN LONDON 'U'

MONDAY TUESDAY WEDNESDAY
Doors 1.25 — — — Last perf. 7.05
John Steinbeck's

EAST OF EDEN

CINEMASCOPE and WARNERCOLOR
JULIE HARRIS JAMES DEAN 'A'
RAYMOND MASSEY 1.50, 5.10, 8.30

Jack Watling Rona Anderson
A TIME TO KILL 'A' 3.45, 7.05

Under the Net is a first novel, and an arrestingly good one. It is not a masterpiece (however loosely one chooses to employ that unyielding word) because it never quite makes up its mind where it is going; but where it does find its feet, and progresses for any distance in one direction, it shows an original talent of great quality. What I suspect Miss Murdoch set out to do was to write a highly intelligent picaresque novel which should be extremely funny: what she has it in her to produce, I believe, is something more—a novel which is not only a novel of action, but one of thought and feeling into the bargain. What convinces me is the individual, unfaltering way in which she presents her first-person hero, Jake Donahue. He is clever, feckless, none too particular as to honesty, egotistical and cold, a would-be writer too lazy to work, a sponger, a man to all intents and purposes worthless. Yet his potential worth is gradually made clear; as he pursues his ludicrous adventures he grows and ripens, and by the last page we know he is on the point of becoming a good writer. This is partly due to the fact that his first-person narrative is so admirably well written. For all his hard, unsentimental manner there is poetry in him, his expression is nervous and economical, his thought masculine. He is the only thing in the book. The minor characters, the adventures, the absurdities one by one fall away, and in the end we are left alone with the intense, the self-absorbed approach of a character to its destiny.

London Magazine
1954

Sadler's Wells. *The Turn of the Screw* (October 6)

The Opera

The ways of the public are strange. *Gloriana* is tying with *Faust* at the moment (in our Opera Competition) as the work that people would least like to see announced at Covent Garden. But Britten's next opera, *The Turn of the Screw*, aroused public enthusiasm such as had not been known before for a new British piece. It was harder to get seats than for the latest musical; each of us had to use his tiny influence with the house, or with the English Opera Group, to try to get in to later performances. A success, oh yes a success with the public. There were only four performances: may we soon see it again.

Opera
1954

POKING his head out of the cab of the three-ton lorry, the driver glowered down at the green saloon which had just nipped ahead of him at the lights. "Who do you think you are—Stirling Moss?" he inquired.

The driver grinned at me companionably. Well, you couldn't be expected to know that it was Stirling Moss, the man who had just pulled off the most-prized and seemingly, unattainable victory for an Englishman—victory in the classic Mille Miglia.

Daily Mail
1955

Steinbeck story

James Dean, the "second Marlon Brando" who was killed in a recent motor accident, shares the leading roles of "East of Eden" (Belle Vue, Weymouth, Monday for three days) with Julie Harris and Raymond Massey.

Film is an adaptation of the John Steinbeck novel and tells of the twin sons of a farmer. One is neurotic and fancies himself unloved while the other is a likeable youngster, interested in farming and his girl.

Julie Harris—who will be remembered for her "I Am a Camera" performance—is the girl.

*Dorset Daily Echo
and Weymouth Dispatch*
1956

BRANDO BANNED

AND THE SPOTLIGHT VIEW IS...

A MARLON BRANDO film has been banned in Britain. The picture is called "The Wild One," and the censor has taken not one but several looks at it.

He has decided that at the moment he cannot give it any certificate at all. Even the censor has difficulty in remembering the last time this happened with a film of a major star.

I am one of the few people in Britain to have seen "The Wild One." I know it is brutal—but it is also brilliant. It ought to be shown.

"The Wild One" is a story of a bunch of young hoodlums who ride their motor-cycles into a small, quiet American town. The local policeman is weak and nervous. The youngsters in black, shining riding jackets roar their machines about the place terrorising the inhabitants. They call themselves "The Black Rebels."

They are only cleared out after a man is killed and the State Troopers are brought in.

The British censor is afraid of the effect the picture might have on some young people here. But the film punches home its moral: take a strong line with young toughs at the beginning and there won't be any trouble.

Hollywood is suggesting a possible new ending. As it stands, a battered Brando—the leader of the cyclists' raid—rides off after being freed on a charge of manslaughter. He has been beaten up by some of the townspeople.

Brando's performance is astonishing. He talks in grunts and jerks. He gives a complete picture of a worried youth needing the false security of gang violence.

In France—where the film is showing uncut—Brando's acting has been picked as the best of the year. "The Wild One" is blazing, entertaining—and it would be a top-talking point wherever teenagers try to act tough.

This brutal, brilliant film should be seen, says DAVID LEWIN

Daily Express 1955

OPERA

Vol 5 No 11   NOVEMBER 1954   2s 6d

Jennifer Vyvyan and David Hemmings

NEW WRITING

By KENNETH TYNAN

Observer 1955

A SPECIAL virtue attaches to plays which remind the drama of how much it can do without and still exist. By all the known criteria, Mr. Samuel Beckett's **Waiting for Godot** (Arts) is a dramatic vacuum: pity the critic who seeks a chink in its armour, for it is all chink. It has no plot, no climax, no *dénouement*; no beginning, no middle and no end. Unavoidably, it has a situation, and it might be accused of having suspense, since it deals with the impatience of two tramps, waiting beneath a tree for a cryptic Mr Godot to keep his appointment with them; but the situation is never developed, and a glance at the programme shows that Mr. Godot is not going to arrive. "Waiting for Godot" frankly jettisons everything by which we recognise theatre. It arrives at the custom-house, as it were, with no luggage, no passport and nothing to declare: yet it gets through, as might a pilgrim from Mars. It does this, I believe, by appealing to a definition of drama much more fundamental than any in the books. A play, it asserts and proves, is basically a means of spending two hours in the dark without being bored.

Submarine TRIDENT

SWIMMING CAP

Such wonderful comfort! It's a joy to wear. Featherlight and stretchy, the internal suction cups cling caressingly to every contour of the head, keeping the hair absolutely dry. Styled in Black, White and 6 gay colours.

OBTAINABLE AT BOOTS, TIMOTHY WHITES, CHEMISTS AND STORES. IN CASE OF DIFFICULTY PLEASE WRITE TO THE MAKERS.

W. W. HAFFENDEN LTD.

RICHBOROUGH RUBBER WORKS, SANDWICH, KENT

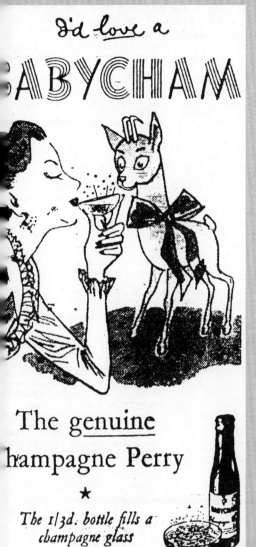

I'd love a

BABYCHAM

The genuine
champagne Perry

★

*The 1/3d. bottle fills a
champagne glass*

E KITCHEN SINK IN
E DRAWING ROOM

ll that criticism can usefully do, therefore, is to be
the lookout for climatic changes, and this year's
rlington House show does indicate quite a consider-
e, though, on reflection, not a surprising change.
r since the end of the war a small but tough group
younger artists, inside the R.A., has been gradually
hering strength. Between them and their seniors
re is a noticeable age-gap—the gap created by the
years. For many years their exhibits have formed
ackbone to the annual exhibition but not until this
r have they been able seriously to change the
demy's policy. This year they have opened the
red doors of Burlington House and beckoned their
unger friends in. And their younger friends have,
general, invaded the premises in a compact body
entrenched themselves in rooms 7 and 8, making
Alfred Munnings feel so sick that he was unable to
end the annual Banquet. Bare, ruined Bratbys and
ddleditches surprisingly occupy the walls where late
sweet thoroughbreds and bluebell glades hung,
minating these two rooms and calling attention to the change
climate by their size and forcefulness.

Art News and Review
1956

Angry Americans say

ROCKY BROKE ALL THE RULES

Hit while Cockell was down

From CHRISTOPHER LUCAS : New York, Tuesday

WORLD heavy-weight champion Rocky
Marciano was today angrily accused by
American sports writers of dirty tactics in his
fight with Britain's brave loser, Don Cockell.

Joe Williams, *New York
World Telegram*, wrote :
" It was a fight which saw
Marciano violate practic-
ally every rule in the book.

" He hit after the bell, used
his elbows and head in
close quarters, several times
punched below the belt, and
once hit Cockell while he was
down.

" The visitor was subjected to
a very rough time, and if as a
result of his experiences out
here he should get the idea that
anything goes in the American
ring short of wielding a knife
or pulling a gun you couldn't
blame him altogether. Not
once did the referee so much as
admonish Marciano.

Such cavalier
treatment

" Inasmuch as the visitors
had received such cavalier
treatment from the boxing
commissars before the fight—
and a few of their requests
seemed reasonable enough—
what subsequently happened in
the ring somehow had the
appearance of piling it on."

Jimmy Cannon, *New York
Post*, said : "It was a dirty
fight and Marciano continually
fouled Cockell.

" He butted him and dug his
elbows into Cockell's face.

" He took a last blow as
Cockell lay like the clotted drip-
pings from an immense candle
against the ropes after the first
knock-down.

" But the British fighter is a
brave man by the standards of
his cruel occupation and few
heavy-weights have taken
more."

Under the headline, " Don :
Champion of Courage " the
New York Journal American
praises Cockell for the " sort of
courage that thrills you."

It says : " He's no champion
of the world. Nor is he ever
likely to be. But he's a man.

Daily Mail
1955

CREW - CUTS

The Crew - Cuts, four young
Canadians who have become
America's most popular vocal
quartet, opened their first British
tour at Liverpool Empire this
week

The Stage 1955

Sporting Life
1956

By TOM NICKALLS

THIS was the most amazing Grand National ever run. Sensation and incredible drama—so fantastic that not even in fiction could such a finish be imagined —but, alas, with a tragic ending. In the 117 years of its history, there have been a great many hard-luck stories, but Saturday's surpassed them all.

After taking the lead between the last two fences the Queen Mother's grand horse, Devon Loch, landed over the last a length and a half in front of E.S.B., and began to draw steadily away up the run-in.

Rounding the elbow a furlong out it was seen that he had the race well won, and a storm of cheering broke out such as I have never heard at Aintree.

Most of the huge crowd had turned to face the Royal box with hats uplifted or thrown in the air, and there was our Queen beside herself with excitement, together with her mother and sister.

Five Lengths Clear

Fate then dealt them the cruellest blow. Devon Loch, with the winning post barely 50 yards ahead, was leading E.S.B. five or six lengths when his hind legs appeared to slip under him.

He staggered, and was nearly down sprawling with Francis striving desperately to keep his seat. They were at a complete full stop, and the roar of cheering ceased in the instant.

Though E.S.B. raced past Devon Loch and won the race, it still seemed that if only Devon Loch could start again he must be second. But he was all at sea and seemed temporarily to have lost the use of his hind legs.

Convinced that something was wrong Dick Francis jumped off as Gentle Moya went past to take second place, followed at ten lengths by Royal Tan, and then, as soon as the girths were loosened, Devon Loch appeared to be himself again, and walked away as sound as a bell.

Poor Francis, distressed beyond measure, flung his whip on the ground, and walked to the stable like a man in a daze with the tears rolling down his cheeks.

By MAURICE FAGENCE

I FOUND Frankie Laine, the American crooner, hiding among garbage cans at London Airport last night while a thousand crazed gramophone fans were tearing railings down to reach him.

"My fans have gone berserk," he told me.

They had. They had bowled over steel barriers, smashed bicycles underfoot, battered Press cameras, even tugged shoes off the feet of people in Laine's party apparently as souvenirs.

Thirty police officers were swept by a tide of a thousand shrieking fans, 70 per cent. teenage girls, the rest youths.

While I talked to Frankie Laine, pale and obviously frightened as he hid in a yard full of garbage, the crowd looked over a fence and saw him.

"I want no more affairs like this," he shouted.

As the crowd swarmed the fence, police smuggled him through a side door and hid him among the milk-bottles of a canteen kitchen.

Injuries

FOUR injured people were carried away for treatment. Several Press photographers had leg injuries.

Daily Herald 1954

Theatre

Look Back in Anger: Osborne. *Royal Court*

LOOK BACK? But not far, and in temper, rather than deep settled rage. This is a young man's first play: it has the tensions of young writing and is often fierce, even shrill in its defiance. Those who have not forgotten how agonizing it is to be young and those who are interested in the surgery of play-projection will find a good deal to hold attention here. But the play in total effect is rather a misfire.

Every new generation believes itself the hardest done by; the next in age group is apt to point out that, itself, it had a harder time. Here, in the squalid, exacerbated, trumpet-playing Bohemia, a sort of British *Streetcar* develops, at least in what affects the husband and wife of Tennessee Williams' drama. The man is a *goujat*, a swine, spoilt, whining, abusive, making a hideous noise on a jazz trumpet and railing at his wife and his mother-in-law, 'a bitch', of course, being the word he chooses. He is much given to 'hating people's guts': very non-U. When the wife walks out, he makes do with one of her 'superior' friends: then she comes grovelling back, having miscarried. Nothing has been settled. The sex battle will go on. Utter disillusion prevails.

Time and Tide 1956

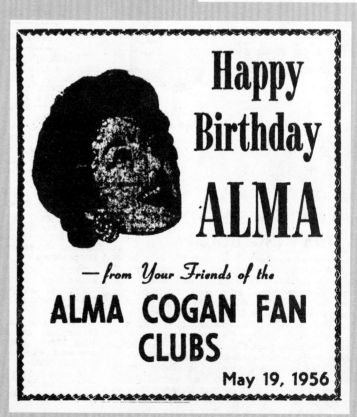

Happy Birthday ALMA

—*from Your Friends of the*

ALMA COGAN FAN CLUBS

May 19, 1956

Melody Maker 1956

BERT WEEDON

plays

DEMONSTRATION

at

**SELMER HOUSE,
SATURDAY, JUNE 2,**

2-4 p.m.

Hofner

*Hear Bert with his
Hofner on*
PARLOPHONE R.4178
playing
**"THE BOY WITH THE
MAGIC GUITAR"**

Selmer   114 CHARING CROSS RD., LONDON, W.C.:

Send for folder H.G.18 from—

Dial me
FOR TEST SCORES
WEBber 8811

ROY WEBBER

GOOD news for cricket fans. You will be able to get the latest scores during the Test matches against Australia at Lord's (June 21—26) and the Oval (August 23—28) simply by dialling WEBber 8811.

This was announced yesterday by Dr. Charles Hill, the Postmaster-General. He said the idea will be experimental.

The fictitious exchange, Webber has been named after Roy Webber, the News Chronicle's famous cricket statistician.

A Post Office spokesman said yesterday: "The letters WEB are the only coherent and easily remembered combination available. From that it was a short and natural step to Webber—everybody knows

the name is synonymous with cricket scores."

A G.P.O. spokesman in Manchester said: "A decision on extending the scheme to the northern Tests at Leeds (July 12-17) and Manchester (July 26-31) will depend on the success of the London experiment."

TAILPIECE: Said Roy Webber last night: "The G.P.O. rang to ask if I would mind. I naturally said 'Not at all.' After all, Webber 8811 looks good to me—I could never score it off my own bat."

News Chronicle 1956

Day of Triumph for Laker

The Ashes Safely in England's Keeping

By Our Cricket Correspondent

Laker, the Surrey off-spinner, took all ten Australian wickets for 53 runs to give England victory in the fourth Test at Old Trafford yesterday by an innings and 170 runs and ensure the retention of the Ashes.

This immense bowling feat, following on the heels of his nine for 37 in the first innings, completed a performance unlikely to be surpassed. Illustrious records fell in splendid flames as Laker ran through the Australian batsmen in an invincible period after lunch.

He is the first man to take all ten wickets in a Test innings. Another distinguished record to go by the board was the highest number of wickets ever taken in a Test Match, which was created by Sidney Barnes against South Africa at Johannesburg in 1913-14.

Laker also passed the record number of 15 wickets taken in an Australian Test, which had been previously accomplished only by Verity at Lord's in 1934 and by Rhodes at Melbourne in 1903-4.

Birmingham Post
1956

Birmingham Bans 'Rock' Film

Sunday Showings Stopped by Rank Organisation

Birmingham, Brighton, Gateshead, Bootle and South Shields have banned the film, *Rock Around The Clock*, and the Rank Organisation has stopped the Sunday showing of this "rock 'n roll" film in all its cinemas. In the words of a Rank spokesman: "Sunday night is regarded as the 'difficult' night in the cinema world."

The decision that the film must not be shown in any Birmingham cinema was made yesterday by the city's Public Entertainments Committee after representations from the Chief Constable, Mr. E. J. Dodd.

The committee chairman, Mr. A. H. Sayer, said that some "Teddy Boys" had announced that they would "show Manchester what Birmingham could do." The film had been causing a lot of trouble, and its showing would have made a greater call on the already-overworked police.

Birmingham Post
1956

HUNTING THE TV 'PIRATES'

ANYONE in the Exeter Post Office area, from Cullompton and Honiton to Dawlish, who owns a television set without a licence will be sleeping uneasily for the next fortnight.

The best thing to do—and this is a tip straight from the Head Postmaster, Mr. R. Phillips—is to get a licence without delay.

Why? Because otherwise they are almost bound to be found out, and that may mean a court conviction and a fine.

A Post Office detector van, looking like "the thing from another world," with three vaguely sinister aerials on the roof, is on the prowl to discover the television "pirates."

"They can't do very much to stop us picking them up, whether they have an indoor or an outdoor aerial," warned Mr. R. Powlesland, of Pinhoe, one of the two operators of the van.

Today he showed a reporter how the signals from television sets are heard. Each of the three aerials has a range of up to 200 feet. As the van cruises down the street, a signal is picked up on the first aerial, which is on the left-hand side of the front of the van.

PORTABLE DETECTOR, TOO

This registers on a meter, and the note is heard on head-phones by one of the operators. The aerial at the back and on the same side then picks up the signal. When the two are of equal strength, the operators know that there is a set somewhere on a line across the centre of the van. The third aerial, at the back on the right, tells them which side of the street it is.

An address list shows whether the owner of the set has a licence or not. A portable detector, which works on the same principle, is used in blocks of flats.

Mr. R. E. Boatman, the Deputy Head Postmaster, recalled that an autumn comb for sound licences made last year resulted in 614 new wireless and 255 television licences being taken out over a six-week period. A total of 44 people were prosecuted. There were 73 cases of evasion.

The number of television licences in the area on January 31 was 5,143. Radio licences totalled 35,656. In the past six weeks 325 new television licences had been issued.

Mr. K. A. Doney, of Saltash, the other operator in the van, stressed that the aim of detection was not primarily to prosecute. But the regional authorities would be notified of any inexcusable breaches of the law. He estimated that between three and five per cent of television-set owners did not have licences.

The van will return to Exeter in April. It is permanently stationed in the South West, and is one of nine in use in the country.

Exeter Express and Echo 1955

HEROIC ENDEAVOUR

J. R. R. TOLKIEN: *The Fellowship of the Ring.* Being the First Part of "The Lord of the Rings." Allen and Unwin. 21s.

In an earlier book, *The Hobbit*, Professor Tolkien portrayed a raw young world, where men crept up empty valleys while in the waste dragons and dwarfs disputed hoarded treasure. In this world dwelt the hobbits, creatures very like men but with furry feet. They are jolly, rather Philistine, creatures whose chief pursuit is " growing food and eating it "; hearty beer-drinkers, heavy smokers, fond of giving parties and making after-dinner speeches. (One reader saw in them the influence of Toad of Toad Hall.)

In *The Fellowship of the Ring* it is as though these Light Programme types had intruded into the domain of the Nibelungs. The result is a system of mythology as coherent, complete and detailed as that constructed by the ancients from the city-cults of the Levant. The author has undertaken a task at which Homer, Hesiod and Ovid laboured, and in this long book, the first volume of a trilogy, their different styles are mirrored by different moods.

The hobbits farm and feast and live for many years; but they are not immortal, and they marry and have offspring. The hero of this happy community of elderly schoolboys is Mr. Bilbo Baggins, who once captured a dragon's hoard; he keeps a magic ring as trophy of this dangerous adventure. But the Shire, the placid home of the hobbits, is set in an ancient and ruinous world; the surrounding waste is dotted with the vestiges of vanished kingdoms, and by half-known roads uncanny wanderers bring rumours of unpleasant doings in the south. Mr. Baggins learns that his ring is more than a trophy. If the great magician can get hold of it, he will rule the world by its evil strength; but its magic is no help to the good, for the wearing of it is harmful to their souls and bodies. So Mr. Baggins retires to live in a wood with the elves, passing on the ring to his nephew and heir, Frodo Baggins. Frodo decides to destroy the ring; though it can only be melted in the fire that forged it, and this fire glows in the depths of the citadel of evil. He sets forth with his dangerous burden, is joined by various brave and gifted magicians, dwarfs, elves and men, and by the end of the volume is about to enter, alone, the very capital of wickedness and danger. Duty has compelled him to undertake his task, and from a greedy young hobbledehobbit he has become a noble paladin.

Only considerable skill in narrative can surmount the difficulty of this complete change of key within the limits of one book. It is a near thing, but Professor Tolkien just pulls it off. The facetious account of banquets in the Shire leads on to gently beautiful descriptions of Rivendell and Lothlorien, the lush greenwood of the elves; later the grim record of the slaying of Balin, son of Fundin, the prince of the dwarfs who attempted to reconquer the underground realm of Moria from the sinister Orcs, echoes deliberately the matter-of-fact despair of the Sagas. The copious invention of background and the excitement of thrilling adventure carry the reader safely from mood to mood.

Yet the plot lacks balance. All right-thinking hobbits, dwarfs, elves and men can combine against Sauron, Lord of Evil; but their only code is the warrior's code of courage, and the author never explains what it is they consider the Good. Lacking the Grail, lacking romantic love, even the world of Malory would seem empty. Perhaps, after all, this is the point of a subtle allegory. Against Russia, the western world can draw together, but if the Iron Curtain vanished the rulers of Yugoslavia and Spain and Britain would find it hard to agree together on the next step. Whether this is its meaning, or whether it has no meaning, *The Fellowship of the Ring* is a book to be read for sound prose and rare imagination.

Times Literary Supplement 1954

Melody Maker 1956

Donegan debut

MONDAY night at a provincial Variety theatre is not often an occasion for cheering.

Last Monday at the Nottingham Empire, however, gave the lie to this generalisation—for Lonnie Donegan's début in British Variety there attained almost the proportion of a Palladium first-night.

Before he was half-way through his act the packed house was clapping on the off-beat; at the end the applause—cheering included—was prolonged and deafening. Lonnie's offering, ably backed by Denny Wright (gtr.), Mickey Ashman (bass) and Nick Nicholls (drs.), concentrated on a compelling beat which rivalled the devastating rhythm of rock 'n roll without ever descending to the vulgarity and paucity of ideas which characterise that current craze.

Brightest stars in a strong supporting bill were pianist-singer Mike McKenzie, comedian Ron Parry and 19-year-old Greek singer Maria Pavlou.—*Peter Leslie.*

LONNIE DONEGAN

Punch 1959

FENELLA FIELDING and KENNETH WILLIAMS

THE 'PLATTERS at the De Montfort Hall, Leicester, last night. Left to right (front) Herb Reed, Zola Taylor and Tony Williams; back: Rupert Branker, David Lynch, James Battieste (manager) and Paul Robi.

Dispensing that old, old 'rock'

DESPITE its comparative infancy, Rock 'n' roll is just about long enough, as it were, in the musical tooth to have been developed and stylised by its exponents—like the original jazz. At least, this was my belief until last night.

Coffee - coloured, crinkly - haired Paul Robi, one-fifth of the top American vocal group, the Platters, who served up two zest-filled shows at Leicester's De Montfort Hall, put an end to that way of thinking.

I discovered from Paul that rock 'n' roll is mighty old—so old, in fact, that the 'rock' should be suffering more than slightly from erosion and the 'roll' getting a little rusty.

DIXIELAND DAYS

"Man," said Paul, his brown eyes full of earnestness, "that started way back in the days of Dixieland music. It was just a case of putting rhythm and blues together and giving it a name.

"Folks have been doing Rock 'n' roll for the past 10 years—the music of the 1920s revised, only they just didn't know what to call it."

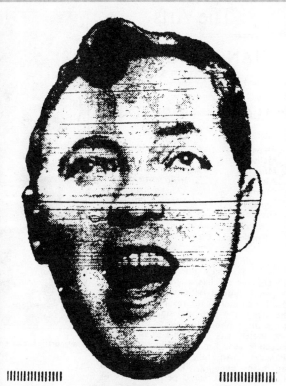

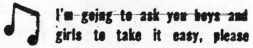

HE SAYS . . .

I'm going to ask you boys and girls to take it easy, please

SO the first night is over. . . . We're glad you liked the show.

This London audience was just great. Last night alone made our whole trip worth while. And I can only hope that some of the folk who "knock the rock" were there at the Dominion Theatre to see how well behaved those youngsters were — both inside and outside.

Their reaction was the same as we have found from audiences all over the world. They clapped with the music, sang, and some jumped up and down—just in a happy sort of way.

But that only goes to prove a strange thing that I've always noticed—nobody likes rock 'n' roll except the people.

Of course, there are always a few people who wish to take a verbal poke at us, whatever we do

There are always some who want to make us out as rabble-rousers and give it around that we don't care what happens

so long as we get the money.

I can only assure you that this is not the case. We are entertainers and we are grateful for applause. We like to see the youngsters jumping up and down, because it means they are happy.

But people who say that anything in the nature of a disturbance is good publicity for us—are talking through their bonnets.

We've never experienced riots (though we've heard a lot about them—and even read the word since we've been here) and there is nothing we would like less.

So I'm going to ask you boys and girls to take it easy, please.

This is your music, and there are plenty of people eager to attack it. But unless they rig disturbances for their own purposes — and I've known that happen —they'll find nothing bad in it.

☆★☆★☆★☆★

The Arts

HANDEL OPERA SOCIETY

"ALCINA" REVIVED AT ST. PANCRAS

Bradamante	MONICA SINCLAIR
Melisso	JOHN NOBLE
Morgana	EMERENTIA SCHEEPERS
Alcina	JOAN SUTHERLAND
Oberto	MILES AMHERST
Ruggiero	JOHN CARVALHO
Oronte	JOHN KENTISH

Producer: ANTHONY BESCH
Conductor: CHARLES FARNCOMBE

Plunging dauntlessly on into the long list of Handel's operas, the Handel Opera Society has alighted on *Alcina*, a piece studded with musical beauties. Half the point of the resurrection would be lost if the principal singers had not agile and euphonious voices; fortunately the society has been able to muster an effective cast for its production at St. Pancras Town Hall, which will be given again this evening. These are believed to be the first stage performances of *Alcina* for 220 years.

Dramatically considered, *Alcina* is a stagnant pond; but Mr. Winton Dean reminded readers of his programme note that dramatic consistency was not required of an opera composer in Handel's day. "The libretto was required to place the leading singers in as many different predicaments as possible, to enable them to show their prowess in arias of every type." The immediate inference is that Handel's operas are ignored because they are obsolete, but *Alcina* can hardly be buried when it contains three or four arias which belong with the great music of the world. The second act in particular sets one captivating aria after another; one of these, a florid aria of rage translated here as "How shall I avenge," stopped the show last night, and Miss Monica Sinclair was compelled to repeat the da capo section.

Dramatic pace or no, the stage performance compelled attention. One point of interest was the appearance of a male soprano as Ruggiero, the enchanted hero. Mr. John Carvalho produced some strong and ringing soprano, or perhaps high alto, tones, but there was also much whooping and a want of long breathed sostenuto in his art. The experiment was far from unsuccessful, even if a humane substitute for the old *castrato* soprano seems as far away as before. The musical and vocal delights of the performance were nicely shared between Miss Joan Sutherland, who looked regal and sang most expressively as Alcina, and the admirable Miss Sinclair.

The Boyd Neel Orchestra played elegantly for Mr. Charles Farncombe, but the harpsichord was too often silent when it was needed. The stage was skilfully peopled by a discreet producer, Mr. Anthony Besch. This is a welcome revival.

The Times 1957

The court scene in Act I of *Alcina*. In the centre (seated) is Alcina (Miss Joan Sutherland), and to her left is Ruggiero (Mr. John Carvalho).

A pin-up calendar hoax on churchmen

DOZENS of businessmen in London were startled and shocked yesterday to receive calendars for 1957 picturing scantily-clad girls —like the one on the right —which purported to come from the Lord's Day Observance Society and the Society for the Propagation of the Gospel.

IT WAS A HOAX. The names of the societies seemed to have been superimposed on the calendars by an amateur printer.

One businessman who received a calendar, Mr. Frank O'Sullivan, of Moorgate, said: "I am a Baptist and a churchgoer, and I think the calendar is offensive."

Mr. Harold Legerton, secretary of the Lord's Day Observance Society, said last night: "I am sure no one will take these calendars seriously. Everyone will see they are a hoax."

The Rev. E. Morgan, of the Society for the Propagation of the Gospel, said: "I would like to assure anyone who received such a calendar that it didn't come from US."

The verse on the calendar reads:

"Of faerie grace and elfin feature She is just the kind of creature Who destroys our resolution— Giving place to— evolution!"

One of the hoax calendars—with pin-up. It bears the name and address of the Lord's Day Observance Society.

Daily Mirror 1957

8.30 THE GOON SHOW
with Peter Sellers Harry Secombe, Spike Milligan
The Ray Ellington Quartet
Max Geldray
Orchestra conducted by Wally Stott
Announcer, Wallace Greenslade
Script by Spike Milligan and Larry Stephens
Production by Charles Chilton
(BBC recording)
Repeated on *Thursday* at 10.0 (Light)

Radio Times 1958

'Player-of-the-year' Finney faces Scots with stitches

By CLIFFORD WEBB

EVERYTHING'S happening to Preston's Tom Finney. He was yesterday elected " Footballer of the Year " —first player to get the award twice.

He was also told that he would have to turn out for England against Scotland at Wembley on Saturday wearing a special pad over the eyebrow he gashed in the League match against Aston Villa last week-end.

Tom came off the field after the England team's work-out at Highbury yesterday morning complaining that the cut was very sore.

Trainer Marshall (Sheffield Wednesday) took a look while Tom winced at every touch, then said: " You won't be able to have the stitches out, Tom. I'll have to fix you a pad that will make it easier when you head the ball."

The hope is that the soreness will decrease during the lighter training sessions today and tomorrow, otherwise this injury will be a handicap to England's attack.

Narrow margin over Edwards and Charles

It was in 1954 that the Preston plumber got his first statuette as " Footballer of the Year." He now completes a notable double by a narrow margin of Football Writers' Association votes over Duncan Edwards (Manchester United) and John Charles (Leeds United).

His brilliant performances since being moved from the wing to centre-forward have pulled Preston from a struggling position near the foot of the table to second place this season

There's another unique situation about this England team. Two of the players had never met until I introduced them over the edge of the Highbury dressing-room bath.

They were 20-year-old Alan Hodgkinson, the Sheffield United goalkeeper, and winger Stanley Matthews, C B E, who played for his country before Alan was born.

Blushing furiously, the chubby-faced goalkeeper told Stan he had first seen him play at Bramall-lane when he (Alan) was 12.

" You'll like it at Wembley," Stan told him. " It's the greatest Soccer arena in the world, and you won't be nervous at all once the match starts."

'Never dreamed the day would come'

The introduction over, Hodgkinson said to me: " I can still hardly believe it. Stanley Matthews was the idol of all the boys at my school and I never dreamed the day would come when I should be playing for the same team in the big international match of the season. It is the most wonderful thing that ever happened to me."

Matthews presented a slightly comic picture during England's practice game against Arsenal. He was wearing an oversized Arsenal shirt (number 3) and shorts borrowed when he reached the ground a full hour before the rest of the team.

STAN HAD STAYED IN LONDON OVERNIGHT INSTEAD OF JOINING THE PARTY AT THEIR HENDON HOTEL AND HE HAD BEEN LAPPING THE HIGHBURY PITCH AND PRACTISING SHORT SPRINTS FOR 45 MINUTES BEFORE THE PRACTICE MATCH STARTED.

George Young, captain and centre-half, and Ian McColl, right-half, did not train with the rest of the Scottish team at Elm Park, Reading, yesterday.

They had played for Rangers in a Scottish League match, travelled overnight and were allowed to sleep late at their Sonning (Berks) hotel.

Daily Herald 1957

Tom Finney . . . . with plaster

6.0 NEWS

6.5 Climb aboard the SIX-FIVE SPECIAL with

Jo Douglas and Pete Murray
introducing among others
Kenny Baker and his Dozen
Michael Holliday
The King Brothers
Pouishnoff
Featuring sport
Freddie Mills
Star Spotlight on
Lisa Gastoni
Script by Trevor Peacock
Designer. Tony Abbott
Produced by
Josephine Douglas and Jack Good
See page 3

Radio Times 1957

They Were Off Their Rockers

WHAT OF OPERATION LEE LEWIS?

OBVIOUSLY THE AMERICAN AND HIS ADVISERS WERE OFF THEIR ROCKERS IN BRINGING A 13-YEAR-OLD, NON-LEGAL-ISED WIFE TO A COUNTRY IN WHICH 13-YEAR-OLD WIVES ARE NON-EXISTENT, AND NON-LEGAL MARRIAGES NOT EXACTLY BRAGGED ABOUT AT THE VICAR'S TEA PARTY.

Worse, they were hardly reticent about it. True, they didn't actually introduce her at a mass meeting in Trafalgar Square. But just the same, when the press started to press, she was made literally available for pictures and interviews, instead of being packed off quick on the next plane to New York.

WHAT THOUGH, HAS ALL THIS TO DO WITH JERRY LEE AS A STAGE PERFORMER?

However much we may disapprove of *de facto* juvenile spouses, the truth remains that if, over the years, all artistes with off-beat private lives had had their contracts cancelled, the total ticket money refunded in consequence would by now have been rather more than enough to buy a packet of fags.

My view, in other words, is that except in grossly heinous cases, an artiste's private life should have no bearing on his or her standing as an entertainer and that Jerry Lee Lewis could have been living with a chimpanzee for all the difference it need have made to his tour of Britain.

Record Mirror 1958

DAILY MIRROR REPORTER

VIEWERS saw how the Swiss spaghetti crop was harvested in a film in the B.B.C. programme, " Panorama," last night.

The spaghetti dangled full length from heavily-laden trees as girls gathered the harvest.

Commentator Richard Dimbleby explained: "Of course the Swiss crop is not as heavy as the Italian. In Switzerland it is more of a back-garden hobby."

While viewers were no doubt asking themselves : " Surely spaghetti doesn't grow on trees ? " they saw the girls laying the spaghetti strands out in the sun " for drying."

Dimbleby went on : " Many people have often wondered how it is that spaghetti is all of the same length. But this is the result of years of careful cultivation and selection."

The 2½-minute film ended with a harvest celebration of spaghetti-eating.

" Just a piece of April Foolery," said the B.B.C when more than 250 viewers telephoned.

" They were anxious to tell us the real facts of spaghetti," said a spokesman, " and roared with delight when told the film was an April Fool joke."

Daily Mirror 1957

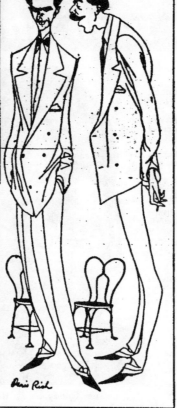

Ten Years of T.I.F.H.

Yes, it was ten years ago—on March 23, 1948, to be exact—that producer Charles Maxwell brought together two up-and-coming comedians — Jimmy Edwards and Dick Bentley—and two promising scriptwriters—Frank Muir and Denis Norden—in a comedy show with the non-committal title of 'Take It From Here.' After an uncertain start, the show became widely popular, and now has the distinction of being the longest-running comedy series ever.

Yet when we called on scriptwriters Muir and Norden (right), they were in no mood for happy reminiscence, nor for forward-looking optimism. 'Will it go on another ten years?' we asked. 'Ten years!' echoed Norden. 'Impossible. But then ten more shows are impossible. The script for the next programme seems impossible. We just plug away at it until it's finished, and don't go home until it is.' 'Yes,' added Muir proudly, 'we've managed to get home eight times in the last ten years.'

Radio Times 1957

Theatre World
195[8]

Skiffle scatters crooks

WRITING one of the first of these columns, more than eleven years ago, about Soho's asphalt jungle I christened it "the naughty square mile."

The name stuck. It has since been used in books and films and plays. But, strolling around my old beat for the first time in many, many months last week, I decided it was out of date.

Soho is no longer London's "naughty square mile." It has become Espresso Land, bright with the coloured neon lights of oddly-named coffee bars—" Heaven and Hell," " Prego," " The Macabre " and " The 2 I's "—and noisy with the yowling screams of the skifflers.

I hardly recognised the neighbourhood that I once knew like the palm of my hand.

Now instead of razor-armed mobsters and cosh boys you meet bearded young men in dufflecoats carrying double basses and washboards and pimply-faced rock-'n'-roll fans in tapered pants.

Their girl friends with pony - tail hair - do's and wearing jeans and ballet shoes have replaced most of the painted prowlers.

And in the cellars where all-night dice and poker taken over and the young-

the spielers once ran their games the skiffle bands have sters are jiving.

In fact, the kids seem to have done what the cops could never do. They have cleaned up the once naughty square mile.

The People 1957

A BATTERED and bruised Brian London, knocked out by Floyd Patterson in the 11th round of his world heavyweight championship bid in Indianapolis last night, said today he might return to the United States "to learn to be a good fighter." One eye slightly swollen from a cut underneath it, the other blackened by Patterson's vicious punching, West Hartlepool-born London was counted out after 51 seconds of the 11th round.

In the previous round he had gone down in a neutral corner from a right which he said hit him on the temple, and he took a count of five before the bell intervened.

London said afterwards it was the first time in the fight that he was really hurt. "I never recovered fully from the punch, and was still dizzy when I went into the 11th round," he said.

Northern Daily Mail 1959

Music and Musicians 1959

LONDON AND MOSCOW OPERA STARS

VISITING Bolshoi Theatre soprano Galina Vishnevskaya (left) went to Covent Garden to hear Lucia di Lammermoor on the last night of the season on February 28, afterwards met Joan Sutherland in her dressing-room with warm congratulations. Vishnevskaya sang in London in the February Tchaikovsky Festival, reviewed on this page. Photo: M & M

LETTERS

Spike Milligan and Vivien Leigh

WAS Vivien Leigh right to protest in the Lords against the proposed demolition of the St. James's Theatre? Was Harry Fieldhouse wrong (this page, Saturday) when he counterblasted: "This Island is overrun with sentimentalists"? For reader reaction, read on . . .

TELEGRAM: YOUR CORRESPONDENT HARRY FIELDHOUSE IS RIGHT. ST. JAMES'S THEATRE IS JUST A MUSEUM PIECE. AWAY WITH IT AND UP WITH OFFICES. CARRYING HIS IDEA A STEP FURTHER AWAY WITH THE OLD CURIOSITY SHOP AND THE CENOTAPH (JUST SILLY SENTIMENT). BURN THE CUTTY SARK AND AS FOR NELSON'S OLD VICTORY, RIP IT OUT AND TURN IT INTO FLATS STONEHENGE SHOULD BE MODERNISED. ANN HATHAWAY'S COTTAGE AN ESPRESSO BAR. I ALSO SUGGEST PULLING DOWN MR. FIELDHOUSE.
SPIKE MILLIGAN, B.B.C., Portland-place, W.

Daily Express 1957

Meetings, Entertainments

GAUMONT
ON THE STAGE
To-day—2.30 6.15, 8.30
The Great American Recording Stars:
Buddy Holly and the Crickets
with All-Star Supporting Artistes.
Seats available: 7/6, 10/6, 12/6.
Sundays—4.30 to 9.30
Glenn Ford Julia Adams
"THE MAN FROM ALAMO" (U)
Colour by Technicolor
Next Week:
Bing Crosby, "MAN ON FIRE" (A)
Ava Gardner, Stewart Granger
"BHOWANI JUNCTION" (A)
CinemaScope and Colour.

LYRIC, HAMMERSMITH

"The Birthday Party"

COMING away from the Lyric Theatre one wondered what it was that had induced Michael Codron, this time in association with David Hall, to include *The Birthday Party* by Harold Pinter in his current season of plays. Was it the success of Beckett, Ionesco, Simpson and Mortimer? This type of play is very much in fashion just at present and one can only suppose that Mr. Codron, after the success of the Mortimer Double Bill, thought he would get away with it again. Unfortunately Mr. Pinter as a writer is not in the same category. Simpson and Mortimer are not obscure; even Ionesco and Beckett for that matter leave scope for argument, but each plays with words and ideas with stimulating effectiveness.

Harold Pinter, a twenty-eight-year-old actor, will not say what his play is about. The dialogue is often amusing, but most of the characters appear to be mentally deficient and what it all means is anyone's guess. That is if you still care by the end of the evening!

Theatre World 1958

Enlightenment

THE DECISION of the Lord Chamberlain to lift the ban on plays concerning the subject of homosexuality is the most welcome pronouncement to be made from St. James's Palace for many a decade. It means that the Lord Chamberlain has adopted a common-sense attitude and is making an honest effort to recognise the enlightened opinions expressed in the Wolfenden Report.

* * *

"THIS SUBJECT is now so widely debated," writes the Earl of Scarbrough, in a letter to Charles Killick, chairman of the Theatres' National Committee, "written about and talked of that its complete exclusion from the stage can no longer be regarded as justifiable. In future, therefore, plays on this subject which are sincere and serious will be admitted, as well as references to the subject which are necessary to the plot and dialogue and which are not salacious or offensive."

* * *

THIS STEP in the right direction will terminate the previous ludicrous situation, whereby a play banned from stage presentation by the Censor could still be heard on the radio, seen on both cinema and television screens and read in book form. This led to a series of bitter and justifiable attacks on the question of censorship, which may have caused this welcome change of front at St. James's Palace.

* * *

The Stage 1958

BRENDAN IS BARRED AT THEATRE

By DEREK LAMBERT

RUMBUSTIOUS Brendan Behan, Irish playwright and professional "broth of a boy," was barred last night from the West End theatre where his play, "The Hostage," is running.

This move followed Brendan's startling appearance at the theatre—Wyndham's—on Wednesday night, when he made a hilarious entry into the stalls and barracked his own play.

"The Quare Fellow"—he has been called that ever since the first night of his play of that name—is in London after a spell in a Dublin hospital for treatment for the effects of excessive drinking.

He turned up at Wyndham's again last night after a convivial day out.... But the theatre's public relations officer, Mr. Duncan Melvin, guided Brendan gently away to the nearest pub.

The beefy Irishman had a drink. Then he again demanded entry to see his play.

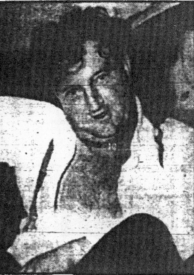

Playwright BRENDAN BEHAN *pictured last night.*

Daily Mirror 1959

Television Weekly 1958

6.0 OH BOY!

An explosion of beat music

TONY HALL
introduces
NEVILLE TAYLOR
CHERRY WAINER
THE DALLAS BOYS
THE VERNONS GIRLS
MARTY WILDE
RONNIE CARROLL
JACKIE DENNIS
The John Barry Seven
Cliff Richard and the Drifters
The Cutters
Lord Rockingham's XI
Red Price
Music direction by
Harry Robinson
Dance direction by
Leslie Cooper
Script by Trevor Peacock
Directed by Rita Gillespie
Produced by Jack Good
An ABC Network Production

6.30 MARY BRITTEN,

Radio Times 195

Calling Morecambe and Wise
★
Jimmy Clitheroe introduces the stars of your radio music-hall
at 9.0

TWO BRITISH DRIVERS WHO SCORED SUCCESSES IN THE MOROCCO GRAND PRIX AT CASABLANCA :
J. M. HAWTHORN (LEFT) AND STIRLING MOSS.
J. M. Hawthorn, in a Ferrari, won the 1958 World Motor Racing Drivers' Championship when he came second in the Morocco Grand Prix at Casablanca on October 19. His score for his best six races of the season was 42 points. He is the first British driver to win the honour. In the same race, Stirling Moss, in a Vanwall, came first, setting up the fastest lap time, and finishing one point behind Hawthorn in the Championship.

Illustrated London News 1958

1960 ★ 1970

PRAISE FOR NORMA PROCTER'S FINE SINGING IN DEBUT

EXCITING £2000 COUNTY SOUP CONTEST

How much do you know about **The Archers?**

B *Walter Gabriel* **D** *Philip Archer*

A *Doris Archer*

E *Tom Forrest*

C *Carol Grey*

F *Dan Archer*

IT'S SO EASY

and such fun to do! See how much you know about that famous country family, "The Archers", and your favourite soup – COUNTY, the soups with real country character!

1ST PRIZE £1,500 CASH

2ND PRIZE £500 CASH

One hundred third prizes of luxury silk squares

CUT OUT AND COMPLETE THIS ENTRY FORM

What you have to do. Here are some of the well-known Archer characters. Below are 8 phrases about County Soups. Simply pick out the phrase you think each character is most likely to have said, and enter its number below the appropriate letter in the panel opposite. For example: If you think Doris Archer is most likely to have said phrase 1 – enter number 1 below letter A on panel.

Now – there is no phrase for Dan Archer (letter F). In not more than 12 words write, in the space provided opposite, what you think he might say about delicious County Soup.

Closing date of this competition is March 31st, 1960. Full competition rules are printed on entry forms obtainable from your grocer. But you can enter now, using the entry form printed here, and enclosing an empty packet of County Soup. You can send as many entries as you like, but each one must be accompanied by an empty packet of County Soup. Plain paper entries will also be accepted.

1. Try County Soups, me old pals – they're just like grannie used to make.
2. In my game, keeping well fed is essential. That's why I say you can't beat County Soups.
3. I like my soups to taste of freshly picked country vegetables – that's why I always choose County.
4. Fresh air makes you peckish – and County Soup is a meal in itself.
5. Nourishing, delicious and so easy to prepare – that's why Ambridge folk choose County.
6. County – the soups with real country character – for me.

7. Plenty of variety – and all of 'em so tasty – that's County.
8. I don't make my own soups now – with County nobody can tell the difference.

A	B	C	D	E
Doris Archer	Walter Gabriel	Carol Grey	Philip Archer	Tom Forrest

F Here is my suggested phrase for Dan Archer ....

....

....

Write your name and address in BLOCK LETTERS in ink, and post this entry form, together with an empty packet of County Soup to:
W. Symington & Co. Ltd. (Comp. A14) Market Harborough, Leicestershire.

NAME ....

ADDRESS ....

....

....

NORMA PROCTER

Ernest Bradbury, Yorkshire Post, wrote: "She made the most telling effects by the simple, unassuming sincerity of her playing, by splendid articulation and by her pure tonal feeling for Gluck's lines . . . the audience threw restraint to the winds at the end, giving Miss Procter the ovation she had undoubtedly earned."

*   *   *

"A really memorable night. I just can't describe how wonderful it was." That was today's comment from Norma Procter herself.

Telegrams and letters of congratulation poured in before the performance, many from her musical friends in Grimsby and Cleethorpes, she told the Evening Telegraph today.

"People have been so wonderful. And the reception from the audience . . . I just can't describe how I felt. Such a mixture and confusion of feeling."

Grimsby Evening Telegraph **1961**

The Pytchley

We were able to hunt three days last week for the first time this season. The fixture from Norton on December 12 produced a busy but uneventful day.

From the meet at Braunston on the Wednesday, a fox found in Ashby St. Ledger's park was hunted slowly up to Braunston Cleves, but leaving it on the right, hounds settled down to run well leaving Braunston on the right, past Middlemore, across the main and by Braunston Covert to run out of scent near Elder Stubbs. A good hunt with a four-mile point.

A misty morning – later to develop into a thick fog – greeted the biggest field of the season at Yelvertoft on December 17. After a fox from Mr. Miller's good covert at Winwick Warren had got to ground, another was found in Colonel Lowther's kale and provided an enjoyable, if somewhat circuitous, hunt before hounds ran out of scent the far side of Cold Ashby. By this time it was three o'clock and the fog was so dense that the Master decided to call it a day.

TACITUS

The Field **1960**

GEORGE FORMBY—the lad from Lancashire who endeared himself to the whole country, the slick-haired George with the water-melon grin, the cracked voice as flat as a cap, the jaunty ukulele and the innocent naughtiness of a cheeky schoolboy—is dead. He was 56.

His heart gave out on the verge of happiness, after covering up 15 years of unhappy marriage to Beryl, the woman who taught him to read and write and helped to build him into one of Britain's biggest and best-loved stars.

For it was the great irony of Formby's life that had it not been for Beryl and the myth of the perfect marriage which he was reluctant to destroy, he might have lived a far happier personal life.

He announced his engagement to 36-year-old Lancashire school-teacher Pat Howson only six weeks after Beryl's death.

SHOCKED

And a few days later shocked the public who had swallowed the stories of a 36-year-old perfect marriage by saying: "For the last 15 years we did not live as man and wife. We tried to keep drink away from her but the damage was done.

Daily Herald 1961

Late star spot poses a package show problem

Colston Hall, Bristol: Everly Brothers, Cherry Wainer, Five Dallas Boys, and others.

"What are we going to tell your ma, what are we going to tell your pa, what are you going to tell your friends . . . ?"

So run the lyrics of one of the Everly Brothers' biggest hits—the one that recalls the plight of the two young conspirators who have stayed out late and realise that explanations will be required.

And many teenage Bristolians, I suspect, found themselves in a similar dilemma last night.

For this was a long show. Despite a fairly prompt start and an admirably brief interval, the star spot in the second performance was not reached until after 10.30 p.m.

TOO LARGE?

Some patrons with buses to catch had to leave without even seeing the Everlys. Many others left after only two or three of their seven songs.

To have paid 15s. and then not to be able to get even a glimpse of your favourites, is "a bit much," and raises again the question of whether some of these package shows are too large.

The bill included no fewer than three small bands, each using a permutation of electric guitars and basses—and all sounding, perhaps not surprisingly in view of their similar instrumentation, pretty much alike.

There were two longish drum solo spots—again, rather too much of a good thing, even allowing for the fact that one of them was a feature of the Dallas Boys' quite outstanding act.

These boys are one of the few vocal groups who take some trouble over their presentation, and it reaped dividends last night.

INDIFFERENT

Miss Wainer entered into the holiday spirit by appearing in a gay red, white and blue striped dress which reminded one of a stick of Weston rock or a rather charming barber's pole.

The lateness of the hour inevitably tempered our appreciation of her work at the Hammond organ—and the indifferent amplification of the instrument did not help. Even from the front row of the balcony, it sounded like a band of bagpipes passing the top of Colston Street.

Two of the newer recording discoveries, Messrs. Danny Hunter and Lance Fortune, had a warm reception, but still have something to learn about correct pitch and intonation.

Miss Wainer, and the American musicians who accompanied the Everlys, apart, the instrumental spots were entrusted to the up-and-coming groups, the Freddy Lloyd Five and the Fabulous Flee-Rakkers.—A. H. R. T.

Bristol Observer 1960

CASH BETTING SHOPS ARE HARD TO FIND

·

CURB ON ADVERTISING

DAILY TELEGRAPH REPORTER

THE Betting and Gaming Act came into force yesterday, but for the punter who wants the novelty of placing a ready-money bet off the course betting shops are not easy to find.

Two aching feet bear painful witness to the fact. The shops are there, of course. Finding them is the trouble.

After a tour of Soho I had acquired considerable knowledge of establishments devoted to "strip" shows, including one that boasts intriguingly that the cast is all female. But I failed to find the betting shop that I am assured is there.

The reason is that bookmakers are legally restricted in the manner in which they may advertise their premises. Their name and "Licensed Betting Office" in 3in high letters is all that is permitted.

Altogether, it was an enforcedly furtive entrance that the cash transaction bookmaker made upon the public scene. If you succeed in finding one you may think the whole business rather impersonal and antiseptic.

You will find lists of runners displayed and will write out your bet and hand your money over the counter in return for a receipt. After the race you will have to go inside again to discover if you have won as the bookmaker cannot put the results in his window.

Loitering is going to be the greatest problem. The Racecourse Betting Control Board is guarding against it at its two London offices by imposing a one-hour interval between the result and the "pay-out."

These two shops work entirely on the Tote system with stakes in units of 4s, 10s and £1. The office at Euston has seven grilles behind a wooden counter something like a modern railway booking office.

Daily Telegraph 1961

WHAT A LIFE!...*by Gilbert Wilkinson*

"Let him stay up for the Army Game—then if they do revive the Call-up, he'll think it's no end of a giggle."

Daily Herald 1961

The worst predator of them all?

WHEN one considers the vast number of predators which live at the expense of the trout, it seems strange that the trout itself should not only be a predator, but probably the worst predator of the lot.

Every trout is a cannibal which regards its own young as an attractive item of diet. When I have watched alevins and fry being swallowed by the hundred I have wondered whether spawning could be dual purpose with a secondary object of providing a rich food item to compensate for the loss of condition which spawning entails. Nature has some strange ways of relating numbers to food supply.

That is, however, only part of Nature's problem, for in addition to numbers, there is the important factor of quality. We are apt to think that every trout is much the same as every other trout. But there surely must be the good, the average, and the below average as in other forms of life. Nature's usual way of eliminating the poor specimens is by predators, and the best eliminator of a poor trout is another trout.

Trout and Salmon 1962

WORLD CHAMPION

This year's Drivers' World Championship, for what it is worth, goes to Jim Clark, *deservedly*. Clark is a polished and very fast G.P. driver; he has proved himself also to be a fearless and versatile racing motorist. His splendid second place at Indianapolis in the Lotus-Ford and subsequent victory at an American banked track endorse his all-round virtuosity. Here is a British World Champion of whom even Floyd Clymer should approve. Congratulations, too, to Lotus, winners of the 1963 Manufacturers' Championship, and Coventry-Climax for aiding Clark to clinch the Championship.

Daily Mirror 1965

A DRAMATIC fall by Christine Truman in the eighth game of the second set helped Torquay's Angela Mortimer to triumphantly lift the women's singles title by 4—6, 6—4, 7—5 on the Centre Court at Wimbledon this afternoon.

Miss Truman, one set up and well placed to break Miss Mortimer's service for a 5—3 lead, fell heavily in reaching for a high ball. When she resumed she obviously had difficulty in turning and Miss Mortimer, amid mounting drama, went on to take the second set and win a desperate battle in the third.

Sports Argus 1961

TOUGH, all-action Terry Downes stormed his way to become world middleweight champion at Wembley last night when he forced Paul Pender, of Boston, Mass., to quit at the end of the ninth round of a savage, ruthless bout.

I have never seen an American of Pender's class quit before, but last night he did QUIT!

Daily Herald 1961

Crusader for music

—THAT WAS 'TOMMY' BEECHAM

By Andrew Smith

S IR THOMAS BEECH-AM, the wit and wag of British music, the idol of concert-goers and opera-lovers in two continents, was a born crusader.

. He spent most of his life trying to awaken British taste for the best in music, yet he could have lived idly on inherited wealth.

Those who dismissed him as "Old Pepperpot" did not understand the purpose behind his many vitriolic outbursts. They were carefully calculated to draw attention to music.

Beecham himself let the cat out of the bag in his autobiography, "A Mingled Chime." A provincial operatic tour was going badly. So he adopted "a method of propaganda which I have since found invaluable."

SPLENDOUR

Before visiting a city he would attack its inhabitants as barbarians. First reaction was a flood of warnings "not to show my face anywhere near the place. The next was a rush to the box office."

Another trick was to attack an institution before exploiting it. Soon after denouncing the Royal Festival Hall exterior as "monstrous," he was conducting a series of concerts in it.

All his apparently irresponsible words were spoken in the cause of good music.

Don't forget, this was the man who gave London operatic seasons of unprecedented splendour when Government help was still a dream. He brought great singers like Melba and Chaliapin to Covent Garden and the Diaghilev Ballet to Drury-lane.

In those days he would spend whole days in the theatre, conducting in the evening, staying till the small hours sorting out production problems.

It has been estimated that this son of a pill millionaire spent nearly £250,000 on such enterprises. He was conductor, producer, impresario, publicity chief, financial backer. His tasks would have killed a man of ordinary constitution.

His phenomenal gifts were discovered as long ago as 1899, when he deputised at the last moment for Hans Richter as conductor of the Hallé in Manchester.

Young people may remember him only as conductor of the Royal Philharmonic Orchestra, which he adopted in 1946 and built up into one of the finest in the world. At home, on the Continent, in America, it drew crowded audiences, who marvelled at the richness of its tones.

Sir Thomas' greatness as a conductor is unchallenged. He was the finest interpreter of Mozart and Delius (for whose recognition he worked tirelessly). And over a wide range of composers, old and new, he had few equals.

Daily Herald 1961

A talk to revue fans at the Festival Fringe Club had to be cancelled to-day when the star speaker, Peter Cook, failed to appear. He is one of the four young men who scored such a hit last night in the late-night revue at the Lyceum.

The lounge of the Club's headquarters in South St Andrew Street was packed to "standing room only" to hear Peter speak on the hit revue, "Beyond The Fringe."

Club secretary and organiser Michael Imison, made an apology to the audience and asked them to be patient as every effort was being made to get in touch with Peter. Half an hour later, with still no sign of Mr Cook, the secretary apologised again — and cancelled the talk.

He said: "We have failed to get in touch with Peter, and I am deeply sorry that his talk will have to be cancelled."

About an hour later Peter arrived at the Club and blamed reporters for his non-appearance. He was accompanied by Jonathan Miller, another star of the show.

Peter said that journalists had invaded his flat seeking interviews after his successful opening night.

Peter Cooke

Edinburgh Evening Dispatch 196(

LATE SPEECH

Peter and Jonathan then spoke to members of the club who were sipping refreshments in the lounge and talked of the new type of revue which "accentuated the off-beat side of life."

Both left about 10 minutes later.

Peter Cook is 22 and has just graduated from Cambridge University. He wrote the London revue "Pieces of Eight."

With him in the Edinburgh show are Jonathan Miller, a 26-year-old doctor; Dudley Moore, Oxford graduate, and former pianist with Johnny Dankworth's band; and Alan Bennett, a 25-year-old junior lecturer in history at Oxford.

These were the goals which sealed the Soccer Double. Top: Smith falls as he shoots into the Leicester goal. Below: the ball flashing past Banks to give Tottenham their second goal.

Yorkshire Post
1961

A SPECIAL MEDAL FOR TOTTENHAM?

By Richard Ulyatt. TOTTENHAM HOTSPUR 2, LEICESTER CITY 0

Within the next day or two there is likely to be pressure brought to bear on the Football Association or the Football League to have medals struck and presented to the Tottenham Hotspur players to commemorate their achievement on Saturday of completing the great Soccer double—the FA Cup and the Football League championship: the first club to do so since Aston Villa in 1897.

Tottenham's manager, Mr. Billy Nicholson, was full of the idea at the club's official reception at Edmonton and Tottenham Town Hall yesterday, and he thought the FA might do something about it. Mr. Joe Richards, president of the Football League, thought there was much in favour: "No doubt if the Management Committee received such a request," he said, "it would be favourably considered because this is a very special occasion."

Don't think about shopping on stage

(says Maggie Smith)

Kensington Post
1961

Until the spell of Anouilh's play "The Rehearsal" had been broken by the plush tip-up seats snapping back Maggie Smith had been a shy, worried and ill-at-ease young woman.

After the show, treading the thick pile carpets to the bare corridors back stage. I half expected to find Maggie Smith speaking haltingly in her struggle to find the right words to express herself.

Instead, I found her relaxed and perfectly at ease. Drawing gratefully on her first cigarette after the three-hour performance she confided: "In summer I usually go out for a walk between the shows."

"But in this weather," she said, shuddering slightly, "I just rest or go to sleep. I usually feel exhausted after a performance."

I sympathised. It was not difficult to imagine the strain involved acting in this highly emotional play which builds up into a crescendo of violence and death.

"Oh, no," said Maggie quickly. "It's not the actual play. It's being on stage all that time saying and doing nothing that's tiring. You must concentrate on your role all the time. Once you start letting your mind wander you find yourself thinking about shopping lists and things like that—and that's fatal," she explained.

Q. Johnny (Brighton). *I've been playing with a Pop Group and have let my hair grow almost to my shoulders like the others. My girl-friend likes it, but my parents say they won't have me in the house if I don't get a hair-cut. I'm more than a bit worried.*

A. What matters most to you, Johnny, the goodwill of parents or girl-friend? A hard choice, but although I, personally, dislike long hair on a man, I realize that if you're still with the Group you'll have to do as they do. You could point out to your parents that it's just a theatrical make-up, like any other, and not permanent, and that if and when you leave the job you will cut your hair short. And, of course, a lot depends on how serious you are about your girl-friend—if her opinion is all that is important to you.

She 1966

● RECORD CLUB
Everybody's twisting

PRESLEY INCLUDED

THE greatest revolution in the pop music world since rock is now upon us —the Twist. And it is sweeping Northamptonshire in the same way that it is catching on everywhere else.

Local bandleaders tell me that they are inundated with requests to play the Twist, and it is the one dance which is certain to get all the dancers on the floor.

We can expect many artistes to be releasing records with a twisting beat, and one of the first is Elvis Presley.

The number, marked "Twist Special" on the label, is "Rock-a-hula, Baby," (RCA), a tremendous swinging side taken from his "Blue Hawaii" film album.

Elvis is backed by the Jordanaires, and belts out a great rock vocal which leads to an exciting finish. It is backed by Elvis singing "Can't Help Falling in Love," an outstanding ballad which is another track from the "Blue Hawaii" album.

Kettering Leader **1962**

☆ ☆

Thinking of Stereo?

For those who are contemplating the additional enjoyment which stereophonic equipment gives to record-listening—and for those who already have that pleasure—I commend "The Stereo Disc."

I recall the effect upon me of the E.M.I. stereophonic demonstration test record, with its amazing sounds—express and goods trains, table tennis, fire engine turn-out, and so on. Now, from Capitol, comes this new revelation of the wonders of stereo, this time with sounds from America — a bowling alley, New Year's Eve in Times-square, a ferry boat and a subway train, to mention a few—and some impressive music, orchestral and vocal.

Very effective and convincing, but we must not forget that the monaural record still has its delights!

THE STEREO DISC
Capitol: SW9032

Dartford, Crayford, Swanley Chronicle and Kentish Times **1963**

THERE may soon be two commercial radio ships broadcasting from just outside Harwich, and if the second vessel takes up its expected position, in the sea area known as the Cork Hole, it will be floating above 500 tons of still active nitro-glycerine.

The explosive was sunk in this deep-water spot after it had been damaged in the floods of 1953 at the Great Oakley explosives works.

Story which has made national news this week was how the pirate radio ship Atlanta was beaten to a pitch on Harwich's doorstep by the pirate radio ship Caroline.

Transistors have been booming out pop music put out from the Caroline nine miles off Harwich, and a "scare" on Tuesday that the ship had been "bumped" by another vessel fizzled out to be just a matter of rock and roll.

For some time, Radio Atlanta had been expected off the coast, to broadcast commercials, but it was the Caroline which burst upon the listening world from the grey North Sea just off Harwich at the weekend.

Latest news is that Atlanta will be taking up a position within a few miles of Caroline!

Harwich, Dovercourt, Manningtree and Mistley Standard **1964**

TV JANICE GIVES THE BIG CITY A 'FOIVE'

By PATRICK DONCASTER

SNUB - NOSED Janice Nichols, I T V's "Oi'll Give it Foive" girl, took her first look at the "flip side" of England at the week-end.

And her verdict, after a dreamy, whirlwind visit to London? She gave it top marks—"Foive."

Sixteen-year-old Janice, a resident panellist on the "Thank Your Lucky Stars" pop disc show, came to London to cut a disc of her own

As a member of the panel she can give five marks to a disc she thinks will be a hit. Hence her phrase: "Oi'll give it foive."

Lights

The record company which signed her put her up at the plush Ritz Hotel. When she saw her room, with hallway and bath, she said: "Coo! It's bigger'n home."

Home is a modest house at Wednesbury, Staffs—and it is Janice's rich Black Country accent that has brought her fame.

After the recording session Janice was shown the town, and the bright lights. Later she went to the chandeliered nightspot, Talk of the Town, where she Twisted with pop singer Craig Douglas.

That record she made? It's called "I'll Give It Five."

Daily Mirror **1962**

SCREAM-AGERS

IT was a night of pop-pandemonium when the tide of Beatlemania surged through East Ham on Saturday. Screaming, hysterical fans—5,000 of them—surrounded the Granada theatre chanting " We want the Beatles," and brought out reinforcements of police, ambulancemen and bouncers.

There were fantastic scenes—inside and outside the theatre, as police fought to control weeping, fainting and shouting girl fans.

There were tears—from teenagers who had waited since early morning to see their pop-idols arrive. They slipped in under police cover at 3.51 p.m.—by a back entrance. Minutes later, fans raced round the back, to find they were too late.

There were fainting cases inside the Granada.

Barking, East Ham and Ilford Advertiser **1963**

Daily Mail 1963

Stop the fight

CASSIUS CLAY
BEFORE THE FIGHT

says Liz

By VINCENT MULCHRONE

IN a sickening welter of blood, the big fight at Wembley last night ended in the fifth round—just as Cassius Clay had said it would.

It was ended, not by the Louisville Lip, but by a screaming Elizabeth Taylor, a horrified crowd and the referee in that order.

Blood covered British heavyweight champion Henry Cooper's face with a grisly, dripping mask. Rhythmically, a cut above his left eye pumped spurts of blood clear of his face.

He looked like the victim of a terrible road accident—a creature from a horror film.

Blood covered his chest, arms and gloves. He was printing bloody glove marks on Clay's body, and with each blow a fine rain of blood splashed on to the white canvas.

The baying crowd, which minutes before had been screaming for Clay's blood and getting it—were almost silenced by the sight.

'No, no, no'

Then they bayed again—but now in protest. The beautiful Elizabeth Taylor, anguished and holding fiercely on to Richard Burton's shoulder, stood in her six-guinea ringside seat and shouted: "No, no, no."

The crowd around her took up the cry. "Stop the fight," they yelled. The blood pumped on.

Men left their seats and crowded towards the ring. A programme sailed out of the darkness and hit a corner post.

Elizabeth Taylor kept on screaming "No, no." Referee Tommy Little looked closely at the blood pump above Cooper's left eye and stopped the contest.

When they cleaned the gore away they found a 2in cut above that eye. Burton escorted a distressed Miss Taylor from the stadium.

The ballyhoo fight ended on a sour note. One of Clay's seconds sprang into the ring with his latest publicity gimmick—the pantomime crown which he had worn on his way to the ring—to place it on his head. But Cassius, sensitive to the mood of the moment, waved him away.

Said Clay afterwards: "It's the hardest I've ever been hit in my life."

Cooper had him down for a count of four before the bell at the end of the fourth round saved a slightly stunned Clay.

Daily Herald 1964

SO SORRY —THE END OF BOND'S STORY

HERALD REPORTER

AUTHOR Ian Fleming died yesterday — a millionaire whose fortune was made by secret agent James Bond, the man he created.

Fleming collapsed at his holiday hotel in Sandwich, Kent. An ambulance took him to hospital in Canterbury—sometimes touching speeds above 70 m.p.h.

But 56-year-old Fleming was never really James Bond, the trained killer, expert womaniser and lover of good living.

The man who was once called "the gentlemanly chronicler of James Bond's ungentlemanly adventures," said to ambulance men: "I am very sorry to trouble you chaps. Anyway, thanks for all your help."

BOOK TRADE DISTURBED BY "FANNY HILL" CASE, SAYS DERBY M.P.

Mr. Niall MacDermot, M.P. for Derby North said in the House of Commons on Wednesday that "the responsible book trade had been disturbed recently by the nature of the proceedings taken about "Fanny Hill."

No one contemplated at the time of the 1959 Bill that a test case for a work with serious literary claims would arise by way of forfeiture proceedings said Mr. MacDermot, who was speaking on the second reading of the Government's Obscene Publications Bill.

It had been assumed, he said, that forfeiture proceedings would be restricted to more obvious pornography, and any serious issue as to obscenity would be decided by jury. Mr. MacDermot said that for the first time for over 100 years a Government was taking the initiative in presenting the obscene publications Bill to Parliament. Clause 1 of the Bill suggested a major change in the Law.

Derbyshire Advertiser 1964

CASINO BLACKLISTS 7,000 CHEATS

MORE than 7,000 gamblers have already been banned from Britain's first casino, which opened at the week-end. They have been blacklisted as "crooked."

The names of 7,000 cheats have been handed to the casino by the French police, who know them from their activities on the Riviera.

And the casino owners also know the identity of 300 English gamblers who have "records" of cheating or who are known to have given cheques that "bounced."

MEMORY MEN

The blacklist is part of elaborate security measures taken by the casino, opened at Brighton by a group of British businessmen.

Said M. Jean Marie Cruciani, the French director general of the casino: "We have two men at the door whose job is to remember faces to make sure that no undesirables get in."

Daily Herald 1962

Ban on play by Osborne

THE Lord Chamberlain has banned two complete scenes in John Osborne's latest play, "A Patriot For Me."

But Osborne said in New York yesterday that he will not re-write the scenes. So the play cannot be performed before the general public.

Daily Mirror 1964

Nancy Spain

Lunch with the last Goon

LUNCHED at the BBC Canteen with the last of the Goons, the one and only (now that Sellers has gone respectable, and Harry Secombe settled down, and Milligan's in programmes like Juke Box Jury) Mike Bentine, who wears an Old Etonian tie and (unlike pretty well all the other comedians) is as funny *off* as he is *on*. The lunch was really a script conference and the laughter among the canteen staff was immoderate.

Fantasies over the boiled beef and dumplings and a touch of the old St. Emilion included a highly remarkable description of Doctor Fu Manchu, living out on the Essex Marsh, sending his totally naked manservant to perform a murder in Wimbledon. "How d'you suppose he'd get there?" mused Bentine. "On a bus? Take a 715 to the corner and then change to a 30? Splendid he'd look in all his war paint."

Then there was the future. 1969? "A great vintage year," said Bentine. "Colour — blue. Precious stone — Gall."

The sinking of the Titanic? "It was impossible for the band to have played *Nearer my God to Thee* with the ship canted over at 50 degrees like that after hitting the iceberg," said Bentine. "Do you know that there is a bronze mantelpiece in the Musicians or Orchestral Union Headquarters, opposite the stage door of the Windmill, that commemorates the members of the band, portraits they are, in bronze?" I murmured I would look at it. "It's a lovely, lovely thing," said Bentine.

He was at Eton with Humphrey Lyttelton and Lord Inchcape, he knows everything there is to know about guns, whaling and, of course, goonery. "The Goon Mind is the simple, child mind," explained Bentine "developed to its logical conclusion. For example, d'you remember a skit we did on Dracula, when someone cried 'He's changed into a bat' and we held up a little tiny cricket bat? That's typical.

That's the sort of thing I mean." Bentine pushed his plate around a bit. "I won't admit we do satire, if satire is what they do on *That Was the Week That Was*. To be funny, to send something up, you've got to love it. I love Fu Manchu, and werewolves and Dracula. D'you realize that Doctor Fu Manchu is nearly 100 and The Saint is 60 something and Tarzan is over 80? It's a sobering thought . . . "

It's GOLDstein

Bob Goldstein, one time president of 20th Century Fox, has a gold umbrella from Cartier, gold handle, gold tips to the ribs, gold ferrule. He takes it everywhere with him, checks it into cloak rooms, where people reel back in joy. On his pyjamas he has his own insignia (crossed Bagels) and when he climbs into his Rolls-Royce he wears special overshoes to tip-toe across the pavement. I find these are sobering thoughts, too . . .

The Difference

● The Queen Mother plays croquet, even when the weather is bad. When the weather is bad she wears a hat, and then another hat and then a veil to lash the whole thing down. Binkie Beaumont of H. M. Tennent plays croquet, too, but only when the weather is fine. *That's* the difference between our Royal family and other people.

Night out with Noël

● I've been with the Nouvelle Vague in the Theatre a lot lately . . . you know, beards, the kitchen sink, sweaters instead of dinner jackets, social consciousness and all. So an evening with Noël Coward came to me lately like a deep, warm, gloriously scented bath. There's a lot to be said for the Vieille Vague, dinner jackets and all. We dined in the Savoy Grill, we ate Haddock à la Arnold Bennett (which is poached haddock surrounded by omelette) and Noël whizzed amongst the tables visiting The Charlie Chaplins and The John Mills—two great theatrical families which seemed to be there in their entirety. Hayley Mills, with her long golden hair, black stockings, red dress, and fresh from filming with Burl Ives in *Summer Magic*, looked as though she *might* conceivably be the new wave . . . but how can one spring from a long line of pros like that and *not* be anything but a blissfully competent old wave, exactly like Charlie Chaplin and her dad? For all her youth, Hayley is the pro of pros . . .

In *our* party was the new, news-making heart throb, James Bond himself, Mr. Sean Connery, still enjoying the success of *Doctor No* which has now topped the box office record of *Ben Hur*. He is about to make *From Russia With Love*, but (when we met) was debating should he go with the movie to make personal appearances in Paris, France. Master Coward shook with silent glee. "If you do that, my dear boy," he said, "you'll have to change your name." (No, I certainly won't explain that one.)

After dinner Master took us up to his gracious and lovely suite and there played us the new tunes and lyrics written for the Harry Koenitz version of the Terry Rattigan play *The Sleeping Prince*, now to emerge as a musical, and the best of British luck. I have to report that anyway one of these numbers—the waltz—will be as big a hit as that old waltz from *Bitter Sweet*. It's the kind of deceptively simple tune that you never can *quite* learn, and is going to be heard for ever more like *Never On a Sunday* and the *Harry Lime Theme*. There's a very witty one called *Long Live the King if he Can*, but my favourite concerns some minor Royalties fidgeting and rumble-tummying in the Abbey at a Coronation while the heroine sings that she is having the time of her life.

Top my Spuggy?

I am collecting remarkable dialect words. Still in use in Essex are "Broomdasher," meaning a poor shabby type, "Nipcheese" for mean, "Pill Garlic," meaning another poor specimen; while if you cry "Clutter Bucket!" at someone you mean "Hop it!" In Northumberland an "Apple Sheeley" is a chaffinch and a "Spuggy" is a sparrow. Anybody else top that?

Fun for Freeman

● My favourite disc jockey, Alan Freeman, otherwise known as the Monster of Wellesley Court, bursts forth in another film this month, a sequel to *Trad, Dad* called *Just for Fun*. In it a new political party is formed, the Teenagers of a mythical Britain, who actually take over the Government. Whereupon the country starts to sink under the strain and has to be towed to the Bahamas.

No doubt with Cliff Richard as Foreign Secretary? That dear boy (whom I last saw whooping it up on Coca-Cola in the Sheraton-Cadillac, Detroit, with The Shads) has still not learned another oath besides "Holy Mackerel!"

Marlene's missing teeth

You never know who's going to be on the other end of my telephone when it rings. This time it was Marlene Dietrich (guess that possibility is why I always answer it) telling me she had been offered the Dame Edith Evans/ Gladys Cooper role in the film of *The Chalk Garden*—Rehearsing starts in March. Her first line (if she accepts) would be, "Maitland, will you bring me my teeth, the lower set, I mean? I left them on the drawing-room table."

Alma in any language

● You know Alma Cogan, the singer in *the* frocks, whose act might best be described as "For my Next Dress I . . ."? Well, she can sing and do her act in French, Italian, German, Spanish, Dutch, Icelandic, Swahili, Africaans and Japanese! How does she attain this linguistic competence? (Get *me* . . .) Well, she studies all the while, in aeroplanes and out, the little coloured books of Mister Hugo. "My latest," she said, "is to translate *Never Do A Tango with an Eskimo* into Japanese. It sounds marvellous."

No doubt it's been said before, but Alma spends so much of the year in Tokyo now that she's beginning to admit that she has a yen for it.

She 1963

FORUM, 51 Chancery Lane WC2 HOL 1927	Lunch only. Italian cuisine with excellent fresh pasta. Try tongue in Madeira, *vitello tonnato* or sole *dugléré*. Good carafe wine and delicious things from the sweet trolley. Must book even in non-expense account days. £2 per head.	A 6 W 8 V f M 5
HUNGRY HORSE, 196 Fulham Rd, SW10 FLA 7757	Lovable restaurateur Bill Staughton - ex-Watergate, ex-Popote, ex-Mrs Beaton's Tent- has quickly assembled his with-it clientele in generous basement and offers his version - a good one - of traditional English food served at cramped chatty tables. Essential to book. Very fashionable. £2 10s per head.	A 8 W 6 V f M 7
THE IVY, 1 West St, WC2 TEM 4751	Still OK for lunch. Sad at night. Fine wines. Try duck pâté and *quenelle de sole mantua*. You can be exacting at The Ivy. £2+ per head.	A 4 W 6 V f M 8
LEONI'S QUO VADIS, 26/29 Dean St, W1 GER 9585/4809	Excellent Italian Soho restaurant on two floors. Plenty of attentive waiters and Leoni himself is always there. Good white carafe wine. Try the tournedos Rossini and fillets of sole with hollandaise sauce. £2 per head.	A 5 W 7 V f M 8
MIRABELLE, 56 Curzon St, W1 GRO 4636	Quite impressively more expensive than any other place. Strictly for Jackie Kennedy and show-biz in third year at Drury Lane. Food and wine can be magnificent but advice to ordinary folk is don't stray off the menu. £5+ per head.	A 8 W 8 V f M 4
PARKES' RESTAURANT, 4 Beauchamp Place, SW3 KEN 1390	Nudges the Mirabelle in expense but very exotic for Kensington basement. The food when you sort out the chrysanthemum leaves is generous, delicate and quite original. Must book. £4 per head.	A 8 W 4 V f M 3

Town 1965

MARY RAND THIRD IN SPORTS POLL

Henley's Mrs. Mary Rand, who last year was elected Sportsview Personality of the Year, was placed third in a national newspaper's search for the Sports Personality of the Year.

According to a Gallup Poll survey undertaken by the *Daily Telegraph*, Jim Clark, the racing driver, came top. Cassius Clay, the boxer, was second.

A representative cross-section of the British public were asked: "Whom do you think has been the outstanding sports personality of the year?" Mrs. Rand was the only woman amongst the top six personalities named.

Henley Standard 1965

Soccer bribes: today we accuse three famous players

DECEMBER 1, 1962. Soccer fans—and all who cherish the good name of British sport — should write that date in bold, black letters. It was The Day of Infamy for British football.

That was the day when the ugly cancer of corruption spread its evil growth right up to the highest strata of Soccer.

THAT WAS THE DAY WHEN TWO INTER-NATIONAL STARS TOOK BRIBES IN A FIRST DIVISION FOOTBALL LEAGUE MATCH.

Association football is Britain's national game—the game we invented and gave to the world. And now, it is our regrettable duty to report, it is the game whose fair name our own players beamirched.

It was almost a year ago that the British football public's confidence in the integrity of the game took its first big knock.

Disturbing facts which came to the notice of this newspaper had to be made public. A handful of players, we disclosed, had succumbed to the temptation of taking bribes to influence the results of matches, so that people in the know could make lucrative betting coups.

The revelations caused a scandal in Soccer circles. There was official action — prosecutions, Football Association inquiries, fines, life suspensions of the guilty players.

The corruption that had reared its ugly head in British Soccer was exposed and purged. At least that's what the Soccer public thankfully believed. Now they could go on watching the matches and filling in their pools coupons confident that the game was being played straight, clean and fair.

Unfortunately it was not. There were a number of disquieting aspects of last year's scandal that still needed looking into. "The People" felt that it was its duty to continue its investigation in the interests of Soccer fans, pools punters and the good name of British football in general.

£60-a-week

And, now, unfortunately, we have to report that the corruption was not confined merely to a handful of players in Third or Fourth Division clubs.

It has spread right up to the very top clubs, famous First Division clubs whose names are by-words in British football, and whose stars can earn £60 a week.

Nearly 30 players, our investigations have revealed, have risked their whole careers and sold their integrity for a handful of silver.

Among them are men who have proudly worn the white shirt of England in international matches.

Today, with the utmost regret, we have to name these three top-flight stars —two of them England "caps"—who are guilty of taking bribes:—

DAVID "BRONCO" LAYNE, Sheffield Wednesday's star centre-forward and leading goal scorer.

PETER SWAN, Sheffield Wednesday and England centre-half and idol of the Hillsborough fans.

TONY KAY, England wing-half, former Sheffield Wednesday star, transferred to Everton for a £55,000 fee last season, now the idol of the Goodison Park crowds.

These three players are together worth more than £150,000 in transfer fees.

Layne, Kay and Swan are guilty of backing Sheffield

By MICHAEL GABBERT
and a team of 'People' investigators

The People 1964

Wednesday to lose in their away match against Ipswich on December 1, 1962—Soccer's Day of Infamy. It was, in effect, a bribe, paid by a man who had arranged a betting coup. For the coup to "pay off" Sheffield had to lose. And all three players knew it.

Ipswich, who were second from bottom of the League before the match, won 2—0.

All the three players got out of "going bent" and risking their whole playing careers was £100 each.

2 Van Heusen 'Vantage'
Non-iron shirts

'Vantage' POPULAR Non-Iron

New model with 'ply-controlled' collar attached designed to meet the demand for a non-iron shirt with popular 'Vantage' qualities at only
39/6

'Vantage' PREMIER Non-Iron

The established favourite, hitherto known as the 'Vantage' now with a 'ply-controlled' collar attached that stays permanently wrinkle-free.
42/6

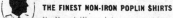

THE FINEST NON-IRON POPLIN SHIRTS

Van Heusen's 'Vantage', the most successful non-iron poplin shirt, is now available in two models— the 'Vantage' PREMIER (hitherto known simply as the 'Vantage') at 42/6, and the new 'Vantage' POPULAR at 39/6. Whichever model you prefer, it is the best non-iron poplin shirt you can buy for the money. Both are available in white, cream and pleasing patterns.

Van Heusen *of Savile Row*
make fine shirts and collars

FIRST MIDLANDS LITERARY LUNCH

A triple effort by Trentham Gardens, W. H. Smith and Sons, and the Martin Black Lecture Agency, to provide for the Midlands what Foyle's do for London and the "Yorkshire Post" for the north, got off to a good start at Trentham last Thursday when the first literary luncheon was held in the Highland suite of the gardens.

Stone Guardian and Eccleshall News 1965

A preponderance of splendidly plumed women made up the bulk of the literary enthusiasts present and while they seemed to respond slowly to the wit and wisdom cascading from the top table, one was assured afterwards that they were really a little self-conscious in the presence of a quartet of well-known names presided over in the most erudite manner by Mr. Lionel Hale.

Mr. Hale, a critic and broadcaster of many years, was full of appropriate quotations and he began, with the aid of Roget's "Thesaurus," by calling a literary luncheon a "bibliophilic regalement" and several other choice concoctions.

DESTRUCTIVE

The principal speaker was Mr. John Braine, the Yorkshire novelist, with an unashamedly Yorkshire accent, author of "Room at the Top," "The Vodi," "Life at the Top," and "The Jealous God."

With typical Yorkshire forthrightness he began: "The worst of being a novelist, you are not just a born liar, you are a professional liar. I have spent all my life not exactly murdering the truth but certainly decorating the truth."

And to make sure the clouds of romance were swept completely out of sight, he went on: "There is no occupation as destructive as that of the novelist."

Daily Mirror 1966

THE man who found the World Cup was wondering last night: "Am I going to get the £6,150 in rewards?"

Mr David Corbett discovered the missing solid gold trophy when his dog Pickles sniffed it out in the garden of a house in Norwood, South London on Sunday.

Last night 26-year-old Mr. Corbett said: "I haven't heard about the rewards officially yet.

"I would thought that the people offering the rewards would have got in touch with me by now.

Radio Times 196

A new comedy series by Johnny Speight

1

7.30

THE series beginning tonight is yet another 'spin-off' from BBC-1's highly successful *Comedy Playhouse*. The star of the series is the script, written by Johnny Speight, who is one of the country's top comedy writers. He wrote the first Eric Sykes-Hattie Jacques series, and has just completed his tenth year of writing for Arthur Haynes.

Till Death Us Do Part is set at the far eastern end of Wapping High Street in London's dockland.

The cast is headed by **Warren Mitchell** who plays the father—Alf Garnett. He is working class, skilled at his trade, three generations behind the times, and is well endowed with most natural human failings. He is narrow-minded, prejudiced, selfish, greedy, cowardly, and very, very proud of himself. He is a self-confessed expert on any subject. He is also a Tory and a Monarchist, but has never forgiven Edward Heath for trying to get us into the Common Market. It need hardly be said, therefore, that Harold Wilson and the Labour Party are utterly wrong as far as he is concerned. The same also goes for General de Gaulle, the Russians, the Chinese—all foreigners—and the gentleman who is in charge of Big Ben 'because the clock's always wrong . . .'

But what wounds Alf's permanently hurt pride most is his young son-in-law Mike (played by **Anthony Booth**). Young, good-looking, virile, strictly of this new generation which rejects all the lovely traditional shibboleths in which Britain has wallowed since Queen Victoria, he tears down every belief that the older man depends upon.

Dandy Nichols plays Else, Alf Garnett's wife, who is a pale echo of her old man, and is vaguely worried as well—by the price of eggs and the fact that the weather hasn't been so good since Labour got in.

There is but one beautiful flower growing in the middle of this compost heap—the Garnetts' daughter Rita (played by **Una Stubbs**). Pretty as a picture, she has no neuroses and is utterly happy as befits a bride of eight weeks. DENNIS MAIN WILSON

The Listener 1965

Sargent at Seventy (BBC-1): with Sir Malcolm are, left to right, Lord Boothby, Sir Alan Herbert, and Sir Thomas Armstrong

England captain
Bobby Moore,
Wembley, 1966.

ALAN BENNETT tells all—about his comedy series which begins tonight

Radio Times 1966

2 **8.5** 'THIS *On the Margin* of yours,' enquired the Head of Light Entertainment, 'is it very sophisticated?' I laughed lightly and tripped heavily over my cigarette-holder. 'By sophisticated we in Light Entertainment mean someone who knows that *vol au vent* doesn't always mean a robbery in a high wind. Because if it is sophisticated I feel that the best time for it would be Sunday at 9.30 a.m.

I flushed with pleasure. Then H.O.L.E. continued suavely: 'I still think it a pity you aren't using jugglers.' He thrust his nose deep into the Golden Rose of Montreux and sniffed appreciatively. 'There was this man I came across,' H.O.L.E. mused meaningfully, 'in an old casting directory. He does incredible things with flags and hamsters. And he's never been used. You want that sort of a lift. Yours is a very limited sort of talent. When I wanted to sign you for six programmes at thirty-year intervals I was doing you a favour. Over-exposure is death.' I half licked his suede boots.

'Anyway now we've made it weekly I think you perhaps ought to tone it down a bit. You know as well as I do that under the BBC Charter we have to be impartial. All these references to skirts will have to be balanced by an equivalent number of references to trousers. Otherwise we're going to be accused of unduly influencing the public in favour of the skirt. Before we know where we are we'll have a nationwide flight from the trouser on our hands. And we don't want that. But at least I'm glad to see there's none of this political nonsense.'

H.O.L.E. ushered me out, 'Just before you go. This Ortega y Gasset woman you keep mentioning. Isn't she the one who won the Eurovision Song Contest a few years back? Or is it me?'

'You,' I said, sycophantically.

Radio Times 1966

THE WEDNESDAY PLAY

CATHY COME HOME

'I reckon it's just us now. Just you and me. Have some kids, eh Cath?'
'I'd like that.'

1 **9.5** CATHY is blonde and attractive with an open, determined face. Just up from the country and in the big city she meets Reg and falls for him. He is so easy-going and relaxed and full of laughs. She dreams of settling down, building a home and having some babies. A natural thing to want, one might think, and something we all have a right to look forward to.

Just a simple love story. But things don't turn out for her quite like that. Events cruelly overtake her and Reg—and later their children. They begin a journey through Britain, but it is a Britain many of us have never seen. What happens to them we may scarcely believe. But it is happening now, and is likely to go on happening to lots of people for a long time.

Everything in tonight's play the author Jeremy Sandford has seen with his own eyes. It is something he feels deeply and his passion and his anger leap out at us from this story of two human beings trying to make a home for themselves and their children. Trying, with humour and love and courage, to live decent lives and keep their self-respect.

Cathy Come Home is directed by Kenneth Loach, whose outstanding contributions to 'The Wednesday Play' last year included *Three Clear Sundays* and *Up the Junction*. Carol White and Ray Brooks play the young people. TONY GARNETT

KISS TO SEAL A PROPHECY FULFILLED

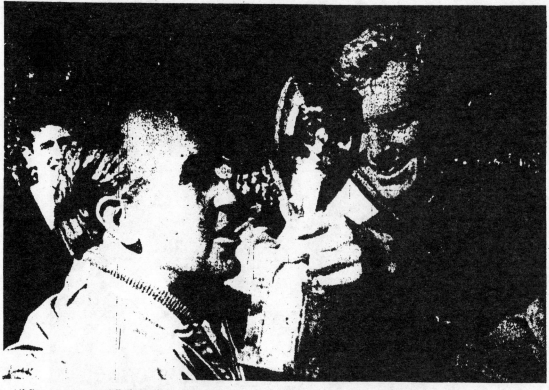

Alf Ramsey, manager of England's footballers, who prophesied three years ago that his team would win the World Cup in 1966, kisses the trophy held up to him by the captain, Bobby Moore.

Observer
1966

London goes wild for Cup victors

by a Staff Reporter

BRITAIN erupted with joy last night after England had won football's World Cup final at Wembley.

Patriotic fervour, unequalled since VE Day, spread all over London in celebration of the 4—2 victory over West Germany.

As the team arrived at the Royal Gardens Hotel in Kensington for a banquet, arm-linked cordons of police popped open like seams when a crowd of more than 6,000 mobbed the players. Cries of "England," "Ramsey," "Moore," "Stiles," "Charlton," greeted them when they came out on a balcony before the Union Jack-waving crowd.

Traffic in the West End was at a complete standstill. Thousands of cars and pedestrians jostled around Leicester Square, Piccadilly Circus and Trafalgar and Parliament Squares.

Teenagers who had not been to the match clambered into the Trafalgar Square fountains singing: "We gave them a bloody good hiding—and so say all of us." The pubs were full and cinemas and theatres empty. Groups of people danced and sang in the streets.

An AA spokesman said: "It's like VE night, election night and New Year's Eve all rolled into one."

Pop group coming

AN American pop group, well up in the charts, has heard about the Hammersmith charity ball planned to raise money for the relatives of the three dead policemen—and have offered to come.

The Chiffons — a group of four coloured girls — heard about the mammoth ball 3,500 miles away in New York, and wrote to organizer, Mr. Barry Powell, offering their services.

"I've written to The Beatles and Bing Crosby," Mr. Powell said, "asking them if they can make it on October 7. I haven't had a reply yet, but I'm hopeful that Bing Crosby can make it."

Shepherds Bush
Gazette
1966

'Pop' pirates told: Ban on Aug. 15

By MARTIN JACKSON

RADIO pirate chiefs were told yesterday that their pop stations face official scuttling next month.

One of them immediately warned the Government that the new regulations would be defied.

Mr. Edward Short, the Postmaster-General, told the Commons that he hoped to bring the Act banning private radio stations into force on August 15.

An Order would make it illegal to work for, supply, or advertise with an unregistered station.

Asked how soon he expected to silence the pirates, Mr. Short said: "This depends a good deal on our European colleagues. Most of these countries have legislated. Holland, I think, is the only one that has not."

Fight

Mr. Ronan O'Rahilly, founder of Radio Caroline—the first and biggest pirate station—said last night: "I am prepared to go to prison to fight for freedom on the air.

Daily Express 1967

Daily Express 1967

BRITAIN'S cycling hero Tommy Simpson died today—a victim of the sun and the savage 13th stage of the Tour de France.

Simpson, 29-year-old former world professional champion, collapsed as he heaved his way up 6,273ft. Mont Ventoux near Avignon.

He was a mile from the top of the 1-in-12 Alpine pass. The temperature was nearing the 100degs. mark. Simpson slumped on to the rough road.

British team officials in the car following went to help. Simpson, though obviously in a bad way, gasped: *"Put me back on the bike."*

He was helped back on, but fell off again, unconscious. The tour's official doctor gave Simpson the kiss-of-life until a helicopter arrived and lifted him to hospital.

But he died within minutes.

Radio Times 1967

Hello, me dearios!

7.35 RADIO 2

'THERE'S a lot of talk about cordwangling these days,' Rambling Syd Rumpo says, 'but very few people know what it really is—and those who practise it don't like to talk about it . . .'

Country Meets Folk at 5.30 on Radio 1? It could be. *Round the Horne* at 1.30 on Radio 4? It certainly will be. But what really gives rise to this reference to Rambling Syd's passionate involvement in country matters is that Kenneth Williams is today picking his *Million Dollar Bill* for Radio 2, and Robin Boyle will persuade him to talk about *that*. Perhaps he will also recall that bosky turve where Syd first woggled his moulie . . .

Radio Times 1967

IN THE THIRD PROGRAMME AT 7.30

THE TRAGEDY OF KING LEAR

by

William Shakespeare

John Gielgud
AS KING LEAR

WITH

John Gielgud as Lear at Stratford in 1950

Virginia McKenna *as Cordelia*
Barbara Jefford *as Goneril*
Timothy Bateson *as the Fool*
Derek Godfrey *as Edmund*
Michael Goodliffe *as Albany*

Howard Marion-Crawford *as Kent*
Barbara Bolton *as Regan*
Mark Dignam *as Gloucester*
Philip Guard *as Edgar*
Roger Delgado *as Cornwall*

Campbell killed 200 yards from triumph

By Daily Mail Reporter

~~DONALD CAMPBELL~~ was only 200 yards and one second from setting a world water-speed record of 300 m.p.h. when he was killed yesterday.

His jet-boat Bluebird leapt from Coniston Water, somersaulted 50ft. into the air then crashed and sank.

The 200 yards was all that remained of Campbell's second kilometre run across the lake to give an average speed.

At the time of the disaster Bluebird was travelling at more than 300 m.p.h.

Mr. Norman Buckley, Campbell's chief observer, said: " Donald could have beaten his own record of 276 m.p.h. and reached the 300 m.p.h. average easily.

" He had only to return at 303 m.p.h. because his first run was completed at 297 m.p.h.

NEWSIGHT and pictures Pages 4 and 5

Daily Mail 1967

Galsworthy's story of a prosperous English family told in twenty-six parts— Saturdays on BBC-2. The Forsytes' watchword is Respectability, Property its God; but Beauty and Passion steal into the family citadel—destroying its solidarity, setting husband against wife, father against son

Radio Times 1967

Donald Wilson, the producer, explains some of the problems involved in dramatising John Galsworthy's huge work for television

8.15

IT may seem superfluous to write a new preface to *The Forsyte Saga,* because John Galsworthy gave us his own, but there are two reasons perhaps good enough to excuse me. The first is that although the novels have never been out of print since they were first published and a whole new generation reads them now, the work will be unfamiliar to many thousands of television viewers. Secondly, what we have produced, and what you will see, is a work wholly different in kind, though not, we believe, in spirit, from the original.

Let me try to explain this. Galsworthy was a playwright—and a good one—as well as a novelist. If the notion had come to him to relate what he calls ' this long tale ' as a series of plays for the stage, he would have gone about the job in a totally different way. The restrictions, and opportunities, of the theatre would have forced upon him a form of construction alien to the novel.

These fascinating descriptive passages of narrative—and *The Forsyte Saga* is mainly narrative—would have been replaced by dialogue scenes because, as Bridie once said, a play is a story told by actors; not told, you observe, by the playwright, who can only speak through the words he puts into the mouths of his personae.

So, in dramatising the *Saga,* we have tried to put ourselves into the mind of Galsworthy the playwright, and retell his story—and what a story!—in purely dramatic form. But with such advantages as the author, bound by the theatre, knowing only the silent cinema and nothing of television, could never have dreamed of.

Our play runs for more than twenty-one hours, spread over twenty-six weeks. Each fifty-minute part is an Act, standing dramatically by itself but holding situations in suspense, and rounded off by a strong ' curtain.'

This is after all the craft of the storyteller, and where our construction varies from the novels, it does so only to serve the dramatic purposes of the television serial, one aspect of which is the fact that each entr'acte lasts for a week. We have simplified and clarified the action, but only one major change has been made.

POPPET ON A FLING

BILL, PHIL and SANDIE fulfil TOM SLOAN'S ambition !

New Musical Express 1967

IT was a truly British triumph in Vienna on Saturday, when practically all Europe (including the East) saw the Eurovision Song Contest and heard Sandie Shaw sing the winning song, " Puppet On A String," written by Ireland's Phil Coulter and Scotland's Bill Martin.

Tom Sloan, head of BBC-TV Light Entertainment, saw his dream come true. For ten years he has been leading Britain's effort to win this international competition, and despite five seconds, this is his first win. Among those who came second have been Matt Monro, Ronnie Carroll, Kathy Kirby, the Allisons, Brian Johnson, Teddy Johnson and Pearl Carr.

Radio Times 1967

ED STEWART

10.0 to 12 noon

MICHAEL ASPEL

12 noon to 2.0

PETE DRUMMOND

2.0 to 5.0

ALAN FREEMAN

5.0 to 7.0

Radio 1 is new and Radio 1 is News

This is its first weekend and the spotlight is on the new people and the new shows.

Tony Blackburn launches it on Saturday at 7.0 a.m. with the first of his Monday to Saturday record programmes; Keith Skues takes over a new-fashioned *Saturday Club*; Emperor Rosko—a colourful character indeed—breezes in from Paris for sixty swinging minutes at noon. Jack Jackson returns with his comedy record show at 1.0; Chris Denning keeps the style and tempo firmly *Where It's At*, and Pete Murray highlights the pick of the week's new records, whether 'pop' or 'middle of the road.' Pete Brady then takes Radio 1 to 5.30 for the rendezvous with the best in Country and Western and Folk music. At 6.32 Johnny Moran presents *Scene and Heard*—a bright sharp look at trends in people, places, and pop. On Saturday evening Radio 2 leads the way with a series of star-studded shows. Then—at 10.0 p.m.—Pete Murray hosts his Party right up to the Midnight News.

* * *

Sunday at 10.0 a.m. brings in Ed Stewart with a brand new successor to *Easy Beat*; at 2.0 p.m., after the expanded world-wide *Family Favourites*, Pete Drummond presents *Top Gear*, seconded by John Peel. This three-hour weekly show will feature the most forward-looking groups and singers in the pop world. At 5.0 Alan Freeman takes over for an extended *Pick of the Pops*—followed at 7.0 by Mike Raven with *R and B*. After the *Jazz Scene* Radio 1 joins Radio 2 at 9.30 for radio's top satirical programme *Listen to this Space*. David Jacobs presents his own show from 10.0 to midnight—with Julie Andrews as the first star guest.

BE A RADIO 1-UPMAN

Black and White Minstrels

 Tonight the BBC's longest-running television spectacular reaches another milestone. It is hard to think of what more could be added to this exciting show. The answer, of course, is colour. The Black and White Minstrels move from BBC 1 to BBC 2, and with them will be all the usual faces, including Leslie Crowther.

RADIO 1
TOP GEAR
John Peel

Like those four other bright boys of Pop he was born in Liverpool. But he began working for radio at Station WRR in Dallas, Texas. He went on to Radio KLMA Oklahoma and Radio KMEN Los Angeles, and came back to Radio London (which was not on the mainland.) This afternoon he joins Pete Drummond in his regular Top Gear spot with four new and up-and-coming groups.

AT 2.0

BIG NEW SINGLE
Gonna give her all the love I've got
TAMLA MOTOWN TMG603

JIMMY RUFFIN

OBITUARIES

Siegfried Sassoon, 1886-1967

It was for his war poems of 1914-18 that Sassoon was best remembered as a poet; but he continued to write poetry for another forty years, and in the tranquil, insighted poetry of his middle years he found a true metier. It may be that posterity will remember him for his prose—the truly marvellous and poetic prose of his autobiographical books. But he was a poet at heart, with a deep and religious concern for the human spirit.

Poetry Review 1967

RADIO 4, 3, 2 .. ONE —GO !

5 a.m. in the Tony Blackburn flat .. BBC alerts the first D.J. on duty

by Michael Nevar

Jacqueline

Tonight's film about the remarkable cellist Jacqueline du Pré is introduced by Christopher Nupen

1
10.25
'I heard it on the radio when I was four and although I don't remember the sound I liked it so much apparently that I asked my mother to give me the thing that made that sound. And she did, she gave me a big, big cello which I learnt to play.'

The story seems too simple—too inevitable. But eighteen years later Jacqueline du Pré is among the most successful musicians this country has produced, and if inevitability is not the keynote then a dramatic sense of vocation certainly is.

She wanted nothing so much as to play the cello and the extravagant natural talent was only a start; she had also the character to develop it and the right environment from the beginning.

Her mother, a pianist, bought her the longed-for cello. Then with great flair she wrote tunes for Jacqueline to play, and illustrated them with enticing drawings.

Not that she needed enticing. Her mother recalls a holiday on Dartmoor where it was thought that the cello would hardly be missed and would probably be out of place; so it was left at home. On the third day she found a tearful

Jacqueline alone on the moor, and on asking her what was the matter learnt very simply that she missed the cello that much.

There has always been a striking contrast between the simplicity of her everyday personality and the fire of her playing—as if when she plays she is possessed by her own talent. To make the most of this she tells her own story in the film and is seen making music at different ages; with her mother, her

teacher William Pleeth, Sir John Barbirolli, and Daniel Barenboim.

She was married to Daniel Barenboim last June; to celebrate the event and provide a climax for the film we invited them to record the Elgar Concerto.

With a spirit that is typical of their music-making they jumped at the chance, chose the New Philharmonia Orchestra, and produced a performance worthy of the occasion.

AFTER MONTHS of planning, worry and conjecture, BBC's Radio 1 today starts pumping out its daily ration of pop.

The last of scores of "dry runs"—heard, digested and modified only by the people making them — finished at midnight. Today millions can make their own assessment.

Tony Blackburn, the first purely Radio 1 disc-jockey to be heard—sharp at 7 am. — did not know until yesterday exactly what records he would play.

He did know that a telephone call to his Knightsbridge flat would get him up at 5 am. and that he would drive in his MGB to the Broadcasting House studio eight minutes away.

Blackburn, a product of Millfield public school and Radio London, has three turntables on his desk. I saw him trying them out yesterday.

Concentration—Jacqueline as concert-goers see her today and with the 'big, big cello' she played as a child

Radio Times 1967

New Statesman 1968

Stanley Kubrick's "nightmare" comedy "Dr. Strangelove, Or: How I Learned to Stop Worrying and Love the Bomb" will be premiered in London just in time for the Christmas rush—December 19. Stars are Peter Sellers, Sterling Hayden, George C. Scott and Keenan Wynn.

Kentish Times 1963

Radio Times 1967

MUSIC PROGRAMME

HAYDN
The Creation

A performance conducted by Eugen Jochum and recorded at the 1966 Munich Summer Festival

AT 1.4

THIRD PROGRAMME

VERDI
Falstaff

A performance on record conducted by Leonard Bernstein with Dietrich Fischer-Dieskau in the title role

AT 8.15

Cecil Day-Lewis is new Poet Laureate

BY OUR OWN REPORTER

Mr Cecil Day-Lewis is to be the new Poet Laureate, it was announced from 10 Downing Street last night. Mr Day-Lewis, aged 63, is a former Professor of Poetry at Oxford.

He and Mr John Betjeman had been widely considered as favourites for the post, which fell vacant last May on the death of Mr John Masefield at the age of 91.

The post has been a regular institution since the 17th century, although its origins are much earlier. It carries an annual stipend of £70 plus £27 in lieu of wine, and minimal official duties. Robert Bridges, in fact, made a precedent of ignoring State occasions.

Long delay

There has been an unusually long delay of seven months in appointing Mr Masefield's successor. This was thought to reflect the controversy surrounding the rôle of a Poet Laureate in today's conditions.

Some critics felt that he should be more of an innovator than he had been in the past. Others thought, after John Masefield's tenure of 37 years, that it should be an appointment with a fixed term.

In the event the Queen has chosen probably the most established figure among the likely candidates. Mr Day-Lewis as well as being a former Professor of Poetry, is a vice-president of the Royal Society of Literature and chairman of the literary panel of the Arts Council.

He was educated at Sherborne School and Wadham College, Oxford, and is a director of the publishers, Chatto and Windus.

Mr Betjeman had been mentioned as a leading contender, though with the proviso that he might not always relish the sincere solemnity required of a Court poet.

The best . .

Robert Graves and Edward Blunden were other names put forward. Mr Day-Lewis commented on the post earlier this year: "It is a curious one. Now that it has ceased to be a Court function, I think the best poet in the country should be selected." "And that," he added, "means Robert Graves."

Mr Day-Lewis, who published his autobiography, "The Buried Day," seven years ago, sees his own poetic roots in Hardy, Yeats, Robert Frost, and Auden. Besides his poetry he has written translations of Virgil, and under the pen name, Nicholas Blake, has produced several detective novels.

Feather in the cap for Ireland, page 4

Guardian 1968

JUST A MINUTE

DAVID HATCH writes:

7.30 RADIO 4

VERY WELL, I'll come clean—it's a panel game. No, no, hang on; don't go flipping off to the television pages. It'll only take a minute—in fact, *Just a Minute*. In a few seconds I'll give you a subject about which you've got to talk for one minute—without hesitating, going off the point (deviating), or repeating yourself.

Before I begin, get a stopwatch and stand by. O.K.? (Oh, you've got to make it funny, too.) All set?

Your subject is ' *Things to do in the bath.*'

Go! . . . Well, go on, it's easy.

THE REGULAR MINUTE-MEN

CLEMENT FREUD

DEREK NIMMO

Radio Times 1967

Mr. W. L. Webb, Manager of the Astoria, Finsbury Park gives a second opinion on patient Charles Hawtrey. This happened at a special screening of "CARRY ON DOCTOR". Also adding to the chaos are (left to right) Barbara Windsor, Kenneth Williams, Peter Butterworth and Frankie Howerd, the stars of the film which is showing at the Astoria, Finsbury Park this week.

Camden, Holborn and Finsbury Guardian 1968

▲
PAUL McCARTNEY (with Martha)
The Beatles
❛I believe that love is the one thing that can supersede everything else.

Love is a groove. It sounds complicated but it's simple. It's just a matter of me sitting here and you sitting there and both of us starting out from the point that we have some things in common, that basically we dig each other. Then we can relax and progress and not get hung up on any useless prejudices. Is there anything wrong with that? Doesn't that make sense?

Love is the only natural thing. Cynicism isn't real. Love is very easy, but cynicism is forced and it hasn't a direction to anything or anyone.

I honestly believe love is more powerful than anything. Yes, I admit it's easier to preach love when you're rich and secure than when you're starving, but I still think people who are hungry, who are sick and dying should try to show love.

I've found it's possible to get on with anyone. I used not to bother with people who seemed boring or difficult, but now I take my time, I try to approach them openly, and then I find that they have their own groove.

Queen 1968

Beatlebores

Sir: Bless you, Bill Grundy. People *do* pay attention to you (13 September), sensible people anyhow, including those unaffected by the present mania for upgrading garbage from the artistic slums.

I particularly welcomed Mr Grundy's article because on seeing the *Sunday Times* would-be appetising announcement of the Beatle memoirs I wrote to the editor expressing my complete disinterest and *sang froid* at their great sales-swelling scoop. A polite reply hazarded the view that after reading the excerpts I might come to share the *Sunday Times*'s view that the reasons for the Beatles' phenomenal rise to fame were well worth examining. To this I could only, of course, reply that as I was not in the least bit interested in the spread of contagious diseases I had not the slightest intention of reading these or any other articles about the Beatles.

In the original announcement what struck me as the high spot of humbug was the claim that despite the orgies of *ersatz* bumptious arrogance the Beatles would be found in the last resort to have retained . . . wait for it . . . their integrity. That, surely, is something to which they, like Hitler, are welcome.

G. Reichardt

12a Mount Pleasant Road, Poole

The Spectator 1968

Stewart wins the big one

—From—
BRIAN GROVES
Watkins Glen, New York,
—Sunday—

JACKIE STEWART turned the 1968 world championship into a three-cornered battle today when he scorched to victory in the American Grand Prix here.

With only next month's Mexican Grand Prix to go he is now second in the title hunt.

Britons took the first three places in today's race. Graham Hill was second in a

AND TAKES £8,300 IN U.S. GRAND PRIX

Lotus Ford. John Surtees was third in a Honda.

It was 29-year-old Stewart's third grand prix victory this season.

He led in his Matra-Ford for almost all the 248 miles, setting a new lap record of 126.57 m.p.h.

He won £8,300 of the race's £40,000 prize money—the richest Formula One event ever.

The Scot said later : 'I had a trouble-free run.'

Daily Mail
1968

The Booker book prize

THERE was welcome confirmation yesterday of my July prediction that Booker Brothers, McConnell Ltd., the £28m. rum, sugar and engineering group with a big toe in the literary world are to launch a £5,000 literary prize—Britain's biggest.

The aim is to provide a financially attractive prize which will also stimulate a significant increase in book sales. The Booker Prize for Fiction will be awarded annually. Judges for the first prize, to be announced next April, are Dame Rebecca West, Stephen Spender, Frank Kermode and David Farrer, under the chairmanship of W. L. Webb, literary editor of The Guardian.

Short List

Any novel by a writer from Britain, the Commonwealth or the republics of Ireland and South Africa which has been published first in Britain will be eligible. The Publishers' Association, who are collaborating with Booker Brothers over the prize, say that a short list of possible winners will be released four to six weeks before the final decision is made so as to arouse speculation and public interest in more than one book and one author.

Booker's generosity was, coincidentally, more than matched yesterday in Paris. Madame Cino del Duca, wife of the Italian-born publisher, has decided to create Europe's biggest literary prize—150,000 NF (£12,500) annually. It will go alternately to a man of letters and a scientist whose work is associated with modern humanism. The first award will be made next June.

The Times **1968**

South Africa exposed

Who is the South African Prime Minister kidding? South Africans presumably.

He pretends that England is to blame for the political fuss surrounding the selection of Basil D'Oliveira, a Cape Coloured, to tour South Africa this winter. But it is clearly South Africa which, by refusing to allow any coloured cricketers to represent South Africa at any time, has created the situation.

What does such a man do? In the case of D'Oliveira he chose to come to England and proved himself, admittedly after an unfortunate amount of indecision, good enough to be selected to tour South Africa. He was good enough to tour the West Indies last year.

Mr. Vorster did not call that a political act. What has happened to D'Oliveira since which should make his selection any more suspect? A century against the Australians?

It really is impossible to separate sport from politics if politicians thus interfere with sport. Sport should, where possible, be a bridge to people who hold political views different from one's own. This is why, on balance, England is right to go on trying to play against the South Africans despite South Africa's abhorrent racial policies.

It now seems certain, however, that this particular tour will be off, even though no official decision has been taken by the MCC. Colin Cowdrey, one feels, is being super-optimistic in thinking that Mr. Vorster has not completely closed the door. One had only to hear the recording of the South African Premier's speech to realise the depth of his bitterness, and it was quite apparent that the door had been slammed.

The blame lies squarely in Mr. Vorster's lap. His extraordinary views and the extent of South African political interference in sport stand exposed for all to see.

Bradford Telegraph and Argus **1968**

SPOTLIGHT

WHAT DO YOU WANT TO BE, BESIDES DISHEVELLED?
"Hair", the most unexpected hit on Broadway, opening in London
at the Shaftesbury Theatre on July 29, and other happenings

Vogue
1968

The Time
196

Sir John Gielgud and Derek Jarman, *above*, producing
and designing Sadler's Wells' new *Don Giovanni*—
Geoffrey Dunn's new English translation, Leonard
Delaney in the lead (London Coliseum, August 21).

David Warner, *above*, Evans in *The Bofors Gun*, the
film from John McGrath's play of the British army
in post-war Germany. Unease, frustrations, Jack Gold
directing, Nicol Williamson,
Ian Holm co-starring (Odeon,
St Martins Lane, August 15).
Katharine Ross, *left*, star
ascendant with newcomer
Dustin Hoffman, Anne
Bancroft in Mike Nichols'
tragi-comic film of parental
conflict, *The Graduate*.
Hoffman involved with wife,
daughter of parents' friend:
seduction, grief, chase, chaos
(London Pavilion, August 8).
Tiny Tim, *left*, America's
newest musical shock. "Face
of a teenage vampire" say
Newsweek. Voice from tenor
to high falsetto and ukulele
hysterically on record here
with *Tiptoe through the Tulips*,
God Bless Tiny Tim,
arriving mid-September for
Apple-organised concerts.

The Queen talking with Mme. Georges Duthuit, daughter of
Henri Matisse, the French painter, after opening the Hayward
Gallery on the South Bank, London, yesterday. The gallery
contains a large Matisse exhibition. Diary, page 10.

SPOTLIGHT
ON THE POP EXPERIENCE

IAN YEOMANS

rian Henri, *above*, a man of many talents oet, painter, musician; father figure of Liverpool scene and a formative figure in ties art. His first volume of poetry, *To- ht at Noon*, just published (Rapp and iting, 21s.); his first one-man show of ntings at the ICA (Nov 1-27) and the first ord by his new group, *The Liverpool ne*, coming out on Nov 15 (RCA). "I want aint A SYSTEMATIC DERANGEMENT ALL THE SENSES in black running ers 50 miles high over Liverpool."

Nuttall, *right*, ubiquitous author of a te outstanding study of post-war arts, *mb Culture* (Nov 18, McGibbon and Kee, .), written with passion, total commit- nt and a fierce insight. A major figure in Underground, Nuttall has variously led a band, exhibited paintings, written poetry and articles and created and produced the *People Show* around the country. At pre- sent teaching a mixed media course at Bradford's Regional Art College, he has just finished a novel, *Pig*, "a collage of fantasies, chopped, shuffled, dispersed, reassembled".

ue 1968

QUIZ TIME

PENNY'S POP POSERS

How much d'you know about the pop scene at the moment? Try answering these questions and find out! Check your answers below.

1 Who is Lily The Pink?
2 Who wrote Lulu's latest hit "I'm A Tiger?"
3 Name the members of the group The Tremeloes, and state their latest record.
4 Where did Dusty Springfield record her latest single, "Son-of-a-Preacher Man"?

5 Who is the singer with Manfred Mann?
6 What is Cilla Black's real name?
7 Where was Barry Ryan born?
8 Can you identify the group pictured above, and name their hit record?
9 Which is the record that took two years to get in the recent Hit Parade?
10 Who had a hit with "Harper Valley P.T.A."?

Penelope 1969

DAVE HEMERY

talks about his career; his thoughts before, during and after the Olympic Final; and his future to Melvyn Watman

How surprised were you by the time of 48.1?
As I was walking down the ramp I had heard 48.1 announced in English but I didn't know if they had made a mistake and meant 49.1. I thought it might have been about 48.9, something like that, because of the wind and the rain. Be- fore the final I thought I might be capable of under 48.8—perhaps 48.4 on a good day. But the cold and rain may have cost me up to half a second.

Athletics Weekly **1968**

EAST CHEAM MADE HIM FAMOUS

SO THE man who made Railway Cuttings, East Cheam, an address familiar to people all over the country, is dead.

Tony Hancock, the modern Pagliacci, the tubby, sad-faced funny man with the broken heart for whom little, lately seemed to go right, was found dead in a Sydney hotel bedroom.

I interviewed him once at a BBC junket to launch an appearance on TV after he abandoned Hancock's Half Hour and split up (amicably) with Sid James.

He seemed then to me to be an unhappy man, striving for something which persistently eluded him after those successful years on TV. He wanted to go it alone, prove he could retain the audiences who loved him then, but retain them without what he perhaps regarded as the props of Sid James and scriptwriters Alan Simpson and Ray Galton.

It was they who invented Railway Cuttings, East Cheam—chose it, Alan Simpson once told me, because to him Cheam epitomised quiet suburbia and lent itself to a little gentle mickey-taking.

But it was Tony who brought it to life and made Cheam a name to turn up the mouth corners and crinkle the eyes of Hancock's Half Hour fans everywhere.

Now he is gone and the world is the poorer for it. Men who can reduce us to paroxysms of mirth as he used to don't come our way too often.

Perhaps he set his eyes on too distant a star and strove too hard to make us laugh.

CATHRYN SANSOM

Sutton and Cheam Herald **1968**

'LAST EXIT' TO BE REPUBLISHED

Conviction is quashed

BY A STAFF REPORTER

The American novel Last Exit to Brooklyn, by Hubert Selby, jun. which was banned in Britain after a jury at the Central Criminal Court had ruled it obscene, may be on sale again later this year.

The publishers, Calder and Boyars Ltd., who brought out a British edition of the book in 1966, won their appeal yesterday against conviction for publishing an obscene article.

Mr. John Calder, a director of the company, said after the hearing: "The book will obviously be republished, but we have not started to think about it yet". Another company official said a new edition would probably appear later this year.

Lord Justice Salmon said in the Court of Appeal judgment that the summing up of the trial judge, Judge Rogers, had certain "fatal flaws". He had failed to put to the jury the defence case on the question of obscenity and failed to give proper directions on whether publication was for the public good.

Mr. Calder said that perhaps publishers would be encouraged to be slightly more courageous.

"But I and other publishers will go on working for the complete abolition of the Act of Parliament under which this case was brought."

The Times **1968**

FRIENDS MOURN BUD FLANAGAN (late of Dolphin Sq.)

MANY of his friends at Dolphin Square, Pimlico, where he lived until 1963, this week mourned the death of Bud Flanagan, who died in hospital at Kingston, Surrey, on Sunday, aged 72.

"He was a great character and we miss him very much," one of the residents said. "He lived in Beatty House for a long time and then went away for a bit but he came back in 1957 and lived in Rodney House until 1963."

But Flanagan was one of the original members of the London Palladium Crazy Gang and was famous for his song, "Underneath the Arches."

In recent years he was in partnership with Mr. Jack Solomons in a chain of betting shops. Only a few months ago they opened one of their shops at Vauxhall Bridge Road, near the New Victoria cinema.

But Flanagan's real name was Robert Winthrop. His stage name was that of an Army sergeant who had "crimed" him for dumb insolence. "I'll make you remember this" he told him.

Flanagan teamed up with Chesney Allen and worked with him for years until Chesney's ill health broke up the partnership.

Flanagan was a Crazy Gang stalwart and appeared in the Gang's farewell show, "The Young in Heart," which opened at the Victoria Palace in December 1960 and ran for 824 performances.

In 1946, Bud Flanagan was elected King Rat of the Grand Order of Water Rats. In 1959 he was given an OBE.

The funeral took place yesterday (Thursday).

Westminster and Pimlico News **1968**

AFTER John Surtees had retired, Graham Hill, Dan Gurney and Jim Clark duelled for the lead. Here they are seen lapping Mike Spence who was having his first Formula 1 drive for Team Lotus. The order in this shot is Hill, Gurney, Clark.

Daily Mail **1968**

MARTY'S TV SHOW GETS TOP AWARDS

By JACK BELL

COMIC Marty Feldman and his B.B.C-TV series "Marty" won three top awards last night.

Marty, 34, was named as TV light entertainment personality of 1968 by the Guild of Television Producers and Directors.

He was presented with the award in London by Earl Mountbatten, himself a TV "star" these days with his life-story series on I T V.

Marty and his co-writer on the "Marty" series, Barry Took, won the award for the best script.

And producer Dennis Main Wilson took the top light entertainment producer title for his work on "Marty" and the B B C's other big comedy hit, "Till Death Us Do Part."

The B B C scooped thirteen of last night's awards with I T V getting four.

Madcap

Wendy Craig, 34, who plays the madcap housewife in the B B C-1 comedy series "Not In Front Of The Children," won the best TV actress award.

Roy Dotrice took the top T V actor title for his 85-minute solo performance in "Brief Lives" on B B C-2.

The Guild supreme prize, the Desmond Davis Award, went to B B C director Ken Russell for "the most original creative contribution to T V."

Report

He has been acclaimed for a "breakthrough" in T V arts documentaries with programmes like "Elgar," "Debussy" and "Isadora Duncan."

The Richard Dimbleby award went to Julian Pettifer for his reports from Vietnam and the United States for B B C-1's "24 Hours."

I T V took two awards for the best factual programmes — "This Week" and Granada's "Cities at War."

The other I T V successes were the A T V documentary "Big Fish, Little Fish" and "News at Ten."

The B B C's Anthony Page won the top drama producer award for "The Parachute," which starred John Osborne.

The foreign television programme award went to the Czech TV service's producers, directors, reporters, cameramen and technicians "for their integrity and courage throughout the past year."

Marty talks to Ken Irwin—See Page 11.

Daily Mirror 1969

Events

ISLE OF WIGHT FESTIVAL

Saturday 30 and Sunday 31 August, at Woodsiue Bay, near Ryde, Isle of Wight.

Saturday

Who, Moody Blues, Fat Mattress, Joe Cocker, Bonzo Dog Band, Family, Free, Pretty Things, Marsha Hunt and White Trash, Battered Orgaments, Aynsley Dunbar Retaliation, Blodwyn Pig, Gipsy, Blonde on Blonde, Edgar Broughton, King Crimson. Tickets 25s.

Sunday

Bob Dylan and the Band, Richie Havens, Tom Paxton, Pentangle, Julie Felix, Garry Farr, Liverpool Scene, Indo-Jazz Fusions, Third Ear Band. Tickets £2.

British Rail are running ferries every 15 minutes between Portsmouth and the Isle of Wight, night-time included, from Thursday night to Sunday night, 10s return tickets. Coaches run from Ryde to the festival; fare not included.
Tickets are available for each day, or for £2 10s the weekend, from Harlequin Record shops:
36 High Holborn, WC1
96 Berwick Street, W 1
129 Cannon Street, EC4
116 Cheapside, EC2
150 Fenchurch Street, EC3
167 Fleet Street, EC4
67 Great Titchfield Street, W1
35½ Haymarket, W1
163a Kilburn High Road, NW6
41 Liverpool Street, EC3
121 Moorgate, EC2
119 New Bond Street, W1
201 Oxford Street, W1
28 Strutton Ground, SW1

WHO 23 AUGUST

From 6.30 to midnight, two separate shows (so that Who and Amen Corner can both be top of the bill!) with 15-minute gap, one ticket for both.
Who, Amen Corner, Aardvark, Andromeda, Freedom, Ipsissimus, Bum, Evolution, Classics. Tickets £1 from A. P. Johnson, 41 Lodge Lane, Grays, Essex, or at gate. Concert at: Marquee Meadow, Brentwood Road, Grays, Essex.

Time Out 1969

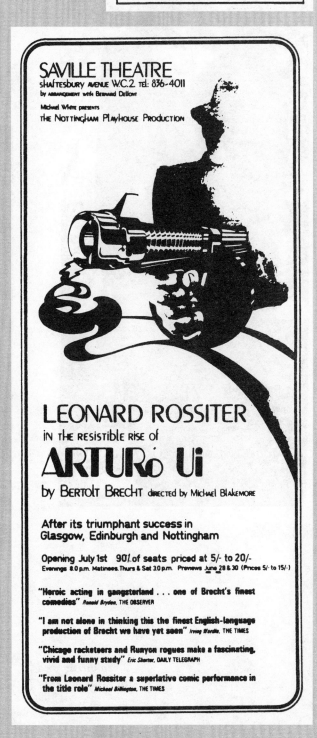

MEN IN VOGUE
MICHAEL YORK AND THE FASHION FOR MEDITATION

Michael York wears three new suits designed by Gordon Deighton for 20th Century-Fox's comedy *The Guru*, filmed in India, opening here in January. He plays a pop star searching for the key to meditation, and finding meditating dolly, Rita Tushingham, instead. (His beard's an anachronism grown for his next film *Alfred the Great*, trimmed by Doug at Sweenys.) And the clothes, made in heavier stuff for a British climate, are at Trend of Simpson.

Vogue 1968

It was odd that Kenneth Horne's sad and sudden death should occur at this particular point in time. As long as *Round the Horne* existed, the case for the continuation of radio comedy needed no further argument. Here—as an ill-fated recent attempt on ITV showed—was something that television could neither duplicate nor imitate. Whether similarly unique radio comedy will be discovered in the future is another matter. It is my lasting regret that somehow I was never able to take up the kind invitations from Douglas Smith (the well-known purveyor of Dobberoids) to attend one of the recordings of *Round the Horne*, which I gather were almost cult occasions. Yet, alone with my transistor, the avuncular suggestiveness of Horne, combined with the outrageousness of Kenneth Williams et al, made me laugh louder than anything on television since Hancock. I only met Horne once, and that was not long after his first heart attack. Its considerable effects on him were noticeable, and were being overcome with a characteristic good grace, determination and professionalism. After this he wisely gave up the business side of his life and concentrated on being an entertainer. He retained the outer air of a managing director, but the sort of managing director who in the middle of the most grave board-meeting could be relied on suddenly to emit a huge raspberry at the absurdity of everything.

The Listener
1969

ROBIN RETURNS

SEEN ON SUNDAY, battling through high seas, solo round the world yachtsman Robin Knox-Johnston sails his ketch Suhaili over the last few miles of his 29,500 miles voyage. Some 100 miles off Lands End, strong headwinds postponed his expected arrival time, as a south-westerly gale which would have speeded his return never materialised, and instead a force 6 sprang from the East.

Even so, Knox-Johnston is the first home in the Sunday Times Golden Globe race, for sailing single-handed non-stop around the

World. On his return to Falmouth, his home and starting-off port, he will be awarded the Golden Globe.

Francis Chichester, one of the race judges, has said that Robin's chief worry is not the weather but that somebody will "plonk something aboard" Suhaili or try to help in some respect, thus disqualifying him from the race.

On Tuesday morning, the minesweeper Warsash set out to escort Suhaili to Falmouth.

Yachting and
Boating Weekly
1969

GENTLE CLOWN PUTS THE BOOT IN

By WILLIAM GREAVES

IT will not have escaped the notice of anybody who enjoys laughing, without knowing why, that Monty Python's Circus is flying tonight (BBC 1, 10.15).

We won't be required to think too much, and we need not bother looking for hidden messages.

It will, of course, be frightfully silly. Daft at times, stupid from start to finish, infantile, zany, and a waste of time. And very funny indeed.

The Circus crept from under a BBC stone last year, and slipped unnoticed into the evening programmes so near the end of Sunday night that it was almost Monday morning.

Those of us who discovered it there found a sort of throwback to the days of meaningless comedy, a refreshing reminder of the simple laughter we enjoyed before Private Eye and That Was The Week.

Yet Monty Python is no carbon copy. Its techniques are new, and its humour unpredictable. There is no knowing what might happen tonight.

Crush

Except, of course, that somewhere along the line Terry Gilliam will be putting the animated boot in.

You will remember, will you not, the boot? That soul-less foot that descends like an income-tax inspector to crush everybody, and everything, through the bottom of the screen.

Terry, a long-haired, lovable American who wouldn't—I am assured—hurt a fly, and who looks after the animation in this particular mad-house, sees it rather differently.

He said: "I think of it as the foot of God coming down from the Heavens and crushing everything it doesn't approve of."

Sun 1970

Terry Gilliam ... behind the foot that descends from the heavens.

'LOST' CARP OF THE NENE

by F. J. WAGSTAFFE

THE large king strain carp of the lower reaches of the Nene around Peterborough, particularly those in the Electricity Cut, are well known to many specimen hunters because they have featured in the news quite regularly since around 1960.

Slightly less known and far less appreciated are the stocks of wild carp around Northampton, about 60 miles upstream from Peterborough. Present in vast numbers in a stretch some seven miles long, these torpedo-shaped fighters roam the lily-choked backwaters in the upper reaches of the river providing sport far exceeding that which you would expect from fish of their size and weight.

In March, 1952, the then Nene and Welland Fishery Board decided to use some funds to buy 5,000 king carp. These arrived from a Surrey fish farm on the 18th of the month in an ex-army truck, and 3,200 of these fish ended their uncomfortable journey in pits, drains, lakes and canals in the area. The remaining 1,800 were distributed along the River Nene, being released at five points. Two hundred were put in at Northampton, 400 near Thorpe Waterville, 400 at Oundle, 400 at Nassington and 400 at Peterborough. Those put in at Northampton were quickly lost among the thousands of "wildies" already present there. Large carp are only caught there very infrequently, but "wildies" from 4 to 8 lb. are taken regularly.

In the river near Peterborough at least 40 carp of over 20 lb. have been caught, including four over 30 lb. Double figure carp are too numerous to mention. The unofficial river carp record was broken there several times and now stands at 34½ lb.; this fish was caught in June, 1965.

Angler's World 1967

The Times 1968

London Bridge souvenirs for sale

Souvenirs made of stone, left after demolition of London Bridge, should bring in about £4,500, the Court of Common Council will be told tomorrow.

The smile of the champion, Ann Jones, M B E

Lawn Tennis 1969

£1,000 A WEEK, BUT
DEAD
AT 26
Brian Jones story of drink and drugs

ANNA WOHLIN, Swedish friend of Brian Jones. She told the coroner of his last hand grip

BRIAN JONES — He had he helped on to the spri board on the night of fatal swim

POP star Brian Jones earned £1,000 a week. But at the age of 26 his heart was enlarged, fat and flabby. His liver was twice the normal weight and in an advanced state of fatty degeneration.

Brian Jones was found drowned in the swimming pool at his home, Cotchford Farm, Hartfield, on Thursday of last week.

At the inquest at East Grinstead on Monday a verdict of misadventure was returned and the East Sussex coroner, Dr. Angus Somerville, said Jones had been under the influence of drink and drugs at the time of his death.

East Grinstead Courier 1969

Lord Eccles calls for higher arts standards

By HENRY STANHOPE

Lord Eccles, Paymaster General, with responsibility for the arts, criticized artistic elitism yesterday and spoke of a campaign to persuade the mass media to improve their quality.

He was speaking from the stage of the new Young Vic Theatre, built on a bombed site and a butcher's shop, which was exuberantly opened by Dame Sybil Thorndike, who is 88. There was even an ode by Sir Laurence Olivier, who was created a life peer in the Birthday Honours.

Lord Eccles, speaking about experimental art, exhorted artists not to be satisfied with writing and performing plays " for only a tiny fraction of the population. Beware of the bearded men who say that only two or three out of 100 of us can understand fine art," he said.

" Remember that each time you play to a full house, for every 100 people in the audience about a million will have been watching drama on television that same evening." The millions watching television could not be squeezed into all the theatres in the world

There was need for a massive increase in active support for the live arts " without which British life will soon be blanketed by the thin trivialities that the communications industry must at present provide if it is to secure the vast audiences it needs." Audiences had to be persuaded to demand better fare.

'This is part of your job as professionals, which in the 1970s you cannot lay aside. The Government is ready to help. Between us we must start a campaign using techniques as new and experimental as many of the plays you will perform", he said.

Dame Sybil spoke highly of youth and their concern for the world, but criticized their speech.

" I do not care what language you speak in—there are so many versions of English—so long as it is clear." She was terribly depressed when she went to most theatres. "My hearing cannot be quite as good as it was . . . ." If young people were protesting—then let them protest with clarity. . . .

Sir Laurence's 44-line ode was read by the actor Edward Woodward because Sir Laurence is recovering from pleurisy. It was quite unforgettable.

The theatre is an all-concrete amphitheatre, seating 450, costing £60,000 (half came from the Arts Council) and catering for people in their teens and early twenties.

It will be an offshoot of the National Theatre and will be run by the National Theatre's administrative director, Frank Dunlop, who said that its shape was the most malleable one could think of.

Yesterday its red wooden benches were still a little thick with dust and the audience sat down gingerly. Tickets for all seats will cost 7s. 6d. for plays and 10s. for musicals. It will open on September 11 with the farce *Scapino*.

The Times 1970

SHOW PAGE

STEAM RADIO COMES TO THE BOIL!

Every day nearly 27 million people in Britain tune in to the four BBC wavelengths, their local radio stations or the foreign stations—and considering we're supposed to be living in a television-dominated age that's fantastic! The main attractions of radio are that you don't have to sit chained to a chair to listen in; you don't have to huddle round the set in semi-darkness to appreciate it, and it's a marvellous background to lighten the chores. Best of all, you can take the radio with you wherever you go—even in a car as you bowl along a motorway or country lane.

For the old and lonely it's far more than just transportable entertainment, it's a real and friendly companion. For those in hospital or for the blind it's a breath of the world outside. For 15 million people it's a way of being cheered up and brought together from opposite ends of the earth by way of Two-Way Family Favourites, and countless young people, blasé about the television, wouldn't step outdoors without their "trannies".

Jack de Manio — the Today man

6 *Pop music—the kind of radio I deal in—isn't serious. It's part of the brighter side of life.* 9
Tony Blackburn — the breakfast show DJ

Woman's Own 1969

FORSYTH GOES STRAIGHT

"I like my act to look like one long ad lib," says Bruce Forsyth . . . and his long, humorous face splits into that slice-of-melon grin which in his Palladium days helped hundreds of eager married couples to Beat The Clock with uninhibited gusto. "That's the way I come over best."

In real-life, Mr. Forsyth makes an even better impact than he does on stage or screen. Taller, more good-looking than he appears at a distance, his springy step, firm handshake and piercingly blue eyes—not to mention a glorious suntan acquired on regular golf sessions—lend him an aura of good health that's instantly attractive.

The famous "busy-body" walk, the clasped hands, the Mr. Punch head thrust ingratiatingly forward—these are not so apparent in the private Forsyth, who is a surprisingly serious man.

"I'm a cautious sort of person," he remarks thoughtfully. "I don't take on anything unless I'm sure I'm ready for it, sure it's exactly right." An attitude born of a long slog to the top in the hard school of showbiz experience. Bruce Forsyth's career began at 14 when he appeared in a song-and-dance pageboy act during World War II. It wasn't until 1958 that he became compere of ATV's Sunday Night At The London Palladium. Now, after a smash hit season at The Talk Of The Town, he has entered a completely new

field: the straight play. Birds On The Wing has opened in the West End, and Bruce was excited about his part.

"After The Talk Of The Town, I couldn't have done more cabaret," he says. "It would have been an anticlimax! I had to go into something quite fresh and different, and when I was sent the play to read I realised it had great potential. Naturally, I'd like it to be a hit and run for ages, but my personal performance goes down if I get stale, so in the spring I'm hoping to launch an act in a brand new musical that I went over to Italy to see—this would be marvellous."

Yet despite this full programme, Bruce Forsyth, who sings, dances, acts and tells jokes, describes himself as "basically lazy". So what happens when he feels *energetic!* SARAH HARRISON

Woman's Own 1969

George Best manages to look happy as he talks to Frank Clough.

BEST BAN KNOCKS UNITED HOPES

By FRANK CLOUGH

MANCHESTER UNITED wing wizard George Best goes into today's FA Cup battle at Ipswich determined to play the game of his life.

That was his mood last night after hearing that he had been banned for a month and fined £100 by the FA

The suspension starts on Monday and means that he will be ruled out of the replay if United force a draw today, and the fourth round in three weeks if United get through

Petulant

Best's ban stems from his petulant outburst at the end of their League Cup semi-final first leg defeat by Manchester City in December when millions of TV viewers saw him strike the ball from the hands of match referee Jack Taylor.

Said Best last night: "When I reported to the ground this morning, and heard the news. I was really shocked. People break legs and get no more

"All I can say is that this makes the Ipswich game extra special as far as I am concerned. I hope I can go out and really turn it on."

● Other decisions announced by the FA today were: J. Larkin (Chelsea) suspended for 21 days and fined £10; P. Turner (Hastings United) suspended for 21 days and fined £10, suspension suspended for 12 months; J. Guymer (Charlton trainer) severely censured, warned as to his future conduct and fined £5; P. Minor (Wembley) suspended for 21 days.

Sun 1970

2.0 THE NAVY LARK
with
Jon Pertwee
Leslie Phillips
Stephen Murray
Repeated: Wednesday at 7.45 p.m. on Radio 1 and Radio 2

Radio Times 1967

Vitapointe gives the Duchess of Bedford shining elegant hair

Woman's Own 1969

Laughable insolence of 'Oh! Calcutta!'

By JOHN BARBER

WHAT is new about "Oh! Calcutta!" at the Round House, Chalk Farm, is its cool insolence. This is an elaborately got-up musical revue that peddles publicly to middle-class audiences the sort of material previously confined to the saloon bar or the sleazier strip club.

Daily Telegraph 1970

By engaging a designer like Farrah, a choreographer like Margo Sappington, and writers like Joe Orton, the deviser Kenneth Tynan has broken through barriers that many people will think better left where they were.

Nevertheless it presents sex as an endearingly improper, absurd and eminently kiddable human activity.

Wendy Craig of Not In Front of the Children

How Ena Sharples was blacked out by a strike

By JOHN STEVENSON

A DISPUTE over bonus payments kept Ena Sharples and *Coronation Street*, one of Britain's most popular TV programme's, off the screens last night.

More than 300 members of the Association of Cinematograph and Television Technicians walked out of Granada's Manchester studios, bringing normal programmes to a halt at 6.30.

The dispute is over bonus payments for next Christmas, and the walk-out came after talks with the management broke down.

The title of last night's unseen episode: *Ena is Lost.*

Daily Mail 1967

It's **Marvellous Beer!**

Tony's Tonic
The Queen Says
'Congratulations'

IT'S A GREAT DAY for British golf as Tony Jacklin wins the US Open. The Queen sent him a telegram, so did Mr. Heath.

His wife Viv was tearful, Jacklin himself suffered cramp, 75,878 people watched play during the week, a total of 3,642 originally entered the event, two qualifiers—Don January and Homero Blancas—refused to play the course because they considered it a monster, and our own Tony came out of the drama a winner by seven shots.

Now he's back in Britain—a hero! Tony didn't just win the US Open, he confirmed he is champion of the world by the biggest margin in 49 years. He put the other world superstars in the shade and the American crowds loved it.

Our pictures show Jacklin and Viv with the cup (and cheque for £12,500), the final putt which dropped for a birdie, some natty trousers for round one, Gary Player with crowd and Jacko in the lead at halfway!

What a win, what a tonic.

Golf Weekly 1970

This England

Prizes: £1 for the first entry and 10s. for each of the others printed. Paste entries on a postcard.

☐ Among Mrs Patricia Hollingsworth's souvenirs are pieces of HM Prison, Dartmoor, and the Notre Dame Cathedral in Paris. For Mrs Hollingsworth has a most unusual hobby – she is a 'chipper'. 'Whenever I go on holiday I take a chisel and toffee hammer with me,' said Mrs Hollingsworth. 'If I see a building or place I like I just chip off a souvenir.' She now has between 40 and 50 bits of stone which ornament her home and garden. – *Coventry Evening Telegraph* (Roberta Hewitt)

New Statesman 1970